The Problem of Production

This book develops a theory of the firm as an economic phenomenon with unique market value grounded in specialisation. In contrast to most existing theories, it places the firm within the context of the evolving market process and as a 'missing' piece of the puzzle of economic development, progress, and wealth creation. The firm here emerges as a means for the implementation of innovative productive solutions that cannot be brought about through market exchange.

This theory successfully places the firm as a function in the market process that helps us explain the dynamics of market progress and economic growth. It also separates economic from legal aspects and therefore produces a theory of the firm that is neither dependent on nor refers to the 'legal firm' (this separates this theory from many others). By doing this, the theory adds a new dimension to the economics of organisations, the economics of institutions, suggests increased applicability of microeconomic theory, and supplies a previously missing piece in the 'Austrian' economic theory of the market.

This book will be of interest to graduate students and researchers interested in industrial and organisational economics, primarily the theory of the firm.

Per L. Bylund is Records-Johnston Professor of Free Enterprise and Assistant Professor of Entrepreneurship, School of Entrepreneurship, Oklahoma State University, USA.

Routledge advances in heterodox economics

Edited by
Wolfram Elsner
University of Bremen
and
Peter Kriesler
University of New South Wales

Over the past two decades, the intellectual agendas of heterodox economists have taken a decidedly pluralist turn. Leading thinkers have begun to move beyond the established paradigms of Austrian, feminist, Institutional-evolutionary, Marxian, Post Keynesian, radical, social, and Sraffian economics – opening up new lines of analysis, criticism, and dialogue among dissenting schools of thought. This cross-fertilisation of ideas is creating a new generation of scholarship in which novel combinations of heterodox ideas are being brought to bear on important contemporary and historical problems.

Routledge advances in heterodox economics aims to promote this new scholarship by publishing innovative books in heterodox economic theory, policy, philosophy, intellectual history, institutional history, and pedagogy. Syntheses or critical engagement of two or more heterodox traditions are especially encouraged.

For a complete list of titles in this series, please visit www.routledge.com.

This series was previously published by University of Michigan Press and the following books are available (please contact UMP for more information):

The Problem of Production

A new theory of the firm

Per L. Bylund

Routledge
Taylor & Francis Group

LONDON AND NEW YORK

First published 2016 by Routledge

2 Park Square, Milton Park, Abingdon, Oxon OX14 4RN
711 Third Avenue, New York, NY 10017, USA

Routledge is an imprint of the Taylor & Francis Group, an informa business

First issued in paperback 2017

British Library Cataloguing in Publication Data
A catalogue record for this book is available from the British Library

Library of Congress Cataloging in Publication Data
Bylund, Per L. (Per Lennart), author.
The problem of production : a new theory of the firm / Per L. Bylund.
Includes bibliographical references and index.
  1. Industrial organization (Economic theory) 2. Production
  (Economic theory) I. Title.
  HD2326.B95 2016
  338.601–dc23   2015027669

ISBN: 978-1-8489-3529-7 (hbk)
ISBN: 978-1-138-29997-9 (pbk)

Typeset in Times New Roman
by Wearset Ltd, Boldon, Tyne and Wear

Contents

Acknowledgements

This book would not have been possible without the support, encouragement, and challenges from numerous people. Among them, I especially want to thank Dr Peter G. Klein of Baylor University for introducing me to the theory of the firm and making me interested in the economic theories of organisation; Dr Randall E. Westgren of the University of Missouri for his never-ending encouragement, interest, and support in my ideas and my work; and Dr Jeffrey M. Herbener of Grove City College for reading, criticising, and thoughtfully commenting on a previous draft of this manuscript. I have gained tremendously from Peter, Randy, and Jeff, but I am most indebted to my wife Susanne for giving me the inspiration, support, and constant push forward; this book would not have been even a remote possibility without her.

Any errors, mistakes, contradictions, or problems with the theory presented in this book are of course completely my own doing.

Introduction

It may not be much of an exaggeration to claim that many of science's great achievements have been of one of two kinds: it has shown that what was believed to be impossibly complex is in fact the result of a rather simple mechanism or process; and it has shown that what was thought of as simple or taken for granted was in fact quite complicated or even beyond our ability to explain. In line with the latter, it indeed seems often to be the case that what appears to be most glaringly obvious may sometimes be the very hardest to explain. The business firm as an economic phenomenon clearly falls in this category.

To the non-academic, the firm presents little problem. Perhaps this is the reason why it was taken for granted for so long also in the study of economics. While the firm has often been present in different forms of analyses and theorising, it has far less often been subject to scrutiny. Adam Smith famously discusses the division of labour exemplified by work within a pin factory and Karl Marx similarly discusses the use and exploitation of labour within factories, to mention only two noteworthy examples. Yet neither of them ask the fundamental question of why there are firms. This, in fact, is almost exclusively the case for economists and social theorists for all but the last century. If the modern account of the recent history of economics is to be trusted, this question remained unasked until a very young Ronald H. Coase posed it in his Nobel-winning article 'The Nature of the Firm' published in 1937.[1] Coase's article was not the first to study firms, but it is generally regarded as the beginning of the modern theory of the firm literature – the tradition that asks why there are firms.

One might think that the 'why' of the business firm should not be a very difficult question to answer. Firms are ubiquitous in the market and have been present in the marketplace for a very long time, so there should be plenty of evidence and cases to study. This is true; there are indeed plenty of data. But even though there are massive amounts of data, the evidence is far from conclusive. In fact, even though we are closing in on the one-hundredth anniversary of Coase's ground-breaking article, and thousands of scholarly books and articles on the topic, we are nowhere near a proper understanding of the firm.

The statement that we are 'nowhere near' an understanding of the firm is likely to be provocative to many if not most theorists of the firm. But it is deliberate on my part. The reason is that there are several notable theories that each provide a different explanation and rationale for the business firm. As we will see later in this book, there are even several different definitions of what the firm supposedly is. The question, of course, is of what use these different definitions are when we try to understand the specific phenomenon. This is more than a rhetorical question. Whatever phenomenon that we study and for which we have several different definitions cannot reasonably be well understood. If there are, say, four different yet seemingly valuable definitions of the firm, they may each capture part of what the firm is. But each one must necessarily be incomplete, since it doesn't capture all of what the other definitions capture. And how do we assess which are better theories of the firm if they attempt to explain different kinds of firm?

Part of the problem is that we as students of the economics of organisations tend towards one of two extremes in our quest to understand the firm: we either start with overly simplified and formalised models of the market, or hope to stumble upon the firm's true essence when going through massive datasets of messy empirical observations. Most of the theorising on the firm has undoubtedly been of the first kind, and Coase's own theory belongs to this category. It is arguably a better approach, since it to a lesser extent depends on interpretations and is therefore easier to assess. From the point of view of modern economic theory, even overly simplified theories of the firm is an improvement. Economic models tend to treat the firm as a 'black box' that can be represented by simply a 'production function', something that transforms inputs to outputs. What happens within firms is disregarded. Theories of the firm, regardless of approach, try to open this 'box' in order to describe what goes on within it – in economic terms. However, rather than examine in detail the type of production that goes on in the firm, they tend to look for a single variable that can describe the firm's rationale. Many of them consequently identify a type of cost that is avoided by having a firm, and the argument is then formulated based on an assertion of what characterises the firm. Coase's theory is an example of this: he defines the firm as production coordinated through authoritative direction, and its rationale follows from the fact that authority avoids the specific costs incurred from coordination using the price mechanism.

This does not mean, of course, that a theory that focuses on finding a simple cost rationale has no value. On the contrary, the vast literature on the theory of the firm has provided many brilliant contributions to our understanding of both the firm and the market. This is the case with Coase's theory too. But one aspect of the business firm tends to be understated in the literature: specialised production.

The firm as production

That the firm has something to do with production is not a surprise to anyone. Indeed, the firm as a 'production function' is all about production, so naturally theories of the firm would need to in one way or the other address this issue. For instance, Coase assumes that production is what happens when resources are allocated, and the theory therefore focuses on the alternative means of coordination of factors rather than on the nature of production as such. The result is a comparative institutional analysis where production is held relatively constant, and the choice of coordinating function thus boils down to a cost comparison.

In what is commonly recognised as an elaboration of Coase's theory, Oliver E. Williamson presents a model for predicting governance choice for economic transactions.[2] Like Coase, Williamson abstracts from the nature of production to focus on cost economising as the basis for matching governance structures with transactional attributes: 'the object is to economize on the *sum* of production and transaction costs'.[3] Unlike Coase, however, Williamson distinguishes between different types of transactions and thereby implicitly opens for discussing implications of production – primarily how they affect governance choice.

In another influential theory of the firm, Armen A. Alchian and Harold Demsetz consider the problems of monitoring individual effort in team production a rationale for the firm.[4] Whereas they place production at the core of the firm, the theory does not go further than to consider effects of generic team production situations such as 'lifting cargo into a truck'. As shirking would be in the interest of each of the individuals working in the team, they would all shirk and therefore collectively be worse off. Team production thus becomes a collective action problem, and in order to find a solution the workers hire someone to monitor and measure their individual efforts, for which the monitor earns the residual rewards of the enterprise.

These theories all point to what firms can do, and it is very likely that there are actual firms that fit these descriptions. But the fundamental question is not what firms do, but how the firm could be defined or understood. If the firm is production, then we should be able to find the essence of what the firm is by studying the type of production that is undertaken within it. The theory outlined in this book attempts to do this.

The theories above were chosen as examples (there are many more) of influential theories of the firm that *relate* to production but do not explore it in detail. What we mean by this is that they assume production is undertaken within the firm (in addition to, we should add, production taking place in the market outside the firm), but assert a specific nature of those relationships or transactions that comprise production. The theories do not venture into discussing what production is or how it is carried out. Granted, this demarcation of the theories' explanatory power is by design. They do not generally make claims to explain more than is supported by the narrow theoretical perspectives adopted. But this is nevertheless problematic since the firm in some sense *is* production, but it is *not* market. This is clearly how the firm is perceived in the 'production function' view, it is evident from empirical observation, and, as we have seen, it is a view more or less explicit in the theories of the firm themselves.

We will here outline a theory of the firm that begins with an analysis of specialised production that is effectuated without firms. This allows us to identify limitations inherent in production, which seem to point to a specific function that can be satisfied by the firm. The firm therefore emerges as a solution to this problem that the market appears to be otherwise unable to deal with. This is not to say that firms do not also economise on transaction costs or monitor effort in team production. But it means that there seems to be a more fundamental function: solving a problem that we will refer to as the specialisation deadlock.

The 'specialisation deadlock'

The specialisation deadlock (discussed in detail in Chapter 3) is used to call attention to the issue of where specialisation comes from. The 'deadlock' follows from the need for compatibility within production in a specialised exchange market. It is easy to see that when production factors are intensively specialised, and therefore used to perform specific tasks in roundabout production processes, they must be compatible with each other. Indeed, a labour worker who performs the first task in a process that comprises a series of necessary steps, each carried out by someone with that specialisation, must produce intermediate goods that are usable in the subsequent task. The labour worker in that stage must then be prepared to use the goods in process produced in the previous step and what is produced must be compatible also with the next step.

Compatibility is not an issue in already established production processes, especially when subject to decentralised market competition and exchange. In decentralised market production, there are often for each producer a number of suppliers of the rather standardised input necessary as well as a number of users demanding the rather standardised output produced. There are, in other words, markets for the intermediate goods used in production. No individual producer is dependent on any one individual to make available the specific inputs used or to buy the specific outputs produced. A producer of steel suited for use in for example automobile manufacturing is not dependent on one specific supplier of the necessary inputs iron ore and coal, and is also not dependent on one specific manufacturer of automobiles to buy the produced steel. Even though long-term contracting relationships may tie parties in a production process such as automobile manufacturing together over time, there is competition between iron ore miners and coal miners to sell their product to the steel producer just like there is competition between automobile manufacturers to buy steel. There is also competition between steel producers, who produce standardised steel using standard iron ore and coal.

The specific process of producing an automobile, here consisting of the three stages iron ore and coal mining, steel production, and automobile manufacturing, requires no further coordination because each of the stages is traded in the market. Each stage may be produced by numerous competing producers, and there may be competing uses for all the intermediate goods used. For instance, steel could also be used in production of shovels and submarines. A decentralised market with autonomous producers of each stage is therefore sufficient to satisfy market demand for automobiles. Should the quantity demanded for automobiles increase, producers of automobiles will pay higher prices to get a larger share of the produced steel. They need more steel to meet the demand. As prices increase up the production chain, resources are reallocated towards automobile production from other types of production. Producers of shovels and submarines will get less steel (unless their market situation allows them to outbid the automobile manufacturers), and the result is more automobiles and fewer shovels and submarines. In other words, production meets demand.

The market's reallocation of resources to satisfy changes in demand happens 'spontaneously' in the sense that it needs no explicit coordination of the process. A decentralised market dealing with standardised intermediate goods is fully equipped to respond to changes as it is in each producer's interest to maximise the profitability of their situation, and this is always in line with satisfying market demand. The price mechanism, therefore, is sufficient for the market to maximise wants satisfaction of consumers.

The reader will recognise that this is a standard model in economics, but we here place emphasis on the fact that production is carried out through specialised stages that depend on heterogeneous resources: labour with specific skills and specific production-aiding capital goods. As long as there is a market with redundant production and thus competition throughout the process, this does not change the story. However, we also find that producers lack the means to step outside the boundaries of the market's standardised production stages. Should any of the individual producers find that they would be more productive by specialising in performing only part of a stage, such as producing half automobiles, they will be unable to do so unless that stage already consists of a series of separate tasks. The reason for this is that they will find their productive efforts incompatible with the existing production structure.

What this means is simply that unless their specialisation efforts are coordinated with another producer, they will suffer from incompleteness. For instance, consider a market that already adequately organises a specific production process consisting of three stages, such as the automobile manufacturing process we mentioned above. What is produced in stage 1 (coal and iron ore) is input to stage 2 (steel production) and what is produced there (steel) is input to stage 3 (automobile manufacturing). Any single producer specialising in part of (but not the entire) stage 2 would fail because the production chain is incomplete – *all* of stage 2 is necessary for stage 3 to begin.

Say this producer chooses to specialise in the first half of stage 2, then this effort will remain compatible with the market through inputs: what is produced in stage 1 (coal and iron ore) can be used to commence production of the first half of stage 2. But the producer, specialising in the first half of the stage, ends with a half-finished stage 2, for which there is no market.

Similarly, if this producer instead specialises in the second half of stage 2, then what is produced would be compatible with the next stage as steel can still be used in automobile manufacturing. But starting half-way through stage 2 means the producer needs to acquire half-finished steel in order to complete the process. Of course, there are no such inputs in the market – the market only trades with coal and iron ore (stage 1's product), steel (stage 2's product), and automobiles (stage 3's product). The only possibility is for the producer of the second half of stage 2 to convince someone to produce only the first half of stage 2. But doing so would make this person dependent on our producer to sell the half-finished stage 2 production. And our producer would be dependent on whoever produces the first half. There are, after all, only two producers in this world specialising to those exact parts of stage 2, so they must trade with each other – no one else will (or can).

What this means is, to reuse Adam Smith's well-known phrase, that the division of labour is limited by the extent of the market. One cannot individually specialise further than what is already implemented in the market so that inputs can be acquired and outputs are saleable in the existing market. It is of course possible to coordinate with others so that a standard, market-saleable task is effectively 'split' into several individual tasks to each, which at least one in the undertaking specialises. This type of solution does not make the innovation incompatible with the existing production structure, since it, combined, replaces a market stage and thus uses standard inputs and produces standard outputs. But it would make each provider of a specialised task strictly dependent on all others. Should any of them fail, the whole effort is practically worthless because its result is incomplete from the point of view of market production, and there therefore is no demand for it. The price one can expect for such partially completed goods should be significantly lower than the proportion completed.

This problem amounts to a 'specialisation deadlock' in the decentralised market, since engaging in extra-market specialisation comes at the cost of significant uncertainty. As there are no prices it also requires detailed coordination, which is not easily brought about in the decentralised market. Individual market actors should therefore be unlikely to specialise outside the market's already supported specialisations, the 'sweet spot' of production, in a manner of speaking. This raises the question of how the market became highly specialised in the first place.

The firm as an 'island of specialisation'

Adam Smith observed that 'The greatest improvement in the productive powers of labour, and the greater part of the skill, dexterity, and judgment with which it is anywhere directed, or applied, seem to have been the effects of the division of labour.'[5] This indeed seems to be the case, and it can be easily observed in the actual market: production in it is quite obviously intensively specialised. More importantly, the more advanced the market the more intensively specialised it appears to be. Advanced markets also appear to adopt increasingly intensive specialisation under the division of labour, so markets must have a means to overcome the specialisation deadlock.

What is argued in this book is that markets, in fact, cannot overcome the specialisation deadlock. Instead, we find the economic function of the firm in implementing production processes that utilise more intensive specialisation than is possible in the market. The firm therefore solves the problem of production.

It is not a means to avoid costs in the market, as many theories of the firm would argue, but is necessarily placed outside the extent of the market as it is a different kind of production. We hold that the firm, in economic terms, is the result of a productive innovation that utilises highly intensive specialisation.

But it is insufficient to assert that the firm provides centralised decision-making and has the authority to enforce such decisions. While this would undoubtedly indicate a solution, though only by assertion, it provides no explanation. What we need to explain is how a decentralised market, which has no basis for authority but must rely solely on exchange and reciprocal contracts, can overcome the specialisation deadlock. In other words, it is unsatisfactory to provide a rationale for a 'firm' that does not also explain the process for how firms are originally formed. It may not be historically accurate to assume a purely decentralised market and then trace what steps may be taken in order to form firms, but it is the appropriate approach for identifying the economic function and formulating a theory of the firm.

We saw in the previous section that the specialisation deadlock makes it very costly to engage in extra-market specialisation. This is the case because, if done alone, the splitting of a standard production stage in the market is not economically feasible due to the necessary incompleteness of that which is produced. Even if done jointly and in coordination, the specialised tasks are strictly interdependent and therefore risk failure should any of them fail. Simply put, any productive activity that is more intensively specialised than is compatible with already existing production, and thus the saleability thereof, falls outside the extent of the market. There is therefore no way of doing this on market terms. The firm, as it here emerges, is an island of specialisation that must be formed outside the extent of the market. It is the observable result of an innovation in production that uses specialisation of a degree and kind that is impossible to establish in the market (that is, through the price mechanism).

What has been said here only outlines the problem of production and the function that the firm serves from the point of view of the decentralised market. There is much more to the argument, the details of which, of course, are found in the chapters to follow.

Notes

1 R. H. Coase, 'The Nature of the Firm', *Economica*, 4:16 (1937), pp. 386–405.
2 See for instance, O. E. Williamson, *Markets and Hierarchies, Analysis and Antitrust Implications: A Study in the Economics of Internal Organization* (New York: Free Press, 1975), O. E. Williamson, *The Economic Institutions of Capitalism* (New York: Free Press, 1985), O. E. Williamson, *The Mechanisms of Governance* (Oxford: Oxford University Press, 1996).
3 O. E. Williamson, 'Transaction Cost Economics: The Governance of Contractual Relations', *Journal of Law and Economics*, 22:2 (1979), pp. 233–261, p. 245.
4 A. A. Alchian and H. Demsetz, 'Production, Information Costs and Economic Organization', *American Economic Review*, 62:5 (1972), pp. 777–795.
5 A. Smith, *An Inquiry into the Nature and Causes of the Wealth of Nations* (1776) (Chicago, IL: University of Chicago Press, 1976), p. 7.

1 What we know and what we don't know about the firm

This book is about what is generally referred to as the 'firm', a phenomenon in the market that appears obvious but that remains difficult to explain. While there is a field of study referred to as the theory of the firm, there are in fact a number of noteworthy theories. All of these theories claim to explain the firm's rationale, value, and purpose. But the theories tend to describe the firm in different ways. The discussion is further complicated as there are several different definitions of this seemingly elusive concept. As a result, our understanding for the economic reality of the firm is inhibited.

The purpose of this book is not to reconcile these theories or definitions, however, but to try a new approach and provide an explanation for the firm by looking at the market setting where we find firms. We start by constructing an economic model of the market as an elaborate yet dynamic system of production without firms. This, in turn, allows us to study the limitations of the economic system of production, and what means are available to overcome them; or, more precisely, how the market deals with this 'problem of production'. The goal is to elaborate on an explanation for the firm by seeking its economic function within the extensive production apparatus of the specialised market.

This chapter positions this book in the extant literature on the economics of organisations and institutions. It does so by summarising and delineating two strands of the academic literature that are separate but should complement each other: strategic management (or, as it is sometimes referred to, organisational economics), especially the theory of the firm, and the Austrian school of economics. While they have things in common and have recently been approaching each other, we will here draw from both strands to produce a theory of the firm. Our theory is based on the Austrian conception of production in the dynamic market process and it takes market-based production and the evolving dynamic of the market process as its point of departure. The perspective is Austrian, but the object for our analysis is borrowed from strategic management. The discussion thereby indirectly attempts to reconcile these literatures by providing a theoretical explanation for particular phenomena in the overlapping space between them. This first chapter is intended to provide background by making the reader familiar with economic theorising on the firm and what the two aforementioned literatures have in common.

Theorising on the firm

Whereas firms are ubiquitous in the economy and therefore often assumed to be a natural component of the market, the concept of a 'firm' poses an interesting question relating to economising, organisation, and production. The question can be stated as simply 'Why are there firms?', but its simplicity is deceiving. The question requires both elaboration and contextualisation to make the problem clear. The 'why' in the question suggests that there must be a rationale for forming firms such that there is a distinct value of coordinating production specifically within firms, which directs our attention to the question of what possible alternatives to firm organising there could be. The commonly assumed alternative is a model of the market as predominantly decentralised exchange-based coordination of production. The theory of the firm literature aims to formulate an economic argument for firm organising in contrast to decentralised market exchange, and under what specific conditions this is of value and therefore can be the predicted outcome. Due to the importance placed on this distinction between firm and market, a significant and important subset of this literature stresses issues relating to the firm's 'boundaries'. A firm's boundary denotes the point where the firm ends and the market begins (and vice versa), which indirectly suggests what makes the firm different from the market. The 'why' of the firm therefore relates to (if not requires) a definition of what constitutes a 'firm', since 'why' must point towards a certain 'what'. Knowing the 'why' and 'what' should also provide insights necessary to investigate the 'how' of the firm, which is another important question at the core of the theory of the firm literature.

The questions of the firm's why, what, and how are generally referred to as the Coasean questions of the firm since they were posed or implied in Ronald H. Coase's ground-breaking, Nobel Prize-winning 1937 article 'The Nature of the Firm'.[1] Coase was not the first to pose questions about the firm's rationale, boundaries, and internal organisation, but his comparative framing was novel and the article's approach has become starting point for the modern study of economic organisation and the firm. Coase's basic question, which asserted a clear theoretical distinction between the firm as a planned hierarchy and the decentralised exchange in the market, was stated rather bluntly: 'in view of the fact that it is usually argued that co-ordination will be done by the price mechanism, why is such organisation [the firm] necessary?'[2] Indeed, as Coase points out, if the market economy is efficient there should be no need for and certainly no value in such alternative means to organise production. Coase answers the question by introducing a cost specific to market exchange – a marketing or transaction cost – that produces a cost-based rationale for organising hierarchies in the place of markets. The firm is according to the Coasean view a means to economise on the market's transaction costs.

From our contemporary perspective, Coase's article appears as the culmination of a vast literature on economic organisation and management of the firm in the 1920s and 1930s. This literature continued the earlier work by primarily Alfred Marshall, who discussed the abstract conception of a 'representative firm'[3] and offered an extensive study of industrial organisation.[4] This line of research, to which Coase's article was likely intended as a challenge but ended up making little if any impact,[5] subsided within mainstream economics in the late 1930s. The economic study of the firm was not revived until Coase's pioneering work was rediscovered in the late 1960s and early 1970s, primarily through the work of Oliver E. Williamson who adopted Coase's comparative institutional analysis ('firm vs. market') as well as the concept of 'transaction costs'. The rediscovery of the Coasean 'make-or-buy' perspective on coordination became the starting point for an extensive literature in economics aiming to explain firm organising, which developed over the course of some twenty years.[6] This literature is still core to the study of the firm.

Austrian economics and the firm

The emergence and development of the literature on economic organisation in the 1920s and 1930s coincides with the Socialist Calculation Debate, one of the great debates in economics. The latter was prompted by the work of Austrian economist Ludwig von Mises, who argued that an economic system based on socialism was both theoretically and practically impossible.[7] Mises was a proponent of the Austrian or 'causal-realist' school of economics founded at the University of Vienna, which focuses on studying the real market through the lens of a deductive theoretical framework. The tradition's focus on the market as it is, rather than – as in modern mainstream economics – highly formalised mathematical models with only occasional relevance to the real workings of the market, suggests it perhaps should have researched the firm. After all, markets both then and now are predominantly populated with firms; most economic activity takes place within or between such organisations. Yet, in contrast to neoclassical economics, which gave the topic a lot of attention in the 1960s, 1970s, and 1980s, the Austrian school did not develop a theory of formal economic organisation, and even less a theory of the firm.

This appears as a conundrum but is also an opportunity. That it is an opportunity is evident from two recent trends in the literature related to the Austrian body of research, on the one hand, and the study of the firm, its governance, and organisation on the other. One trend is the growing interest for issues relating to economic organisation from within the Austrian school and by Austrian scholars. Since the 1990s, articles and books have been published as part of the Austrian research programme that propose approaches to and directions for developing an Austrian theory of the firm.[8] The other trend is evident by the (re)discovery of and then growing use and influence of Austrian economic concepts and theory in strategic management and entrepreneurship research.[9] These two trends, while addressing similar issues, have different starting points and approaches, and build off different theoretical frameworks. But, as we will see, they nevertheless have similar theory implications, however with different emphases, and therefore suggest a possible future convergence.

For scholars in management and entrepreneurship, Austrian economics has offered an opportunity to open new venues for research. While the formal models in mainstream economics, especially industrial organisation (IO), originally laid ground for the study of strategic management, they are deficient for producing predictions and advice in a dynamic world. The formalised economic approach offers little support for more practically oriented or realistic research aiming to understand or aid in the creation or management of real firms. In contrast, the Austrian view of the market as a dynamic, entrepreneurship-driven competitive discovery process, and its focus on realism in aiming to explain real empirical phenomena, has considerable potential to enhance research and practice in both management and entrepreneurship. As we shall see, modern research in these fields has already adopted several core Austrian concepts and insights.

The study of strategic management was originally an offshoot of the so-called Bain/Mason paradigm of IO. While IO focused on the overall efficiency of the economic system as compared to the perfectly competitive model, strategic management developed strategies for the individual firm to exploit the efficiency logic and so establish monopoly power through which it can earn above-normal returns.[10] But the empirical market in which business leaders draft strategies and make decisions is scarcely similar to the perfectly competitive model. Also, in stark contrast to the model, real production is neither perfectly optimised nor instantaneous (which is often the case in formal economic models), and business decisions are always made under uncertain conditions. The market, in other words, is dynamic and uncertain, it is in a constant flux, and is fundamentally less than perfectly foreseeable. Businesses consequently operate in a changing world – that is, disequilibrium – that is rather far from a stable equilibrium state, and this makes the formalised models describing maximising behaviour of rational actors with perfect information quite inapplicable in real business management.

It should therefore have been an obvious and expected development within strategic management to move towards adopting and analysing a more dynamic conception of the market and the firm. The change to focusing on the analysis of a more dynamic and 'messier' view of the market constituted a shift from the formal models of mainstream economics towards an Austrian conception of the market as a competitive and equilibrating *process*. As Robert Jacobson observed in the early 1990s, there are 'relatively few strategy researchers [who] explicitly attribute or link their analysis to Austrian economics', but 'the influence of Austrian thinking is more widespread than this lack of attribution might suggest'. He continued by noting that much of the then-recent strategy research 'fit[s] squarely into the Austrian school of thought' and that this work even 'can be seen as forming an "Austrian School of Strategy"'.[11]

A similar shift has occurred in the study of entrepreneurship, though this field (at least the research done outside economics departments) never adopted as fully the streamlined economic models on which strategic management was originally based. Entrepreneurship is here commonly perceived as some form of open-ended *change*, whether it is the fundamental 'driving force of the whole market system', as Mises puts it,[12] or simply the act of creating firms.[13] As it constitutes a process of change, the concept and its impact on the market are profoundly difficult to express in formal notation. As a result, entrepreneurship could never rely on the models of modern economic theory as was the case in strategic management. This may be a reason why, as William J. Baumol noted, '[t]he theoretical firm is entrepreneurless – the Prince of Denmark has been expunged from the discussion of *Hamlet*'.[14]

Expunged is probably a proper description. Since at least the early eighteenth century, studies in economic theory have placed the entrepreneur at the centre. Richard Cantillon, for instance, defines entrepreneurship as working for non-fixed income (and therefore the bearing of uncertainty)[15] and saw in the entrepreneur the force that brings equilibrium to the market.[16] Adam Smith, commonly regarded as the 'father' of economics, saw in the 'undertaker' an agent that transforms demand into supply.[17] Jean-Baptiste Say saw the entrepreneur as a speculator who runs the firm for profit.[18] The common denominator of these classical approaches to entrepreneurship is that the concept is considered primarily in terms of the role or function it plays in the economy. Modern entrepreneurship, in contrast, has to a great extent approached entrepreneurship as an empirical phenomenon, in which entrepreneurship is measured as 'self-employment' or as the degree of non-concentration in an industry.[19]

It was not until the work of Scott A. Shane and Sankaran Venkataraman,[20] who suggested the study and implications of the entrepreneurial opportunity as common denominator for studies in entrepreneurship, that theorising without direct basis in empirical observation regained its foothold in the field of entrepreneurship. Shane and Venkataraman relied heavily on the work of Israel M. Kirzner in reformulating the study of entrepreneurship, and contrasted Kirzner's 'alert' entrepreneur with a conception of Joseph A. Schumpeter's 'disruptive' innovator-entrepreneur.[21] This has ultimately led to Austrian economics having a strong influence in entrepreneurship.

The use of Austrian concepts in strategic management is as prevalent as in entrepreneurship, but far from as explicitly attributed. Whereas entrepreneurship theory was built on an openly Austrian foundation, strategic management research only infrequently recognises that many of the field's core concepts have already been used, elaborated on, and scrutinised by the Austrians. While there are indeed a number of studies in strategic management that explicitly use an Austrian approach or even adopt Austrian theory, the measurable relative influence of Austrian economics has not increased. Instead, concepts such as resource heterogeneity, uncertainty, and dispersed knowledge – and their implications – are reinvented and drafted anew, and used as means to deal with problems arising due to the reliance on formal economic models. This may at times give a thoroughly strategic management flavour to these concepts that can seem to create a distinct paradigm, but it also subjects the field to costs as already developed theoretical concepts, which can be common knowledge in the Austrian tradition, are reinvented and suffer problems achieving consistency. The latter, in fact, is in line with a warning drafted by Jacobson, who cautioned that while Austrian economics is a mature theoretical framework and therefore both useful and valuable, it is also highly integrated due to its strictly deductive method; this means that 'inconsistencies can arise when attempting to integrate other frameworks with Austrian paradigms'.[22] This may turn out to be a severe problem in strategic management as the field borrows, whether or not intentionally or even knowingly, several core concepts from Austrian economics, and it can equally become a problem in entrepreneurship theory as it originated as an application but not elaboration of Austrian theory. But, as we shall see in the next section, the same type of problem is latent also in Austrian theories of the firm.

Coase and the Austrians

Austrian approaches to studying the firm face similar problems as those we just discussed with respect to theories in strategic management including Austrian concepts and constructs. The approach, however, is the obverse: they take Austrian theory as starting point and then add concepts, theoretical devices, and reasoning from mainstream (non-Austrian) theories of the firm to it.[23] In contrast to typical Austrian theorising then, which maintains consistency through strict deductive reasoning, Austrian approaches to the firm place mainstream conceptualisations within an Austrian 'market process' framework. In order to make the pieces fit, the framework is often made out to hinge on a single or couple of Austrian core concepts (such as knowledge, capital theory, entrepreneurship, or uncertainty). Consequently, we see Austrian theories that discuss how concepts in mainstream economic theories of the firm, like transaction costs, incomplete contracting, monitoring costs, and so on, relate to, can be combined through, are supported, or otherwise further explained by utilising an approach that at least in part is or derives from Austrian thinking. By placing 'bridging' Austrian concepts at the core of the theory, which supposedly adds an explanatory dimension to existent mainstream theories, an argument is indirectly generated for the value of incorporating core components of Austrian economics in mainstream theory development. But doing so could also introduce inconsistencies. The product is in any case a theoretical amalgamation that appears to be mainstream in many ways and therefore builds on strengths perceived in the already established theories, but is presented with a distinctly Austrian flavour.

Whereas these approaches purport to indicate steps towards an integrated framework that can explain economic organisation on Austrian terms, they predominantly attempt to achieve this goal by relying on the unorthodox method of 'combining' Austrian with decidedly non-Austrian theoretical constructs. As these constructs have different histories, are from different bodies of theory, and commonly are formulated using very distinct (and, at least to some extent, incommensurable) assumptions and reasoning, they risk appearing more as a jumble of concepts inspired or held together by an Austrian-style market process argument than an integrated theory. As I concluded elsewhere, 'the existing [Austrian] attempts fail to convincingly explain why there are firms because they are too narrowly focused on specific characteristics rather than on the firm in the market'.[24] It should, in fact, be difficult to imagine an Austrian approach to explaining economic organisation that does not see the firm as having or supplying a distinct and important function to the integrated market system in which it is thoroughly embedded. The firm should be both affected by and effectuate change in the market process. In this sense, the firm cannot be seen as 'only' a governance choice for certain types of transactions or applicable under a certain set of conditions or in specific situations (as several theories suggest), but should – considering the firm's relative omnipresence in the market – play a more substantial role in how the market process works. The firm, seen from an Austrian point of view, should provide a function that fits in the broader scheme of things.

At this point it may be appropriate to address the question of how we define a 'firm'. But this is exactly the problem with existing theories of economic organisation, whether they are Austrian or mainstream – there is no established definition of the phenomenon, so common in the market, that we refer to as a 'firm'. Instead, the theoretical literature suggests (at least) four distinct definitions or rationales for the firm: as a technological necessity, as having a nature that is distinct from the market, as a means for avoiding costs of using the price mechanism, or as an accumulated collection of resources.[25] As can easily be seen, there is no reason to assume that all four rationales are necessarily and always present where there is a firm, which makes the situation theoretically unsatisfying. If we for a moment assume that firms are more than simple 'legal fictions',[26] by which we mean that economic organisation provides an actual and real economic function regardless of legal status, it should be clear that the empirical observation that firms are ubiquitous in advanced markets cannot properly guide the development of Austrian theory. This is not to say that empirical observations are unimportant, but quite the opposite. The fact that business firms are practically 'everywhere' should to theorists of the firm indicate that there may be more to this phenomenon than suggested by either of the simple rationales relied on in the extant literature, and that it therefore could play a more important role in the market process than, for example, offering a means for avoiding some costs of market transacting. Cost minimisation through choosing the 'cheaper' means of coordination can of course be a benefit of the firm, as is Coase's argument, but the full out adoption of the mainstream market/hierarchy duality as one's theoretical point of departure does not necessarily follow from this statement.

Despite this, many Austrian theories adopt Coase's transaction cost theory of the firm, or in any case its argument or assumptions, as starting point. While it is true that Coase introduced the comparative institutional analysis of economic organisation in a nice way, there is reason to think that Coase's framework is incompatible with Austrian theory. His theory of the firm was intended as a defence of economic planning, and it was in support of planning in the market (Coase's conception of the firm) that he introduced the concept of transaction costs – a kind of cost affecting market exchange yet that somehow exists outside economic actors' opportunity cost assessments and therefore has no effect on efficient resource allocation.[27] Coase's point was that the market is 'costly' because resources are heterogeneous and market coordination is not rationally planned, and it follows from this that rational planning (by definition unaffected by this cost) would tend to be less costly. Coase explains that this is the reason such a 'large sphere' of the Western market economies are not coordinated through market exchange but are instead planned within firms, and contrasts this 'decentralised planning' through firms in the market with the centralised economic planning in Soviet Russia (as Coase notes, Lenin had said the country would 'be run as one big factory').

Setting the political connotations aside, Coase's economic argument stands in stark contrast to how Austrian economists understand the market and how they conceive of capital heterogeneity and the implications thereof. To Austrians, as to Coase, it is ultimately the fact that resources in production are heterogeneous, produced, and non-permanent that makes economic planning costly (if not impossible). But Austrians would argue, along the lines of Mises's argument against socialist economic planning, that this is what makes the market an unbeatable (though still, it must be emphasised, *imperfect*) coordination mechanism for advanced specialised production – not the other way around. It is Coase's decidedly un-Austrian framework that allows him to conclude that 'planning' is superior to and therefore a multitude of firms are formed to supersede the market's price mechanism.

Whereas Coase's analytical approach of comparative institutionalism is rightly accepted and appreciated by Austrians, it is difficult to see why the rest of his argument should be. Rather than using a theoretically streamlined but otherwise realistic 'imaginary construction' (the common method in Austrian theorising) to isolate causal links and interdependencies in the real economy, Coase's assumptions intentionally do away with any structural differences so that only the means of coordination remains to distinguish the firm from the market. The conclusion that the choice (which to Coase appears to be made by the economy rather than by an actual actor) of coordinating force between price mechanism and manager is a matter of selecting the least costly alternative is neither interesting nor important – it follows directly from the stated assumptions. This is an important difference between Coase's analysis and the deductive theoretical framework of Austrian economics. Coase relies on a set of strong assumptions without obvious grounding in theory, whereas the Austrian approach incorporates assumptions within a causal-realist framework that provides a bulwark against arbitrariness.

An Austrian theory of economic organisation

Coase's theory ultimately challenged the theory of economic organisation at the time and thereby the body of literature in economic organisation that developed in the 1920s and 1930s. While inspired by E. Austin G. Robinson, an influential Cambridge economist who had written on the logic of industrial organisation,[28] Coase's approach deviated from Robinson's in one important respect: he assumed that the firm's internal organisation is practically a carbon copy of the market's allocation of resources,[29] which facilitated his marginal transaction analysis and allowed him to conclude that there is a strict cost rationale for the firm. The common starting point in the literature at the time, in contrast, was that the firm is defined *contra* the market by its more intensive division of labour. This difference means that the boundary of the firm, according to Coase's theory, is the result of a simple cost comparison between different means for allocating resources, whereas 'pre-Coaseans' like Robinson derived organisational boundaries from real differences in productivity through resource heterogeneity and specialisation intensiveness.

The latter view was further developed in the works of Edith Penrose,[30] who with mentoring assistance by Austrian economist Fritz Machlup,[31] authored an influential book on the evolution and growth of firms. The modern resource-based view of the firm, which applies a strict strategic management perspective on the value creation and value capture problems that arise due to resource heterogeneity, is based on Penrose's non-Coasean approach as derived from the work of Robinson and Machlup. As will emerge through the discussion in subsequent chapters, this legacy of Robinson – and the classical economics approach to the study of the firm that it was based on – should be a much more appropriate starting point for developing a dynamic theory of the firm. Not only is this particular approach evolutionary and dynamic in the same sense that Austrian economics provides a framework for studying and understanding the market as a process, but it already includes several concepts that are compatible with the Austrian approach.

Nevertheless, an Austrian theory of the firm should probably not assume it as a starting point. Considering the deductive and integrative nature of Austrian theory, it would be a mistake to do more than take inspiration from other schools of thought – especially if they are based on different (or even incommensurable) assumptions. Despite how it is commonly approached, the economic theory of the firm is not a specialisation, but an elaboration and extension of the existent body of economic theory aimed at providing an answer specifically to the question of economic organisation. This answer cannot, obviously, contradict the theoretical framework, but can suggest a potential theoretical challenge to existing emphases or applications. In order to be true, a deductive theoretical framework and all its parts need to constitute a consistent whole; what remains, therefore, for Austrian theory to properly provide an answer to the so-called Coasean questions of the firm's rationale, boundaries, and internal organisation is to extend the theory by applying it on and emphasising the particular issues that pertain to organisation. Indeed, as Mises notes, '[t]here is no specialization [in economics], as all problems are linked with one another. In dealing with any part of the body of knowledge one deals actually with the whole.'[32] The point of departure for producing an Austrian theory of economic organisation, therefore, must be the existent body of Austrian theory and consequently the Austrian understanding for what constitutes and drives the market process. It follows that an Austrian theory of the firm should be based on or, at a minimum, be related to core Austrian concepts such as knowledge, capital theory, entrepreneurship, and uncertainty. It should also fit with the theoretical framework – and in fact constitute a missing piece of the puzzle.

As finding and theorising on this piece is the task for this book, our focus must first and foremost be on what specific problem the firm can solve in the market process, by which we mean that organising certain economic activity within the firm must have a value for those involved in the firm as well as the market process as a whole. The former is a question of how the firm attracts labour and capital factors, and the latter addresses the overall value of the structure to the market as such. It is not sufficient to address either of these aspects without also addressing the other ones, as it is not sufficient to address either of the Coasean questions separately, since what then emerges as a potential solution may not fit with the overall theoretical framework. The take-home here is that the theory of economic organisation must be built on yet be ultimately delimited (if not restricted) by the theory of the market.

It should be noted that existing approaches to explaining the firm from an Austrian perspective usefully adopt a similar problem-focused methodology. From our perspective, however, they do so in a very limited sense by phrasing the question to be answered in terms of a gap in the theoretical framework rather than a real economic problem. The integrated economic function of organisation for market actors in the market process becomes an implication rather than a core contribution of the theory. Granted, this allows for the approaches to focus primarily or even exclusively on a specific concept or sub-theoretical orientation (such as capital theory or entrepreneurial discovery or judgment) while purporting to – at least indirectly – inquire into the nature of relationships that exist in the market (or, if we wish, between firms and markets). But the approach in effect emphasises trees at the cost of failing to appreciate the extent of – or even see – the forest. But the nature of economics is such that we are unlikely to fully understand the tree, as a phenomenon that arises within an economic or market context, without first considering the tree as embedded within and part of the forest. In other words, we have to deal with the market embeddedness of the firm in order to understand it, and we therefore need to target its function within the broader market context. This is the point of departure for this book.

Summing up

The discussion above indicates not only that there is a seemingly unoccupied space for a theory to explain the firm from the point of view of the market process, but also that there are several theories, approaches, and frameworks that we can draw from. While a new theory of the firm can provide important insights, and it is indeed the purpose of this book to draft one, it is unnecessary to adopt a completely different approach and 'reinvent the wheel' completely. Yet to take the firm's embeddedness seriously, it is necessary to derive the firm's function from limitations that the market suffers without it. In this sense, we start from the beginning by discussing the market process and how it functions without firms. We look specifically at production as the core activity within the market process, and then elaborate on whether market production is subject to a fundamental problem or shortcoming, which can potentially be solved by entrepreneurs only through economic organising. The next chapter discusses the market as a dynamic process.

Notes

1 R. H. Coase, 'The Nature of the Firm', *Economica*, 4:16 (1937), pp. 386–405.
2 Coase, 'The Nature of the Firm', p. 388.
3 This highly abstract concept was criticised by Lionel Robbins, one of Coase's professors at the London School of Economics, to whom the concept of 'a long-period average business unit, representative of the organisation of a given line of production' is both 'superfluous' and 'misleading'. This concept, which 'lurks in the obscurer corners of Book V [of Marshall's *Principles*] like some pale visitant from the world of the unborn waiting in vain for the comforts of complete tangibility', had nevertheless garnered 'discernible' influence in 'certain recent discussions of applied economics'. L. C. Robbins, 'The Representative Firm', *Economic Journal*, 38:151 (1928), pp. 387–404, pp. 391, 399, 387.
4 See Book IV, A. Marshall, *Principles of Economics*, 8th edition (1890) (New York: Macmillan, 1920).
5 I have made the argument that Coase's contribution should be considered a challenge to, and also attempt to undermine, this literature elsewhere. See P. L. Bylund, 'Ronald Coase's "Nature of the Firm" and the Argument for Economic Planning', *Journal of the History of Economic Thought*, 36:3 (2014), pp. 305–329.
6 Notable contributions to this literature include: A. A. Alchian and H. Demsetz, 'Production, Information Costs and Economic Organization', *American Economic Review*, 62:5 (1972), pp. 777–795; S. J. Grossman and O. D. Hart, 'The Costs and Benefits of Ownership: A Theory of Vertical and Lateral Integration', *Journal of Political Economy*, 94:4 (1986), pp. 691–719; O. D. Hart, 'An Economist's Perspective on the Theory of the Firm', *Columbia Law Review*, (1989), pp. 1757–1774; M. C. Jensen and W. H. Meckling, 'Theory of the Firm: Managerial Behavior, Agency Costs, and Capital Structure', *Journal of Financial Economics*, 3:4 (1976), pp. 305–360; B. Klein, R. A. Crawford, and A. A. Alchian, 'Vertical Integration, Appropriable Rents, and the Competitive Contracting Process', *Journal of Law and Economics*, 21:2 (1978), pp. 297–326; O. E. Williamson, *Markets and Hierarchies, Analysis and Antitrust Implications: A Study in the Economics of Internal Organization* (New York: Free Press, 1975); O. E. Williamson, *The Economic Institutions of Capitalism* (New York: Free Press, 1985).
7 L. v. Mises, 'Economic Calculation in the Socialist Commonwealth', in F. A. v. Hayek (ed.) *Collectivist Economic Planning* (London: George Routledge & Sons, 1935), pp. 87–130; L. v. Mises, *Socialism: An Economic and Sociological Analysis* (1936) (New Haven, CT: Yale University Press, 1951). For a connection between Mises's and Coase's arguments, see Bylund, 'Ronald Coase's "Nature of the Firm" and the Argument for Economic Planning'.
8 Noteworthy examples include: N. J. Foss and P. G. Klein, *Organizing Entrepreneurial Judgment: A New Approach to the Firm* (Cambridge: Cambridge University Press, 2012); P. Lewin, *Capital in Disequilibrium: The Role of Capital in a Changing World* (London and New York: Routledge, 1999); F. E. Sautet, *An Entrepreneurial Theory of the Firm* (London: Routledge, 2000).
9 P. L. Bylund, 'Toward a Framework for Behavioral Strategy: What We Can Learn

from Austrian Economics', in T. K. Das (ed.) *Behavioral Strategy: Emerging Perspectives* (Charlotte, NC: Information Age Publishing, 2014), pp. 205–232; P. G. Klein and P. L. Bylund, 'The Place of Austrian Economics in Contemporary Entrepreneurship Research', *Review of Austrian Economics*, 27:3 (2014), pp. 259–279.

10 M. E. Porter, *Competitive Strategy: Techniques for Analyzing Industries and Competitors* (New York: Free Press, 1980); M. E. Porter, 'The Contributions of Industrial Organization to Strategic Management', *Academy of Management Review*, 6:4 (1981), pp. 609–620; M. E. Porter, *Competitive Advantage: Creating and Sustaining Superior Performance* (New York: Free Press, 1985).

11 R. Jacobson, 'The "Austrian" School of Strategy', *Academy of Management Review*, 17:4 (1992), pp. 782–807, pp. 784, 802.

12 L. v. Mises, *Human Action: A Treatise on Economics. The Scholar's Edition* (1949) (Auburn, AL: Ludwig von Mises Institute, 1998), p. 249.

13 Daniel F. Spulber, *The Theory of the Firm: Microeconomics with Endogenous Entrepreneurs, Firms, Markets, and Organizations* (Cambridge: Cambridge University Press, 2008).

14 W. J. Baumol, 'Entrepreneurship in Economic Theory', *American Economic Review*, 58:2 (1968), pp. 64–71, p. 66.

15 R. Cantillon, *Essai sur la Nature du Commerce en Général* (1755) (London: Macmillan & Co., 1931).

16 M. N. Rothbard, *An Austrian Perspective on the History of Economic Thought, Volume I: Economic Thought before Adam Smith* (Auburn, AL: Ludwig von Mises Institute, 1995), p. 352.

17 A. Smith, *An Inquiry into the Nature and Causes of the Wealth of Nations* (1776).

18 J.-B. Say, *A Treatise on Political Economy or the Production, Distribution and Consumption of Wealth* (1821) (Auburn, AL: Ludwig von Mises Institute, 2008); see also M. N. Rothbard, *An Austrian Perspective on the History of Economic Thought, Volume II: Classical Economics* (Auburn, AL: Ludwig von Mises Institute, 1995), pp. 25–27.

19 See P. G. Klein, 'Opportunity Discovery, Entrepreneurial Action, and Economic Organization', *Strategic Entrepreneurship Journal*, 2:3 (2008), pp. 175–190.

20 See especially S. A. Shane and S. Venkataraman, 'The Promise of Entrepreneurship as a Field of Research', *Academy of Management Review*, 25:1 (2000), pp. 217–226; S. A. Shane, *A General Theory of Entrepreneurship: The Individual–Opportunity Nexus* (Cheltenham, UK: Edward Elgar, 2003).

21 I. M. Kirzner, *Competition and Entrepreneurship* (Chicago, IL: University of Chicago Press, 1973); J. A. Schumpeter, *The Theory of Economic Development: An Inquiry into Profits, Capital, Credit, Interest, and the Business Cycle* (1911) (Cambridge, MA: Harvard University Press, 1934).

22 Jacobson, 'The "Austrian" School of Strategy', p. 803.

23 P. L. Bylund, 'Division of Labor and the Firm: An Austrian Attempt at Explaining the Firm in the Market', *Quarterly Journal of Austrian Economics*, 14:2 (2011), pp. 188–215.

24 Bylund, 'Division of Labor and the Firm: An Austrian Attempt at Explaining the Firm in the Market', p. 191.

25 Sautet, *An Entrepreneurial Theory of the Firm*, pp. 5–6.

26 Jensen and Meckling, 'Theory of the Firm: Managerial Behavior, Agency Costs, and Capital Structure'.

27 Bylund, 'Ronald Coase's "Nature of the Firm" and the Argument for Economic Planning'; see also, H. Demsetz, 'R. H. Coase and the Neoclassical Model of the Economic System', *Journal of Law and Economics*, 54:4 (2011), pp. S7–S13.

28 See e.g., E. A. G. Robinson, *The Structure of Competitive Industry* (London: Nisbet, 1931); for a discussion on Robinson's influence on Coase, see L. R. Jacobsen, 'On Robinson, Coase and "The Nature of the Firm"', *Journal of the History of Economic*

Thought, 30:1 (2008), pp. 65–80. See also E. A. G. Robinson, 'The Problem of Management and the Size of Firms', *Economic Journal*, 44:174 (1934), pp. 242–257.

29 Indeed, Coase argued that the 'object of the organization was to reproduce market conditions', that is to say 'to reproduce [its] distribution of factors ... within the business unit'. R. H. Coase, 'The Nature of the Firm: Origin', *Journal of Law, Economics and Organization*, 4:1 (1988), pp. 3–17, p. 4.

30 For Robinson's influence, see L. R. Jacobsen, 'On Robinson, Penrose, and the Resource-based View', *European Journal of the History of Economic Thought*, 20:1 (2011), pp. 125–147; see also E. T. Penrose, *The Theory of the Growth of the Firm* (New York: John Wiley & Sons, 1959).

31 C. M. Connell, 'Fritz Machlup's Methodology and the Theory of the Growth of the Firm', *Quarterly Journal of Austrian Economics*, 10:4 (2007), pp. 300–312.

32 Mises, *Human Action: A Treatise on Economics. The Scholar's Edition*, p. 869.

2 The extent of the market process

This chapter introduces a model of the market as a dynamic process with actors incentivised in their market positions to respond to changes and thereby adjust their activities as well as positions in the marketplace. The model is intended to capture the ceaseless processes and forces of a specialised market in which production is coordinated exclusively through decentralised exchange. These exchange transactions constitute the backbone for allocation of resources throughout the economy's production apparatus and are also the means by which market prices are determined. Market production is specialised under the division of labour and market actors consequently assume specific roles in advanced production processes. In this model, actors rely fully on decentralised market exchange and price discovery to procure inputs and sell produced outputs. The price mechanism is therefore the sole coordinator of tasks within, and resource allocation between, existing advanced production processes in the market.

The discussion places emphasis on the role of productive capital in the market and how it relates to and is facilitated by specialisation under the division of labour. The last section before summing up the chapter elaborates on the dynamic and distinctively responsive nature of this decentralised market model, in which trade facilitates actors' particular contributions to and provides the means to coordinate existing advanced production processes. Production in this model therefore benefits from intensive specialisation, as is the case also in Coase's theorised market situation. In contrast to Coase, however, we make no assertions regarding the function or benefit of firm organising or how it comes about. Instead, we let the firmless market process play out in order to identify potential limitations, the topic of the subsequent chapter, and then, when and where we find such limitations, elaborate on possible means by which market actors can overcome them or at least lessen their effect. The market model thereby supports our inquiry into the rationale, nature, boundaries, and function of the firm.

Our basic assumption in this inquiry is that the firm is a market occurrence and institution. From this follows that we cannot explain the function of the firm without first knowing something about the market that specifies the setting where firms may emerge. Firms, we assert, must form and operate (and potentially dissolve) in specific market contexts. Individual firms, then, are outcomes of specific actions and instituted for certain purposes in their particular market context.

The function and value of the firm, consequently, is derived from the market setting and – more importantly – contingent on the (primarily production facilitating) value it contributes in the specific situation. To properly identify the function of the firm in a dynamic market setting, we must identify and study the market not as equilibrium or stasis but as a process.

Our approach is based on the market process analysis common to Austrian economics, which aims to explain the process dynamics and the interrelatedness between levels of analysis in an economic system. While focus for Austrians is generally on the individual economic actor, the effects of individual actions can be observed as structural changes to the institutions, incentives, and processes that form the economic system. The market therefore becomes a web of interactions between actors positioned in different market settings, which compose an adaptive system in constant flux that corrects for errors and responds to change in particular ways.

Whereas the method recognises that the individual is the actor and is therefore based in methodological individualism, it also acknowledges that the actor is fully embedded within a market context and influenced by it. There is therefore a fundamental and ongoing interaction between the actor and structure, which in aggregate produces an overall market process. The method is for this reason very well suited for studying and working through the process of firm formation. Firms, from this point of view, emerge as the result of either some individual pursuit or concerted, coordinated actions of several individuals. We will see in subsequent chapters how this method helps establish a logic for firm formation that is based on the function provided by firms in the market. This chapter, specifically, drafts the model for a decentralised, dynamic exchange market in which reasons to form firms can emerge.

Market process analysis

Market process analysis is perhaps best explained by providing an example of how it can be used. We have already seen that it will here be used for the purpose of explaining the firm's function in the market by illuminating what specific problem can be solved by a conception of the firm. To do this, the following sections of the chapter discuss the basic, firmless market model. But, more importantly, what we focus on in this and subsequent chapters is the processes and evolution of the market context in which there may emerge a reason for firm formation. The model of the market that serves as starting point for our reasoning is dynamic rather than static, which is to say that it is both realistic and 'thick'; it bears very little resemblance, therefore, with the streamlined and 'perfect' models used in comparative static equilibrium analysis. It is still a simplification, however, as any model necessarily is.

An illuminating example of the power of market process analysis in economic theorising can be found in Carl Menger's classic 1892 essay 'On the Origin of Money'. As we do here, Menger sets out to explain a market phenomenon – money – by deliberating on its role or function and possible origins: how it emerged and took its present form. States Menger:

It must not be supposed that the *form* of coin, or document, employed as current-money, constitutes the enigma in this phenomenon. We may look away from these forms and go back to earlier stages of economic development, or indeed to what still obtains in countries here and there, where we find the precious metals in an uncoined state serving as the medium of exchange, and even certain other commodities, cattle, skins, cubes of tea, slabs of salt, cowrie-shells, etc.; still we are confronted by this phenomenon, still we have to explain why it is that the economic man is ready to accept a certain kind of commodity, *even if he does not need it, or if his need of it is already supplied*, in exchange for all the goods he has brought to market, while it is none the less what he needs that he consults in the first instance, with respect to the goods he intends to acquire in the course of his transactions.[1]

Menger hypothesises an original situation in which economic man, presumably self-sufficient, awakens to the gains possible to him through 'primitive traffic' of goods with others. Even primitive man has an incentive for engaging in trade, and it is, he notes, 'obvious even to the most ordinary intelligence, that a commodity should be given up by its owner in exchange for another more useful to him'. This constitutes Menger's basic model of an exchange market prior to (without) money. He then identifies that development in line with the interests of economic actors faces a fundamental obstacle in the very rare occurrence of the double coincidence of wants. In this situation, Menger says,

> each man is intent to get by way of exchange just such goods as he directly needs, and to reject those of which he has no need at all, or with which he is already sufficiently provided. It is clear then, that in these circumstances the number of bargains actually concluded must lie within very narrow limits.[2]

Without an existing institutional framework or formal organisations to facilitate the introduction and universal adoption of a currency, how does money – the generally accepted means of exchange – emerge? Menger notes that goods have different degrees of 'saleableness' and that this provides economic actors with the means to bypass the requirement for double coincidence of wants. Indeed, it is easily realised that 'the person who wishes to acquire certain definite goods in exchange for his own is in a more favourable position, if he brings commodities of this [more saleable] kind to market'. So due to the fact that goods have different 'saleableness', economic man is induced to engage in *indirect* exchange. He thus procures not what he personally values but what is more easily traded in the market. This way, he becomes better able to offer in exchange what is valued by those selling what he directly values. As people more and more turn to indirect exchange to satisfy their wants, the relative saleableness of the goods commonly chosen for indirect exchange increases and they therefore become more attractive for this purpose. Hence, a medium of exchange emerges from indirect barter trade. And so it is, writes Menger, clear that nothing may have been so favourable to the genesis of a medium of exchange as the acceptance, on the part of the most discerning and capable economic subjects, for their own economic gain, and over a considerable period of time, of eminently saleable goods in preference to all others. In this way practice and habit have certainly contributed not a little to cause goods, which were most saleable at any time, to be accepted not only by many, but finally by all, economic subjects in exchange for their less saleable goods: and not only so, but to be accepted from the first with the intention of exchanging them away again.[3]

And, *voilà*, a generally accepted medium of exchange – money – arises unintendedly out of a mass of individual self-interested actions. The existence of an accepted currency then facilitates trade and functions as a store of value that makes possible productive investments. A modern-style money economy thus arises from barter trade through the institution of money.

Our approach to explaining the function (and emergence) of the firm is similar to Menger's and uses the same method, but the model of the market is different in that it assumes a specialised exchange economy with elaborate production processes. Reasoning from a firmless model of the market is common practice in theories of the firm, since it provides a counterfactual against which a rationale for organising a firm can be identified. This is also the starting point in Ronald Coase's ground-breaking essay on the firm, though Coase did not elaborate on the specifics of the firmless (or even the firm-inclusive) market structure. Where he referred to economic theory as contrasting model – an economic system that 'works itself', presumably the model of perfect competition – we shall here in line with Menger's approach provide a fuller picture by drafting the particular characteristics of the firmless market process.

The reason for this is that in order to provide a satisfactory argument that explains why there are business firms in the market, it is not sufficient to assume a viable and unchanging equilibrium state. Doing so can at best produce a simple and under-contextualised static rationale for organising, as with the four distinct rationales for the firm we revisited in the previous chapter, either as a reason for establishing firms in an otherwise firmless market state or for why firms have value in a market already populated with firms. Yet an equilibrium explanation consisting solely of an independent rationale is likely to be both arbitrary and irrelevant. The reason for this is that a rationale without indicated implications for individual economic actions, as well as value for the market structure in the aggregate, may be inapplicable and extraneous, and therefore spurious. For this reason, an argument for *why* there are firms, such as the theoretical rationale provided by Coase and others, must also at least indicate a reasonable explanation that applies also to the progression from non-firm to firm. That is, it must suggest a process or method that describes *how* firms come to be and, by extension, why they prevail (if they do) or dwindle. Without addressing the 'how', the economic rationale explains little if anything; it may be an explanation valid only *ex post*.[4]

At a minimum, therefore, an explanation of why there are firms must include two states: the market state prior to the existence of the firm, and that subsequent to its founding. Without both states, we cannot explain how firms are formed and therefore cannot produce a sufficient rationale or argument for why and how there are (or would be) firms. This is the reason for Coase's contrast between the economic theory version of the market that 'works itself' and the empirical market with an abundance of firms, and also for Oliver E. Williamson's conjecture that 'in the beginning there were markets'. But with two states, the argument must properly fill the void between them and so must take account of the step by step process of organising, without which a market fails to move from the previous to the latter state. The task is therefore to produce an image of what this process looks like, which can only be done by first drafting the before state, postulate the after, and tracing the economic actions that constitute and bring about the aggregate transformation of the market from the one to the other. The states must be consistent, rely on similar assumptions, be subject to the same argumentation, and be realistic in order to be persuasive and relevant. These requirements do not pose a big problem, however, since the transformation follows from the original state, and the end state follows from the transformation. What matters is therefore that the starting point presents a theoretically rigorous structure based on realistic assumptions.

Yet assuming two states, whether or not they are considered stable equilibria, with an in-between process of change, suggests that the object of our study by definition must be the *process*. This can be conceived of as a process from an otherwise stable original state. But this assumption makes little sense, and should add little if any value, since the very purpose and intent of the analysis is to introduce a process of change that brings about a new state – in the same way Menger did with money. Also in line with Menger's analysis, it is important to recognise that the change process must be constituted by actions taken by individual economic actors (presumably for their own benefit). It would therefore be absurd to consider the original state to be a static equilibrium. Rather, it should be neither stable nor unchanging, since the very purpose of the exercise is to trace the effects of actions taken and how they change the market structure. There should be little rationale for actors to bring about change from within a state of equilibrium, since the concept indicates stasis and thus disallows action. This is indeed a problem with Coase's model, which contrasts two presumably stable but not necessarily unchanging market states (perfect competition and the empirical market) without a bridging process. It consequently requires a force affecting (or introducing) transaction costs in such a way that the cost comparison between coordination mechanisms change – and firms therefore are formed or dissolved. But we cannot reasonably assume that the creation of market organisations is caused solely by exogenous forces, and therefore the model must allow for and indeed support endogenously initiated and produced emergence of firms. Two things follow from this: we must assume the market is an ongoing *process*, and the firm then becomes a solution to some problem experienced in this market and therefore it should have a specific economic *function*.

It is also not clear that the new state, following the creation of firms, can in fact be considered a state at all, since it is by definition the effect of the change process that is the object of our study – with actions at different levels of maturity – and therefore should be in a flux. Whether or not the market *post*-firm creation could be thought of as eventually settling or stabilising around a certain number of firms, a certain market-equilibrating, standard, firm size, or with a particular market structure (which, with some imagination, the Marxian analysis of capitalism may entail), such a 'final state' is beyond the scope of this discussion. Of interest here are the economic forces that bring about integration in business firms, and therefore the function of the firm; it matters not if the firm creation process will eventually result in a particular pattern. In fact, if the firm can be thought of as fulfilling a specific economic function, then it is not unreasonable to assume that this function – especially in its specific implementation in a particular firm – may be temporary rather than permanent. Yet this is a discussion for later chapters.

The only reasonable starting point is therefore to assume a market in a disequilibrium state: a market that is continuously changing but includes no formal organisation. This does not presuppose that this original market model is the ultimate starting point for economic activity per se. On the contrary, in order to explain the function of economic organisation in the marketplace, the starting point must rather be an advanced, specialised exchange economy where firms do not yet exist. This is indeed the model adopted by Coase as well as more recent theorists on the firm. Assuming an advanced market state *sans* business firms offers the advantage of intensifying the comparative problem that the firm supposedly solves and thereby simplifying the identification of its function. However, we must keep in mind that the firm's function could be core to the development of the market itself and therefore make sure to allow for this possibility in the model. For this reason, the model of the market prior to the creation of firms must be 'thick' rather than 'thin', and therefore better specified than streamlined formal models in the sense that it takes into account existing theoretical and empirical evidence. This means the model should be realistic so that it resembles, at least in terms of function and procedure, the real market and is characterised by intensive division of labour and therefore specialisation. Consequently, our starting point is a 'real' market in terms of its core characteristics, and processes, only without formal organisations.

Heterogeneity of the capital stock

The existence of a market entails the existence of specialisation through an intensive division of labour. Specialisation allows production tasks to be performed more productively, and as production processes are divided into specific and separable tasks they can be carried out by independent labour workers. This division of labour results in a number of specialisations that are dependent on each other to complete production processes. Our model of the market therefore comprises a web of exchanges between unorganised, specialised labour workers.

Their performed work together composes the economy's production through what Ludwig von Mises referred to as 'social cooperation'. Of interest here is the interdependence of labour workers carrying out individual stages of a particular production process in this 'web', what we might denote vertical rather than horizontal. The product of one worker's labour is used as the input of another's, but while the flow of intermediate products through production processes tends to be unilinear, the workers throughout the process are *mutually* dependent. Any labour worker who produces an intermediate stage is dependent both on the producer of the previous stage for supplying their input, on any producer of necessary tools to assist in production, and on the producer of the subsequent stage for demanding and procuring their output. Without either, the labourer is unable to carry out its task and must find another means to earn a living as this specific market position fails the market test.

To the extent that a production process is divided into minute tasks of very limited scope, those parts of the process are simplified to such a degree that work previously carried out by a skilful labourer can, at least in part, be automated and therefore replaced by machinery. It is the highly intensive division of labour and thus the splitting up of a production process into very limited and simplified tasks that facilitates the development and use of capital goods. As Mises identified:

> The division of labor splits the various processes of production into minute tasks, many of which can be performed by mechanical devices. It is this fact that made the use of machinery possible and brought about the amazing improvements in technical methods of production. Mechanization is the fruit of the division of labor, its most beneficial achievement, not its motive and fountain spring.[5]

Considering this explanation, it is difficult to imagine an intensively specialised market that does not also include a large body of specific capital goods that support its intricate production processes. It may even be necessary to develop a highly advanced exchange economy. The automated production apparatus, generally referred to as simply 'capital', is what facilitates the increased productivity of labour that entails economic growth beyond its initial division into separate tasks. The generation of productive capital, developed specifically to support labour workers or relieve them of the already separate and thereby simple and oftentimes repetitive tasks of production, constitutes 'a "division of capital," a specialization of individual capital items, which enables us to resist the law of diminishing returns'.[6] This division, however, builds on and develops the already existent division of labour, and we can think of the two 'divisions' as facilitating each other's further intensifying and thereby overall continuous productivity improvements in the market.

Our model of the specialised exchange market captures this mutual facilitation by assuming a particular intensiveness of the division of labour throughout the market's production apparatus along with the corresponding (or, if I may, enabling) division of capital. We hence assume that production processes have already been decomposed into specific productive tasks carried out by differently specialised workers using tools and machinery developed to be suitable in assisting workers who carry out these or related tasks. There is, therefore, an existing market for both specific labour factors and capital, which are both readily available and so procurable in the open market at market prices.[7] This is similar to the market model implied in Coase's work, even though he does not explicitly discuss the nature of capital. That capital is heterogeneous, however, is a necessary condition for Coase's argument about transaction costs to apply.[8]

Our model of the open market is functional only to the extent that there are multiple possible uses for heterogeneous resources. Should this not be the case, by which we mean that all assets are purely or perfectly specific, then the market is severely limited in its fundamental allocative function since any particular asset will have only one specific use or usage.[9] Where this is the case, the perfect specificity of a resource completely undermines the allocative function of the market. Indeed, perfect specificity implies that there can be only *perfect* substitutes, which is the case where there is a supply in excess of one of any particular resource, since any conceivable deviation between resources' composition or usability suggests a different use specificity. Under perfect specificity the only possible use of a resource is either discovered or not, and its only use represents its full market value. Consequently, under such circumstances where pure specificity is the prevailing condition of capital, the market is needed neither for allocating resources nor estimating their use value.[10] The conclusion that it is necessary that resources are less than perfectly specific for the market to carry out its allocative function properly, whether or not this is done at a cost (as in Coase's model), is therefore not simply an empirical observation – imperfect resource specificity is a necessary precondition for the market.

Perfect capital specificity is however inconceivable, other than possibly for brief moments and for certain capital goods, since the usability limits of a resource are not exclusively based on its physical composition. Whereas there are physical limitations that limit technological uses for a resource, capital is fundamentally *use* specific and therefore the crucial limitation lies in the imagination of those persons willing to put it to use. What makes a resource usable is what also makes it an economic good: its perceived value in imagined specific uses. Specific capital goods, whether or not they are developed for carrying out a single and highly specific task, must therefore in general have multiple specificities,[11] which means that they can be used in several different ways and for different purposes.

A simple tool like a wooden cane is sufficiently unspecific to be usable as a measuring rod and a walking stick as well as for fencing, fishing, pointing, poking, drawing in the sand, and so on. A surgical instrument, developed for a very specific use and purpose, may have a much more limited number of valuable uses. But it is not the level of sophistication and detail in how a particular resource is produced or designed that determines its possible uses and, therefore, value. While any object has distinct physical attributes, only some are of economic significance. While observable physical attributes may define the resource to buyers and sellers in the market, it is the possible uses or functions of the resource, which are subjectively perceived and therefore existent in the eyes (or, rather, the mind) of the beholder, that makes it valuable. These imagined uses ultimately make the resource serviceable towards certain ends as well as re-combinable with other resources, and this is what characterises productive capital from an economic point of view. As Ludwig Lachmann puts it:

> Beer barrels and blast furnaces, harbour installations and hotel-room furni-ture are capital not by virtue of their physical properties but by virtue of their economic functions. Something is capital because the market, the con-sensus of entrepreneurial minds, regards it as capable of yielding an income.[12]

Since uses are perceived by actors in the market, who are different in many ways (that is, with differing experiences, knowledge, imagination, judgment, and so on) and have different ends in mind, it follows that all uses may not yet be known and hence some of them are yet to be discovered. What limits the use of a resource is both its physical composition and the imagination of the person wishing to use it. This means that different resources as well as their distinct uses should also be *combinable*. In fact, most resources available in the market are composites that were themselves created by combining other, possibly less advanced, resources. For instance, a wooden beer barrel, to use Lachmann's example above, can be produced by combining other capital goods in process (wood staves, iron hoops, and barrel lids) using expert labour assisted by specific capital goods that aid production (tools such as a mallet, handsaw, sandpaper, and so on). Each of these capital goods, components used in production, are themselves resources with sets of uses that exceed that of barrel-making. Whereas wood staves are in beer barrel production goods in process, they may be production-aiding capital goods in other production pro-cesses. Ultimately, all resources in the market are products of mixing untouched nature (or what economists call 'land') with some amount of labour. We can therefore think of capital goods as the 'produced' means of production.[13]

Coase's market model appears to treat production as simply a problem of coordinating the necessary allocation of heterogeneous (but rather generic) 'factors' of production (capital goods in process, production-aiding capital, and labour). His coordination problem is therefore limited to finding the proper force to direct resources towards maximising economic uses – price mechanism or manager – but excludes the generation and maintenance of advanced capital structures to aid production. The combinability of resources suggests that they can be combined into structures to produce new and – if successful – even more productive capital. A market's productive apparatus can then be thought of as a capital structure, which is decomposable to particular capital structures produced with specific purposes in mind. Not only does the combination of capital resources bring about structures that support highly specific production processes (both in terms of function and aim), but this process also changes the landscape for economic action. Some combinations are irreducibly combined such that the implementation of the structure changes their physical composition (and there-fore also their imagined uses) – perhaps to such extent that they can never again be returned to their previous state. Part of this reason is due to the non-permanent nature of capital goods, which – even if they are relatively durable – as they are used begin to diminish in terms of serviceableness and ultimately may lose it altogether. More importantly, perhaps, is that the act of combining – the imple-mentation of the combination – causes or necessitates changes to the physical composition of the individual components that may only be reversible at high cost or are completely irreversible. It may not be possible to again put wooden staves to their previously available alternative uses when they have already been combined into beer barrels (for example, if they have been cut, soaked in beer, etc.). This limits or thwarts their use as production-aiding capital goods in other production.

Also, even disregarding changes to the physical composition of goods due to combining, the creation of new capital to support specific production changes goods prices throughout the market. The new capital structure, when aimed at replacing less effective capital, changes both the perceived produc-tive value of its substitutes and the quantity supplied of the structure's output; it may also change requirements for labour factors operating it as well as maintenance and upkeep. Such innovations therefore always to some extent skew and otherwise affect the fabric of the market structure, which changes prices as well as resource allocation throughout. This change should be expected, since the creation of capital effectively *heterogenises* the capital stock in the market. In a market for wood staves and iron hoops, the innova-tion of the beer barrel both adds to the uses for wood staves and iron hoops and creates sub-categories of different usability (perhaps only certain sizes can be usefully employed in barrel-making, and perhaps wood staves with knot-holes cannot so that this new use creates two separate classes of wood staves where there used to be only one). This development also supports production of goods previously unseen, which can be produced using beer barrels or the combination of beer barrels and the previously existent wood staves or iron hoops. This new market situation, which includes wood staves, iron hoops, and beer barrels along with tools to support barrel production (and, possibly, other intermediate products used in the process), offers more types of resources for sale through the creation of the new, specific resource (the beer barrel). It has also established a new productive relationship between certain types of wood staves and iron hoops and the tools used: they are now, from the point of view of use in beer barrel production, complements.

We need not delve further into capital theory, even though it is a fascinat-ing and highly important (but underdeveloped) topic.[14] It is sufficient for our purposes to emphasise that the productive structure in a market is interdepend-ent through its division of labour and therefore also its division of capital, as the latter is ultimately produced to assist and facilitate the former, and there-fore reactive to change. This dimension of dynamic, capital-generating market production is completely absent from Coase's and other theories of the firm. But we here observe that the market's production capital consists of hetero-geneous capital resources that have been and probably can still be combined in order to bring about specific capital structures aimed at particular produc-tion processes and tasks. We also acknowledge that, from the perspective of a specific production process, capital exists in two types: goods in process (wood staves, iron hoops) and capital goods used to aid production (tools, skilled labour). The purpose and use of the latter type is to assist labour factors in production of goods valued by consumers; it is the means by which the pro-ductivity of labour is improved. As can easily be seen, the effectiveness of a labour worker focused on beer barrel production without tools is considerably lower than a labour worker with proper tools. The specific characteristics of a produced capital structure (advanced tools, machinery, etc.) that aids the pro-duction of other capital goods or consumer goods determines what can be pro-duced and how, and facilitates further development as well as limits existing choices. As capital is traded in the market, whose function is to allocate resources towards their most productive uses, even seemingly minor changes to the composition of capital goods affect the capital stock[15] via entrepreneurs and capitalists bidding for resources they consider suitable to their productive ends and, consequently, support their aim for profits.

The effect of the beer barrel above is that the market now has information of more uses for wood staves and iron hoops in production, which affect previously existing production structures. The market availability of these resources dimin-ishes as their overall demand increases with the discovered uses, which brings about a reallocation of capital from the less productive structures to those that are more efficient from the consumers' point of view. While there may not, at least in our limited illustration, be any immediately available substitutes for the only just invented beer barrel, the increased relative demand for wood staves and iron hoops and tools used in barrel production causes their respective prices, as well as the prices of their substitutes, to go up. For this reason, production pro-cesses throughout the market are eventually affected by this change, though in differing degrees.

This market-based interdependence *between* structures of particular produc-tion processes within the capital stock suggests a curious problem that is the topic of the following chapter. But in order to elaborate on this problem and attempt a solution, we must first delineate the nature of and process through which structures of particular production processes throughout the market are affected by a change in the composition of capital used in other production pro-cesses. This is necessary since the discussion so far seems to imply that any extension of the divisions of labour and capital constitute an improvement in overall wealth production through increased productivity throughout. While this is true in general terms, the structure of the market impedes and ultimately resists implementation of further divisions.

The structure and extent of the market

Adam Smith notably opens *The Wealth of Nations*[16] with a discussion on the productive powers of the division of labour. The splitting of a production process into parts, and the specialisation of labour to these separate, more narrowly defined tasks, he writes, 'occasions ... a proportional increase of the productive powers of labour'.[17] As we saw above with the development of capital to replace or assist labour in production, the productivity of labour can be further increased so as to even 'resist the law of diminishing returns'. Yet the market structure poses a constraint on this development and therefore a limitation to what efficiency in production is practically and economically feasible. Adam Smith formulated this constraint thusly:

> As it is the power of exchanging that gives occasion to the division of labour, so the extent of this division must always be limited by the extent of that power, or, in other words, by the extent of the market. When the market is very small, no person can have any encouragement to dedicate himself entirely to one employment, for want of the power to exchange all that surplus part of the produce of his own labour, which is over and above his own consumption, for such parts of the produce of other men's labour as he has occasion for.[18]

Smith here points to an important limitation, but fails to properly understand it. This can easily be seen when considering his discussion on the spontaneous and unintended process of intensifying the division of labour, which is the result of individual decisions incentivised by man's 'propensity to truck, barter, and exchange':

> The division of labour, from which so many advantages are derived, is not originally the effect of any human wisdom, which foresees and intends that general opulence to which it gives occasion. It is the necessary, though very slow and gradual, consequence of a certain propensity in human nature which has in view no such extensive utility; the propensity to truck, barter, and exchange one thing for another.[19]

But in order to act on their propensity and so engage in specialisation, there must already exist a market of sufficient size to support their specialised employment. Such a market can scarcely exist until other labourers have already engaged in similar specialisation and thereby created demand for the specialised output. It is not sufficient for an aspiring specialist labour worker to anticipate a market for the specific goods produced unless there is also a market supplying necessary inputs. To again make use of the example of beer barrel production discussed above, it is possible, and potentially profitable, to specialise in producing beer barrels from wood staves and iron hoops. But this requires a market (or at least the expectation of a market) for beer barrels and an existing market for the capital goods in process and the capital goods to aid production. (More on this in Chapter 3.)

Smith finds a similar paradox as the one above in terms of accumulating the stock of goods necessary for the division of labour, which is the prerequisite for accumulating such stock:

> As the accumulation of stock must, in the nature of things, be previous to the division of labour, so labour can be more and more subdivided in proportion only as stock is previously more and more accumulated. The quantity of materials which the same number of people can work up, increases in a great proportion as labour comes to be more and more subdivided; and as the operations of each workman are gradually reduced to a greater degree of simplicity, a variety of new machines come to be invented for facilitating and abridging those operations. As the division of labour advances, therefore, in order to give constant employment to an equal number of workmen, an equal stock of provisions, and a greater stock of materials and tools than what would have been necessary in a ruder state of things, must be accumulated beforehand. But the number of workmen in every branch of business generally increases with the division of labour in that branch, or rather it is the increase of their number which enables them to class and subdivide themselves in this manner.[20]

Smith here rather blatantly avoids the crux of the problem by assuming both that there is a firm in which labour workers are employed, and through which productive tasks are 'subdivided' and coordinated, and that 'new machines come to be invented' to support this directed division of labour. These assumptions only beg the question, since the real problems are in effect avoided by assumption. Further, it is clear that Smith does not talk about productive innovation in terms of task-splitting or Schumpeterian entrepreneurship (as we will in subsequent chapters), but continuous and quite undramatic change. In fact, judging from the discussion he seems to treat production tasks almost as continuous functions that can be easily narrowed so that operations can be '*gradually* reduced to a greater degree of simplicity' (emphasis added). This all suggests that Smith, while identifying an important limitation, failed to realise the problem of specialisation in the absence of authoritative direction.

All the same, it is for our purposes sufficient to note that a labour worker's specialisation in a single task ultimately can relieve other labourers of the necessity to carry out this particular task and therefore facilitates their specialisation – not the other way around. This should be especially obvious within integrated and highly specialised production processes within 'manufactures' such as a pin factory, Smith's well-known illustration of the productive power of the division of labour. We will return to the process of intensifying specialisation below, as it is core to our understanding of the function of the firm.

While Smith ultimately appears to place the cart before the horse in theorising on the intensification of the division of labour, the limitation of productive specialising by the extent of the market is nevertheless real. Productivity increases with specialisation, especially when supported by the development of aiding capital goods, but the increased heterogeneity in the employments of labour and development of capital requires improved coordination as the individual factors of production become more limitedly compatible. This suggests the benefits of specialisation are neither automatic nor unlimited. Indeed, the intensity and feasibility of the divisions of labour and capital appear limited by the extent of the market for those capital goods used within the particular production process. This is particularly the case when taking the perspective of the individual labour worker who specialises, and thus the market extent as it appears from his or her particular market position – both in terms of supply of necessary capital, demand for intermediate goods produced, and demand for the final product.

Emile Durkheim elaborates on Smith's observation and explains that this market access limitation lies primarily in the perceived economic *density* between factors. The availability of potential trading partners both constitutes the opportunity and limits a labour worker's 'power of exchanging': this 'power' consists of, as we noted above in response to Smith, the total availability of suppliers of inputs and purchasers of produced output, the preconditions for both production and market exchange through specialised production processes. Density is then defined as an actor's reach or the ability 'to act and react upon one another ... and the active commerce resulting from it'.[21] Market production under the division of labour should here be understood as an intricate web of mutually beneficial exchange relationships – or, in the words of Mises, the 'social cooperation' that emerges under the division of labour. The market's density is not fixed or without variation. For instance, Durkheim notes that there may be a higher specialisation intensity in cities than in rural areas. Cities may have greater diversity in the pattern of consumer demands, but what concerns us here is primarily the great variety of production that typically takes place in and around cities – the extent of the market within specialised production processes.

Within any production process, high levels of density imply a situation of increased capital substitutability since in general the economic 'distance' to (and consequently the cost to discover) equivalent or alternative capital resources is shorter (lower). This also has implications for Coase's model, in which transaction costs are a function of the relative economic distance between factors used in a transaction.[22] In other words, in dense market situations (where density refers to the relative availability of compatible exchange partners within or across production processes) any market actor is in a position where he or she can choose from several or many suppliers of inputs and simultaneously has access to a sufficiently sized market for the sale of produced outputs (intermediate goods used in continued production or finished consumer goods). This state of affairs greatly increases the ability to make economically beneficial choices based on the better (more data points as well as providers of) information through market prices, but it also entails more intense competition as any labourer's position in the production structure is fully substitutable through readily available competing suppliers of the specific task or service. This results in a market that is highly dependent on and realised through simple exchange and it is therefore reasonable to think that the velocity of exchange, the number of exchange transactions in any time period, in a dense market greatly exceeds that of sparsely populated markets. It is, in other words, more fiercely competitive but also prospectively enables greater overall responsiveness to exogenous changes such as in consumer tastes or preferences.

But while the dense market should more smoothly carry out its allocative function and therefore establish more efficient structures of particular production processes sooner (at lower cost), dense markets are also – due to competitive discovery (see Chapters 8 and 9) – extensively standardised. Indeed, as competitive pressure increases there is less opportunity (and it may even be unfeasible) to deviate from the market's standard division of labour. The costs of incompatibility with competitively priced inputs as well as the markets for standard outputs may be prohibitively high.[23] Such deviation from the market standard, which can be a result of individual and uncoordinated specialisation, is simply not economically feasible where the lack of density is too persistent. Even minor deviations can have a severe impact on the individual labour worker, since limited substitutability may entail or give rise to incompatibility for cost reasons. Greater deviations may cause outright incompatibility and therefore exclusion from the market.

A lacking market density establishes limits of the market, but the primary effect of density is otherwise to enable and make possible a division of labour. Without sufficient density, labour and capital cannot develop or adopt highly specific uses and therefore there can be no division of a production process into narrowly defined (and highly interdependent) tasks and functions. This is problematic since the very process of extending the division of labour, which increases heterogeneity to the degree of uniqueness through intensive specialisation, requires an already established density for exchange of the specialised outcome. This appears to turn the Smithian logic on its head. It also suggests a paradox where the act itself undoes the conditions necessary for its viability: a labour worker choosing to specialise further than others have already done places him- or herself outside the extent of the market's production, since there is no compatible supply of necessary input or demand of produced outputs.

This can be illustrated by the pin factory example in Adam Smith's *The Wealth of Nations*. Smith observes in his example that within the pin factory a company of ten workers, each specialised to performing 'two or three distinct operations', can 'make among them upwards of forty-eight thousand pins in a day' whereas 'separately and independently' they 'certainly could not each of them have made twenty, perhaps not one pin in a day'.[24] The high degree of resource complementarity within the pin factory is due to the resources already being 'jointly employed' as 'means to the same end'.[25] But such highly complementary production structures, with relatively low (if any, at the outset) substitutability, are feasible only where sufficient resource availability and density is already provided. In fact, the awesome productivity observed in the pin factory is possible only because the factory satisfies and controls the availability of inputs and outputs for each separate and highly specialised task.

While a telling illustration, the generality of which we will have occasion to analyse further below, specialisation does not, of course, only exist within the 'manufactory'. Indeed, Smith's example would make little sense were it not for specialisation already being implemented in the market within which the pin factory is placed. Pin-making is itself a specialisation, so the pin factory has only further intensified the division of labour by splitting the market standard task of pin-making into several distinct serially dependent specialisations. This difference is at this point of little concern to us, since our original model of the market does not include business firms such as pin factories and the issue therefore falls outside the scope of the discussion at present. But it is important to note that specialisation, whether or not there are business firms, can potentially exist at different intensities throughout the market – both between disparate industries and between implementations of similar production processes. Already implemented levels of specialisation intensiveness would tend to harmonise over time due to competitive pressures. But this tendency constitutes an incentive for the development and thus introduction of more intensive divisions of labour, since individual actors could increase earnings by specialising further to take advantage of achieved productivity gains.

We should keep in mind, however, that specialisation is dependent on a previously existent level of perceived market density. This dependence ultimately limits the possibilities of utilising the productive power of specialisation, and poses an interesting contradiction since the adoption of more intensive specialisation is dependent on having already realised the fruits of specialising (both the development of necessary capital and the generation of market density to support further specialising). We shall now expound on the dynamics of the market under specialisation, which will reveal how the divisions of labour and capital are mutually constituting and necessary for the adoption of more highly specialised production structures. Even though the market is characterised as a dynamic entrepreneurial process, it will become clear how the market's density constitutes a real limitation to its further development.

Entrepreneurial adjustments of production

The starting point for this discussion is an advanced exchange market that suffers from some degree of imperfection in the allocation of productive resources. The production apparatus is divided into numerous specialised production processes that utilise specific capital to support labour in carrying out productive tasks. However, the market is not perfectly competitive; it is imperfect in the sense that it is not in a stable efficient equilibrium state, but in disequilibrium. We can think of this market as a previously equilibrated developed market that has not yet fully adapted to the effects of change caused by some disruptive force (exogenous or endogenous). In other words, some number of exchange transactions remain to re-establish fully coordinated and aligned production and therefore equilibrium. The remaining imperfections in this market state have the form of underutilised labour or capital in existing production processes, opportunities for reorganising existing or establishing new production processes, introducing new capital or products, and so on. We further assume that some equilibration has already taken place so that the market is not completely uncoordinated but includes some properly coordinated elements. A market without coordination is not a market, since a market is based on exchange and therefore has some form of price mechanism that coordinates production. The alternative is self-sufficiency and non-specialisation. The market we consider here is specialised and relies on exchange to allocate resources, but it has not reached its end state. In other words, there are opportunities for profit and thus room for improvement. What remains is for profit incentives to play out through free market exchange towards the efficient equilibrium state.

Assuming there are no changes to the market data except for progress made by adjustments in resource allocation through exchange, the market as a whole is involved in the activity of reallocating scarce resources to their better or best possible ends. As underlying market data do not change, there is no real economic problem other than finding maximising uses of specific resources. To the degree that these uses are obvious, which is the case under perfect information where market actors simply react to known prices and arbitrage between price discrepancies, this is neither costly nor difficult. Where the information available is imperfect, it may not be possible to fully equilibrate the market and market actors may make mistakes simply because they do not have access to sufficient information. Coase's theory of the firm assumes that productive resources are allocated efficiently in the market, but that the market is a costly means to coordinate production. His claim is that the discovery of relevant prices, which guide market actors in their exchanges and therefore bring about reallocation of resources, is costly when relying on the price mechanism in the market. This cost does not apply within firms, which is the Coasean rationale for forming a firm.

Our model of the market is imperfectly coordinated and subject to reoccurring exogenous change, which alters the conditions for market coordination by changing the underlying market data and therefore relative prices. It also includes open-endedness and therefore unknowability about future market conditions. Were this not the case but future states of the market were known to actors, then resource allocation would not be much of a problem. Certainly, as conditions change, discrepancies occur between the previously established allocations and their new maximising allocation. This produces opportunities for market actors to reallocate resources through exchange and thereby bring about a more productive resource allocation. With perfect information about ends, which are revealed in consumer valuations of products and services, this type of constant 'adaptation' of the market's production structure presents a comparatively simple problem. Israel M. Kirzner refers to it as 'Robbinsian maximising', where given resources are put to such uses that maximise the outcome from a given and known set of ends.

While this 'problem' may be an interesting mathematical exercise, Kirzner notes that '[a] multitude of economizing individuals each choosing with respect to given ends cannot ... generate a market process'.[26] Indeed, a market consisting of given and known sets of means and ends from which actors simply choose, whether or not the market is affected by exogenous changes, poses no real economic problem. Where both means and ends are known, which means all market data are readily available for the actor, all actions are necessarily maximising. There are no unknowns and therefore no open-endedness with respect to choices in the market. We cannot therefore expect actors to make errors, which would be made against better knowledge, since doing so will most severely hurt themselves in the competitive marketplace – and they would know this outcome.

In a market with Robbinsian maximising we also cannot expect to find an economic reason for establishing formal organisations, since resource allocation is already maximised through exchange. Organisations can provide no advantage when all relevant information is known and therefore there is no uncertainty and, consequently, no coordination problem. The market under Robbinsian maximising is in this sense 'perfectly' competitive, though occasionally (or perhaps frequently) affected by exogenous changes that alter the market data, and it is therefore in effect devoid of competition. The proper and known response to exogenous changes is to reshuffle and reconfigure production processes through exchange, and the market should therefore quickly re-establish efficient allocation, that is, equilibrium. Needless to say, this type of market bears little resemblance with the real market's immense coordination problem with unavailable or tacit knowledge, uncertainty, and open-endedness.

If we introduce variability in the means available and ends sought such that new means–ends combinations can be discovered, it follows that market actors can no longer simply be maximising the outcome of choices among a set of alternatives. This suggests that people suffer from a knowledge problem, since they are no longer able to figure out or calculate what the best means towards specific ends are, and that the market process becomes, in effect, a solution to the knowledge problem. If consumer preferences can change over time, which is a relevant as well as empirically necessary assumption, consumers cannot know what possible ends will maximise their economic situation. In effect, they should at the time of choosing be at least partly ignorant of what ends will be economically feasible, since much of the market data that *ex post* maximising depends on are not yet in existence. Action takes time, and production under specialisation is quite time consuming (imagine setting up a new automobile manufacturing plant, which can take several years). This introduces uncertainty and open-endedness, which means *ex ante* maximising may no longer converge with *ex post* maximising, and Robbinsian maximising therefore becomes impossible. The problem becomes acting based on access to data that are available *ex ante* and therefore may only be limitedly relevant to the market situation at the time the action is completed. This lack of knowledge makes the outcome of market action uncertain.

It should be no surprise, then, that many actions taken in the market will result in errors of some kind: improper choice of means, unknowingly aiming for faulty or impossible ends, or a combination. The errors will be revealed only when the relevant data become available *ex post facto*, and then these errors become opportunities for profit.[27]

These emergent errors, whether they are greater or smaller in magnitude than those occurring in the market prior to the actions taken, present profit opportunities for entrepreneurs willing to invest in adaptation of established production processes. These further adaptations, which take place in a market setting brought about by previous entrepreneurial action, will be profitable only to the extent they constitute improvements to the existing capital structure from the point of view of satisfying *future* consumer preferences. One role of entrepreneurship is therefore to adjust and adapt production, which is the result of prior entrepreneurship, as conditions change or new data become available. Kirzner suggests a similar entrepreneurship-on-entrepreneurship market dynamic when he states that the

> pattern of decisions in any market period differs from the pattern in the preceding period as market participants become aware of new opportunities. As they exploit these opportunities, their competition pushes prices in directions which gradually squeeze out opportunities for further profit-making.[28]

However, this 'squeezing out' of profit opportunities by successful entrepreneurship seems to be unsupported under the stated assumptions. For Kirzner's above-quoted statement to be true, it is necessary to hold consumer preferences constant. Because if consumer preferences are unchanging, whether or not they are known, entrepreneurship amounts to a collective trial and error process towards fixed but unknown ends. Even if the market is subject to exogenous changes that change the conditions for market action, fixed consumer preferences limit the entrepreneurial problem to finding the maximising allocation of resources in production. Entrepreneurs can then make improvements to the capital structure that was established through previous (imperfect) entrepreneurship, and opportunities for profit will be 'squeezed out' as more successful entrepreneurship is added and thereby brings the market process closer to maximised consumer satisfaction. Changing conditions only create speed bumps in this equilibration process by altering the data on which production was established.

In fact, we can make the case that, under constant consumer preferences, the market process in the aggregate will be equilibrating even where entrepreneurial activity overall is guided by profits but specific entrepreneurial decisions are made at random. Random investments in production processes will tend to improve productivity overall as long as feedback is available through profits. The reason for this is that the relatively more accurate production processes will generate greater profits and therefore facilitate increased investment and attract more entrepreneurs, and vice versa. Over time, this produces an equilibrating (increasingly productive) production structure even if processes are tried at random but evaluated by their ability to satisfy consumer wants. Entrepreneurship here boils down to simple arbitrage between processes, which even without qualities such as foresight or 'alertness' will tend to eventually 'squeeze out' opportunities for further improvements. The profit–loss system therefore brings about a market process that is equilibrating. Entrepreneurs do not need to do more than simply follow revealed profit opportunities or identify existing price discrepancies, since the end is unchanging even if the means are not.

The picture is different under changing consumer preferences, where entrepreneurs no longer aim for a fixed (though unknown) target. With a moving target, what worked yesterday may be an error today, and may therefore need adaptation. On the other hand, what did not work yesterday, may work today. Arbitrage activities that take time (that is, all actions, and especially those that for their success rely on first instituting some change to the capital structure) is estimated using two bases, of which only one can possibly be known *ex ante*. An entrepreneur at time t will make a decision for entrepreneurial action based on some knowledge of the existing capital structure $c(t)$ and the existing consumer preferences $p(t)$. His or her knowledge of the present may indicate a means-ends mismatch to the extent $p(t)$ will not be fully satisfied by $c(t)$, which is an opportunity for further improvement. However, the preferred entrepreneurial action cannot be finished until time $t+1$, at which time the capital structure has changed to $c(t+1)$ as a consequence of other entrepreneurs' attempts to improve the production structure to earn profits. Consumer preferences have also changed during this time, to $p(t+1)$. As the entrepreneur at the time of making the decision is not yet at time $t+1$, the nature of the market at this future point in time is unknown. While the entrepreneur does not have the full capital structure at his disposal, at least part of it can be acquired at present market prices and adapted towards satisfying an anticipated end at $t+1$. Yet this end, as Frank H. Knight recognised, is at best 'an estimate of an estimate' where the entrepreneur not only 'forms the best estimate he can of the outcome of his actions, but he is likely also to estimate the probability that his estimate is correct'.[29]

The outcome of the entrepreneurial actions, since they are intended to change the capital structure, is $c(t+1)$ – a combination of his own actions including adaptations made to the share of the capital structure that he controls and the actions of other entrepreneurs. Profitability is achieved where the part of the capital structure controlled by the individual entrepreneur, $c'(t+1)$, corresponds to some subset of consumer preferences at that time $p'(t+1)$. Of course, the individual entrepreneur's achieved profit is also a function of the degree to which other entrepreneurs are equally successful, that is the correspondence between the overall capital structure $c(t+1)$ and consumer preferences $p(t+1)$. The realisable value of the imagined opportunity is an added uncertainty to the entrepreneur's imagined opportunity, since the value is based not solely on his actions to change the capital structure and the created capital configuration's correspondence to consumer preferences, but also the degree to which other entrepreneurs have not successfully exploited this previously not existing opportunity space.

The process of changing the capital structure from $c(t)$ to $c(t+1)$ can be thought of as capital 'regrouping' for the sake of better serving consumers' needs on a macro scale.[30] It consists of entrepreneurs aiming their acquired or by other means controlled capital towards maximising its estimated value in production by satisfying consumer wants. While such decentralised decision-making generates numerous errors, and therefore entrepreneurial losses, from the point of view of the yet to be revealed future market, it is not a random but guided process. Capital is always configured to produce goods and services that entrepreneurs imagine will be serviceable to consumers. This 'imagination' is based on the entrepreneur's personal experiences as well as a developed understanding of consumers and what they need, want, or cherish. The latter is ultimately an expression of the entrepreneur's own life experience and a function of his understanding and comprehension of humanity and human life, likely based on revealed preference through previous market actions, verbally expressed preference or discontentment, and conjecture. The entrepreneur's inability to think outside his humanness results in a path-dependency in market production that limits the scope and frequency of errors.

Over time, failing entrepreneurs in the market amass losses that make continued market action impossible and they are as a result replaced by those who have exercised better entrepreneurial judgment. The market will for this reason in the long run tend towards increased wants satisfaction even though the market may not at all times be equilibrating. The development of productive capital, non-permanent but durable, increases the overall productivity of the market for some time. This lasting increase in productivity, a sort of inertia of capital's structure, retains a level of productivity even in the face of clusters of entrepreneurial error. It also makes the economy vulnerable to radical, exogenous change that fundamentally alters market institutions and thereby changes the play of the market and, ultimately, the 'rules of the game'.

More importantly, this indicates a limitation to the unfolding of the market process where the inertia of created capital structures cannot easily or costlessly be changed. Furthermore, the regrouping and reconfiguration of capital, part of which may include the creation of new capital, pushes the boundary for the path-dependent evolution of the capital structure. Capital is ultimately heterogenised through the creation of novel combinations, which initially places the new capital good outside the boundary of the market since it neither has nor can have buyers and sellers. The market for a newly created capital good is initially non-existent as it is not a substitute for any already used capital good, and has yet to prove its contribution in production. Its creator therefore risks losing the full investment as the good's second best productive use may be of very limited market value – if one exists. The problem of creating capital is in this sense similar to the relationship-specific investments that engender asset specificity in Oliver Williamson's transaction cost analysis of integration,[31] but it here emerges as of a more general nature. While a created capital good's specificity to a particular transactional relationship may aggravate the economic problem in cases where actors are expected to act opportunistically (as in Williamson's system), this is not necessary to make the situation problematic from a specialisation and market compatibility view. Indeed, both Adam Smith and Durkheim would agree that a new capital good without obvious substitutes would fall outside the extent of the market since it has no viable alternative uses within the market production structure. It is for this reason neither demanded nor offered in the market for capital goods, has no obvious or proven independent production value, and consequently lacks a determined market price. What exists is the entrepreneur's anticipated contribution to market value as it is eventually taken into use within existing production processes.

This limitation translates to a more general as well as fundamental market problem since the development of capital is a necessary precondition for and dependent on the further division of labour. While we can think of innovative entrepreneurs willing to assume the risk of creating new capital beyond the extent of the market (that is, where the produced capital lacks an existing market), a division of labour and therefore the development of more productive production processes requires the availability of labourers willing to specialise to production tasks that are *also* beyond the market boundary. Such specialised tasks would be fully dependent on the creation of specific capital as well as other labourers willing simultaneously to assume a similarly vulnerable position.

Summing up

To summarise our discussion in this chapter, we described a dynamic market process that is self-regulating by offering the means to respond to change through decentralised decision-making. While they appear to be uncoordinated, individual actions are guided by the price mechanism towards allocating a resource to better uses. In essence, exogenous changes cause price discrepancies that entrepreneurs exploit for profit. The market process can thereby adequately respond to, and consequently deal with, changes in the conditions for market exchange, even though capital assets are heterogeneous and therefore have different uses.

Whereas arbitrage transactions can be quick, production is a time-consuming endeavour; it is therefore necessarily temporal, and consequently subject to 'Knightian' uncertainty. We further found that production in the market benefits from intensive specialisation under the division of labour, which increases overall productivity and facilitates exchange. Yet whereas specialisation increases productivity, the division of labour is limited by the extent of the market. The market is thus subject to its established economic density, which means it is unable to facilitate production solutions that are not already saleable in the open market – they fall outside the extent of the market. This, as we shall see in the next chapter, poses an intriguing and potentially important problem in the market process.

Notes

1 C. Menger, 'On the Origin of Money', *Economic Journal*, 2:6 (1892), pp. 239–255, p. 239.
2 Menger, 'On the Origin of Money', p. 242.
3 Menger, 'On the Origin of Money', p. 249.

4 In published simulation tests, Coase's theory of the firm provide a rationale that may only be applicable *ex post*. See P. L. Bylund, 'Signifying Williamson's Contribution to the Transaction Cost Approach: An Agent-based Simulation of Coasean Transaction Costs and Specialization', *Journal of Management Studies*, 52:1 (2015), pp. 148–174.

5 L. v. Mises, *Human Action: A Treatise on Economics. The Scholar's Edition* (1949) (Auburn, AL: Ludwig von Mises Institute, 1998), p. 164.

6 L. M. Lachmann, *Capital and Its Structure* (1956) (Kansas City, MO: Sheed Andrews & McMeel, 1978), p. 79.

7 These prices are ultimately determined by entrepreneurs and capitalists, who, in accordance with their judgment of what type of production will generate future profits, bid for particular resources that they intend for specific uses in imagined or already realised production structures and processes. The derived valuation of these resources, on which their bidding is based, is in turn based on their appraisement of the value of final goods for the consumer. This type of dynamic market price determination through 'imputation' is discussed in, e.g. L. v. Mises, 'Economic Calculation in the Socialist Commonwealth', in F. A. v. Hayek (ed.) *Collectivist Economic Planning* (London: George Routledge & Sons, 1935), pp. 87–130; L. v. Mises, 'Profit and Loss', in *Planning for Freedom: Let the Market System Work* (Indianapolis, IN: Liberty Fund, 2008), pp. 143–172.

8 P. L. Bylund, 'Ronald Coase's "Nature of the Firm" and the Argument for Economic Planning', *Journal of the History of Economic Thought*, 36:3 (2014), pp. 305–329.

9 For a discussion on production in a world with only specific factors, see M. N. Rothbard, *Man, Economy, and State with Power and Market. Scholar's Edition* (1962) (Auburn, AL: Ludwig von Mises Institute, 2004), pp. 329–333.

10 Complete and rational planning may not lead to calculative chaos in this situation, since the market value of a resource, which is equal to the physical contribution to production of a specific consumption good, can be perfectly imputed from the value imbued by consumers. For a discussion on calculative chaos due to rational planning, see L. v. Mises, *Planned Chaos* (Irvington-on-Hudson, NY: Foundation for Economic Education, 1947). See also Mises, 'Economic Calculation in the Socialist Commonwealth'; L. v. Mises, *Socialism: An Economic and Sociological Analysis* (1936) (New Haven, CT: Yale University Press, 1951).

11 Lachmann, *Capital and Its Structure*; L. M. Lachmann, 'Complementarity and Substitution in the Theory of Capital', *Economica*, 14:54 (1947), pp. 108–119.

12 Lachmann, *Capital and Its Structure*, p. xv.

13 It is technically more accurately to see capital as 'non-permanent' rather than 'produced', since the problem of capital is not simply its production but its maintenance and upkeep to permanently increase the production of valuable output (and hence income). See F. A. v. Hayek, *The Pure Theory of Capital* (London: Routledge and Kegan Paul, 1941).

14 For important contributions to capital theory, see E. v. Böhm-Bawerk, *Positive Theory of Capital* (1889) (South Holland, IL: Libertarian Press, 1959); Hayek, *The Pure Theory of Capital*; I. M. Kirzner, *An Essay on Capital* (New York: Augustus M Kelley Publishers, 1966); Lachmann, *Capital and Its Structure*; P. Lewin, *Capital in Disequilibrium: The Role of Capital in a Changing World* (Auburn, AL: Ludwig von Mises Institute, 2011); M. Skousen, *The Structure of Production* (New York: New York University Press, 1990); R. v. Strigl, *Capital & Production* (1934) (Auburn, AL: Ludwig von Mises Institute, 2000).

15 The capital stock of a market or society is sometimes referred to as its 'subsistence fund'. See Hayek, *The Pure Theory of Capital*, ch. VII.

16 A. Smith, *An Inquiry into the Nature and Causes of the Wealth of Nations* (1776) (Chicago, IL: University of Chicago Press, 1976).

17 Smith, *An Inquiry into the Nature and Causes of the Wealth of Nations*, p. 9.

18 Smith, *An Inquiry into the Nature and Causes of the Wealth of Nations*, p. 21.
19 Smith, *An Inquiry into the Nature and Causes of the Wealth of Nations*, p. 17.
20 Smith, *An Inquiry into the Nature and Causes of the Wealth of Nations*, pp. 291–292.
21 E. Durkheim, *The Division of Labor in Society* (1892) (New York: Free Press, 1933), p. 257.
22 As Coase notes,

> Inventions which tend to bring factors of production nearer together, by lessening spatial distribution, tend to increase the size of the firm. Changes like the telephone and the telegraph which tend to reduce the cost of organising spatially will tend to increase the size of the firm.

R. H. Coase, 'The Nature of the Firm', *Economica*, 4:16 (1937), pp. 386–405, p. 397.
23 P. L. Bylund, 'Explaining Firm Emergence: Specialization, Transaction Costs, and the Integration Process', *Managerial and Decision Economics*, 36:4 (2015), pp. 221–238.
24 Smith, *An Inquiry into the Nature and Causes of the Wealth of Nations*, p. 9.
25 L. M. Lachmann, 'Complementarity and Substitution in the Theory of Capital', *Economica*, 14:54 (1947), pp. 108–119, p. 111.
26 I. M. Kirzner, *Competition and Entrepreneurship* (Chicago, IL: University of Chicago Press, 1973), p. 33.
27 I. M. Kirzner, 'Economics and Error', in L. M. Spadaro (ed.) *New Directions in Austrian Economics* (Kansas City, MO: Sheed Andrews & McMeel, 1978), pp. 57–76.
28 Kirzner, *Competition and Entrepreneurship*, p. 15.
29 F. H. Knight, *Risk, Uncertainty and Profit* (1921) (Chicago, IL: University of Chicago Press, 1985), pp. 227, 226.
30 Lachmann, *Capital and Its Structure*, pp. 35–52; Lewin, *Capital in Disequilibrium: The Role of Capital in a Changing World*, p. 134.
31 See e.g. O. E. Williamson, *The Economic Institutions of Capitalism* (New York: Free Press, 1985).

3   The 'specialisation deadlock'

The previous chapter presented a model of the market as a highly specialised production structure under the division of labour. The production apparatus is coordinated through the price mechanism, and adjustments to production as well as resource reallocation between processes undertaken through exchange and entrepreneurship. This produces a dynamic model with a production structure that is responsive to exogenous change and that properly adjusts production processes to changing market conditions. But we also found a firm limitation to the extent of this dynamic akin to the limitation identified already by Adam Smith: entrepreneurial adjustments, improvements, and innovations are limited to actions within the extent of the market.

Chapter 2 only cursorily discussed this limitation, as it appeared as an implication of the market model rather than a component of its design. This chapter looks in greater detail into how market action in general, and adjustments throughout its interconnected web of productive actions, is curbed by the extent of the market. Specifically, the discussion revolves around the constraint facing all productive actions – including, and perhaps most importantly, innovative entrepreneurship – as they need be compatible with already existing specialisations in the production structure. This is an important perspective, since it elucidates the productive interdependence and therefore vulnerability of highly specialised production processes under the division of labour. It is central to the argument in this book, and is an aspect of the market that is often overlooked – but, as subsequent chapters will show, has important implications for organisation. Our focus remains on specialised production processes under the division of labour. Actors are assumed to be intensively specialised to carrying out one or a few specific and narrowly defined tasks within particular production processes.

To illustrate the problem hinted at in the previous chapter, let us again turn to Adam Smith's well-known example of the division of labour in pin production within the pin factory. Though, in accordance with our assumptions, we shall consider the production process per se and, at least for the present chapter, pay no attention to the fact that it is, in Smith's depiction, carried out specifically within a 'manufactory'. Our market model remains firmless and decentralised, and to focus on production rather than financing it is also assumed that each labour worker fully owns the capital goods used in the production stage.

Smith describes the production process as follows:

> One man draws out the wire, another straights it, a third cuts, a fourth points it, a fifth grinds it at the top for receiving the head; to make the head requires two or three distinct operations; to put it on, is a peculiar business, to whiten the pins is another; it is even a trade by itself to put them into the paper; and the important business of making a pin is, in this manner, divided into about eighteen distinct operations, which, in some manufactories, are all performed by distinct hands, though in others the same man will sometimes perform two or three of them.[1]

For the sake of simplicity, we assume with Smith that a total of ten people are involved in the production process and that each of them contributes with one or more highly specific tasks necessary to the process. For now, let us also assume that any and all inputs and tools used in pin-making are readily and freely available. It is easy to see that production in this market necessitates that each labourer aligns with the nine workers of other specialisations to form a production chain of ten workers, one of each specialisation. If all of the workers do this, which they of course have an incentive to do, the effect is that the market fully utilises its productive resources. This situation allows us to make several important observations about how this market for production functions.

With this single pin-making process there is no competition among workers as there is no redundancy in the execution of individual production stages within the aligned process. Assuming a constant and even flow of goods in process, production is completely dependent on each task being carried out in a timely manner. All labour workers in the process thus depend on all other workers in that process to do their part; if anyone fails to do so, the whole process fails as it cannot complete production. If someone is sick for a day, workers 'upstream' from the sick worker's specialisation can continue production of the intermediate products used as input for this stage. But the 'downstream' workers in this process will lack the inputs necessary for their stages since the outputs of the sick worker's stage are not being produced. This indicates that the 'social cooperation' through this productive division of labour also implies a rather severe vulnerability as each worker is fundamentally dependent on the workers carrying out the other stages.

Interdependence and market adjustment

Assume that we have a society consisting of 100 equally able workers, all of which are involved in pin-making, and that they are evenly distributed across tasks. We then have a market for pin production where the process is divided into ten separate production 'stages' and where there are a total of ten labourers specialised to carry out each of these stages. In other words, production comprises ten full pin-making processes like the one above. Production in this market is now redundant since there are ten workers in each specialisation, which means the failure of any one worker may not turn out to be a problem – there are still nine able workers producing the same stage in the production process. The production process does not necessarily come to a halt. However, since 10 per cent of production of one stage is lost if a worker is sick there will be excess supply of the produced inputs for this stage while, at the same time, the demand for the stage's output exceeds the produced quantity. The effect is similar to that above, but it is – due to productive redundancy – partial rather than comprehensive. Thus, those producing the 'upstream' stage will find it in their interests to compete to sell their output to the remaining nine buyers (who, in line with our assumptions, are willing and able to use only 90 per cent of the inputs used by all ten workers in this stage), so the price of the nine's input will fall. Correspondingly, there are ten workers in the 'downstream' stage competing for the output of the nine remaining workers, so the price of the nine's output will go up.

To some extent, an immediate change in prices may lead to a slight reduction in the magnitude of the market shortage that we may expect as the remaining nine workers could choose to work overtime to exploit this opportunity for increased income. But how much lost work can the remaining workers replace through working overtime? If we allow workers quickly to change their specialisation, so that workers from the specialisations at other stages can 'chip in' when necessary, the market may become less vulnerable to loss of specific manpower (but the effect, of course, is that labour is no longer as specific). The same is true if we let the market keep a surplus of workers so that there are replacements standing by where needed. But such flexibility-increasing measures are costly since the unemployed reserve is unable to earn a living.

Another option to deal with such problems is if ten parallel production processes in effect constitute overcapacity in the market, and therefore that the market in the event of disturbance can choose to increase resource utilisation to counter the loss of a worker. This would be the case if, for example, there is market demand that is lower than the productive capacity so that all workers normally are able to sell products representing only, say, 90 per cent of full capacity. In this case, the loss of one worker in one particular stage means the remaining workers specialised in this specific stage would need to increase resource utilisation through increasing production and thereby keep overall production at a constant level. Producers of other stages would continue to produce at 90 per cent of capacity. But this too is costly since resources are kept unused, and is not really different from the example above. There is no economic difference between having every tenth worker be idle and all ten workers work at 90 per cent. Both amount to 10 per cent underutilisation of existing resources and therefore loss of potential output.

An alternative means for labour workers to deal with this is to hold inventory. However, holding inventory increases the necessity for producers to bear uncertainty by postponing the income from production. Uncertainty in the present or near future can be mitigated with the use of accumulated inventory, but inventory comes at the cost of postponed (or lost) future income since goods in process are held without being completed. If all labour workers were so inclined, the completion of the production process – and therefore income, which we will see below – would take much longer. The outputs of the labour worker producing the first stage would not be made available to the second-stage worker until satisfactory inventory is accumulated, the outputs of the second-stage worker would be kept in inventory and not be available for the producer of the third stage until second-stage demand for inventory is fulfilled, and so on. Even if a fraction of produced goods in process, rather than the quantity first produced, is held in inventory, the process is burdened with the cost of production for goods held in inventory.

Inventory may be a solution for loss of production in already established and proven production processes, but is hardly possible in its inception. As we will see below, there are major costs involved in establishing a novel production process. Adding the cost of accumulating and holding inventory should be infeasible without external or centralised financing of the process. Regardless of inventory, the solutions mentioned above are unsustainable in a decentralised market setting. With a reserve labour force, there is nothing stopping an unemployed worker from slightly underbidding those already employed in producing a particular stage. There is also nothing keeping underutilised but producing workers from increasing their output to capture a greater part of the market and therefore increase their revenue. In both cases, the leisure of production-willing individuals is traded for labour and for this reason the market's overall production is increased. This, in turn, forces unit prices down and, consequently, reduces the total income of those who choose not to increase their production; similarly, those who produce more get a larger share of total income.

Let us now consider the case where the labour workers in pin production have varying productive abilities (skills). While we have described the production dynamic in terms of cooperation, this is most obvious vertically (through the production chain) whereas the dynamic horizontally, within each production stage, is synonymous with competitive distribution of effort and income. Thinking of the latter in terms of competitive distribution may help in understanding the dynamic within a stage where workers are heterogeneous in their ability to produce. Instead of each worker choosing between labour and leisure on the basis of equal productive ability, we now have a situation where more able workers have greater latitude. The reason for this is that if production volume is equally distributed across workers within a stage, the more able workers get more leisure time than the less able at the same income level. If, instead, production time (invested productive effort) is equally distributed across workers, the more able workers will be able to produce more and thus earn a greater income while having the same leisure time as those less able.

In the former case (equal production volume), the more able workers may choose to increase production for greater income. Correspondingly, in the latter case (equal production effort), the more able workers may choose to increase leisure time while still earning at least as much as the lesser able workers. (We abstract from differences in preferences for now.) Both cases are economically equal since the more able workers make the choice between labour and leisure at comparatively lower cost than the less able. This is why, in the open market, we see a general tendency towards production being carried out by those better suited for a specific type of production – which increases overall production in the economy or, alternatively, increases the time available for other activities (whether leisure or labour) while production output is stable. In other words, this law of comparative advantage shows how society as a whole is better off by letting individuals specialise in producing what they are relatively better at producing, and the individuals are at the same time incentivised to make individual choices in accordance with this rule since it makes them better off. The social cooperation under the division of labour is ultimately strengthened by people's differing abilities, since heterogeneity simplifies and improves our individual specialisation choices.

These adjustments across production processes can also be described in terms of competition between workers specialised to perform the same standard tasks in a particular production stage. These competing workers are the ones who, acting in their own interests and seeking to make themselves better off, assist in the market's social cooperation by bringing about a resource allocation that better benefits society as a whole. The latter is an unintended result of their individual actions, but is brought about as were they led by an invisible hand.

All production processes in this market are 'spontaneously' coordinated through exchange, so there is no issue of formal employment; the issue is only who buys/sells from/to whom. This is why the temporary loss of a sick worker in one of the production stages does not affect a particular production process (of the ten), but has a general effect – if any – across the market. As we started out describing the market in terms of standard tasks in standard production processes, competition is limited to the intra-stage allocation of resources through standard exchange across stages. Consequently, we have so far focused on the production process and the sequential nature of its standard stages, and the dynamic by which a particular production stage 'deals with' changes to keep production intact and avoid losses due to incompleteness (that is, by failing to carry out the whole process and thereby not delivering the end product).

Changing production stage boundaries

The model has so far only focused on adjustments and, to use Kirzner's term, 'arbitrage' across production processes within a particular production stage. We saw that our limited market of 100 people dynamically adjust to changing circumstances and, to some extent, make up for lost production through 'overtime' work. Prices change to reflect shortages and surpluses in such a way that the loss of one-tenth of producers in one stage makes the price of inputs for this stage go down and the price of its outputs similarly goes up. The 'automatic' response by the market to the loss of one worker in a particular stage is to redistribute some of the profits from the 'upstream' and 'downstream' stages (by lowering the selling price and increasing the buying price, respectively) to the affected stage.

In this sense, the price changes incentivise workers to give up their current position to take a place in this stage. It is easy to imagine that if such price changes are of sufficient magnitude, workers may consider retraining in order to earn profits by filling positions in stages that have suffered, say, a loss of two or three or more workers. And the greater the loss, the stronger the incentive becomes. As long as prices are allowed to adjust freely throughout the complete production apparatus so that they reflect real market conditions, the overall allocation of resources will tend to properly adjust to 'maximise' the outcome.

Consequently, even though the discussion above concentrated on changes to and within a single production stage, other stages were affected and involved, so to speak, in bringing about a better allocation of productive resources (workers). There is in this sense effective competitive forces between production stages that help even out existing misallocations over time. But whereas what we have heretofore focused on is the horizontal dynamic within a production process, there is also competition between (and within) stages that is primarily *vertical*. Competition within the production apparatus is indeed between independent workers who compete for positions in the entire division of labour.

Vertical competition, which shifts the boundaries of market-traded production specialisations (and this is the reason we give it attention), can take several typical forms, which have distinct theoretical implications. However, as we will see, the occurrence of one such form does not exclude other forms but can instigate another; likewise, there is a compounding effect such that the impact of one form of vertical competition on the structure of a production process is reinforced by the occurrence of another. A very simple type of vertical competition within a production process is a 'tug of war' between those performing the stages. In the discussion above, we initially assumed the workers are equally skilled (both in terms of performance of chosen tasks and ability scope) and that they engage in standard activities traded in the market. It is very possible that a world with heterogeneously skilled workers sees one or more comparatively very skilful workers who deal directly with workers of comparatively limited skill. To the extent that the skilful worker is higher performing than other workers labouring with the same stage, the skilful worker may be able to take over part of the production volume and thereby free resources for alternative uses (as discussed above). To the extent that he or she is effective more broadly than the market-sized stage, which means having the ability to perform part of the task(s) in an adjacent stage with the same or better skill as those specialised there already, the skilful worker can engage in productive 'imperialism' by for example continuing to produce beyond the boundary of the standard production stage and thus sell a more completed type of intermediate good. The skilful worker can then choose profitably to do part of what in standard market production 'should' belong to another stage and thereby either buy inputs from the 'upstream' stage earlier (in a less developed form) or sell outputs to the 'downstream' stage later (more developed). In both cases, this worker would then ultimately relieve less skilful workers in adjacent stages of part of their standard market undertaking.

The effect of this would be, on the one hand, that less skilful workers get to specialise to more narrowly defined stages (since the more skilful worker is doing part of the 'their' stage) and therefore may be able to become more productive in what remains. But this also heterogenises and ultimately undermines the standard division of labour adopted by the market towards the existent production stages, the workers abandon the standard production process by redefining its stages. This increases the frictions in the market as workers focus their labour towards productive activities that deviate from the market standard. Let us assume that one of the workers specialised to producing the fifth stage in pin production is competitively skilful also in the finishing touches normally carried out as part of the 'upstream' fourth production stage. Since this worker can do this part of the fourth stage at least as well as some of the workers specialised to this stage, it is possible for workers to renegotiate the boundaries of the standard stages they carry out. There may therefore be an opportunity for the skilful worker to expand their vertical productive scope and for the less skilful worker to contract theirs in a similar manner.

Say worker E is the highly skilful worker in stage five, and that E is at least as efficient in producing the last part of stage four as two of the workers presently specialised to it. For the first eight in the order of skill or ability, let us refer to them as D_{1-8}, E is no match – D_{1-8} are more skilful and thus more productive. But for the remaining two, D_9 and D_{10}, E is as good as or better than they are in terms of economic productivity. They may therefore consider selling the intermediate product at an earlier point in time (production-wise), for example when it is only finished to 85 per cent of the standard intermediate product traded, and it is possible that E may consider buying if the price is right. But establishing this type of exchange relationship effectively creates a situation where the two parties must negotiate the price. While this may not be much of a problem for E, who can still procure the standard intermediate product from other workers should this seem like a more economic play, it can possibly become a problem for D_9 or D_{10}, who may have already produced 85 per cent-finished goods to deliver to E when requested. The market for almost finished goods is very limited – in this example it consists of only E – so the unfinished intermediate goods must, if E no longer chooses to buy them, be prepared for and reintroduced in D_9 or D_{10}'s productive activities, meanwhile generating costs of stocking and capital through delayed income. As the remaining 15 per cent of the stage's productive tasks is likely what D_9 or D_{10} are least productive in performing (their reason to 'outsource' this part to E) resuming production may become a highly costly endeavour. If substantial time has passed since E started buying 'earlier', it is likely that the cost for D_9 or D_{10} to resume this type of production has increased.

This example serves to illustrate a problem of deviating from the market standard, since whereas production in standard processes entails interdependence between stages any deviation therefrom will entail interdependence of a much narrower scope (possibly dependence on a single market participant, as in the example above). By deviating, D_9 or D_{10} not only relinquished revenue by in effect 'paying'[2] E to produce the remainder of the intermediate product offered in the market, but forced upon themselves a highly restricted density (only one possible purchaser of their output) and therefore a highly vulnerable market position. And, at the same time, they risked high cost of resuming production using skills potentially lost due to not carrying out certain parts of the standard task (since this was 'sold' to E) should the decision be reversed.

The situation above can also be caused by more effective use of productive capital, which can produce a slightly different dynamic as it may set in motion both horizontal and vertical adjustments. Instead of being naturally more skilful, let us assume that E is one of ten somewhat equally skilled workers producing stage five in the ten-stage pin production process, but that E finds a more productive way of utilising the tools and other capital readily available (and perhaps already in use in this particular production activity). We can think of this as a limited form of innovation in which E reconfigures or adjusts the way in which these capital resources are used to perform the tasks in this standard production stage. As what we are interested in here is tracing the effect of productive capital innovation on the existing structure of production between and across production stages, we further assume that this innovation is the result simply of new thinking and so there is no significant cost involved to implement it.

The result of this innovation is that E, thanks to the greater assistance of capital in production, emerges as more productive than previously. To the degree E used to be equally productive as other workers carrying out this production stage (for simplicity, we may assume that workers used capital in a standardised way), E's increased productivity entails an ability to – at least partially – outcompete other performers of this production stage. There may therefore be an initial shift of volume from the other performers of this stage to E. But E's higher profitability incentivises the other workers to adopt similar innovations in productive capital, which eventually evens out productivity differences in the production stage.

E 'disrupts' the structure of production within the stage (that is, horizontally across production processes) by introducing the simple innovation in production-aiding capital. Whether or not this is a limited or strictly temporary effect, this also upsets the market balance *between* stages (vertically) within the specific process as well as the production structure within the whole ten-process productive undertaking. The reason for this is that the market through competition tends to balance returns between production stages such that they enjoy the same (or at least similar) profitability and return on capital. Where this is not the case, say if workers in the fourth stage earn overall double the rate of return as compared to those in other stages, we should expect at least some workers in other stages to abandon their current positions for production in the stage providing a higher rate of return. Workers will have an incentive to specialise in production of the stage with the relatively higher yield just as they have an incentive to adopt productivity-increasing capital good innovations. The resultant increased competition within the higher-return production stage diminishes its profitability while the stages abandoned by these workers will see a concomitant rise.

Overall, the tendency in the market is towards equal rates of return throughout the production process.

Profitability in and across stages is of course relative to the cost structure of capital usage in production, so for this analysis to be accurate we must also consider changes to market prices of specific capital configurations as workers bid for the more productive capital. However, we assumed that E's innovation is very simple (a discovered new configuration or use of existent and readily available capital) and therefore that it can rather easily be emulated by other workers. Changes to the cost structure of production are therefore very limited in this example market producing only pins. In a real market, this may not always be the case. Also, there may be competition from outside the production process as workers migrate from other types of production – especially where similar skills are utilised and thus demanded in many situations. This makes the picture much more complex, especially if we also involve the uncertainty of selling the end product in the consumers' market, but does not change the forces at play or the tendencies they engender. The market as a whole does not tend to even out the number of workers employed in each stage, but allocates resources according to the efficiency of tasks carried out throughout the production process. It would therefore be inaccurate to assume a production process would utilise the same number of labour workers in each stage, though it can serve as a valid starting point for theorising on market dynamics. As shown above, changes in relative productivity (whether on the individual or stage levels) incentivise corresponding changes throughout the production process, and therefore brings about a more efficient resource allocation. This affects the boundaries between standard market stages, the tasks carried out in each stage, and the number of workers contributing to a stage's production.

Adjustments across production stages

In an extreme case of the previous example of the pin-making market, in which E 'innovated' a new way of using existent capital, it is possible to imagine how the new use of capital increases productivity to such a degree that the production stage attracts and can provide for a very large number of workers. These entrant workers previously utilised their labour powers in other stages, but chose in great numbers (relatively speaking) to abandon their positions in order to capture some of the extraordinary returns enjoyed in stage five of the production process. Assume all workers in stage five have already adopted (or emulated) E's particular capital use and that, as a result of their achieved profitability per invested labour hour, one worker from each of the other stages is enticed to abandon their present position for a share of the profits in stage five.

Continuing the example, the inflow of workers from other stages means the number of workers in stage five is now approximately double that of all other stages (nineteen as compared to nine). As long as there is sufficient space, so that these workers do not step on each other's toes, and – as we assumed above – that there is abundant supply of costless capital, we can trace the effects on the production structure. The new situation may alter the boundaries somewhat (as above), but the massive increase in production capacity primarily increases demand for input as well as, to the degree this demand can be satisfied, increases output to be sold to the subsequent stage. As stage five workers bid for inputs, the prices increase and their profitability therefore diminishes with the increased productivity as well as the inflow of workers. Meanwhile, the higher prices received make profits in stage four increase. The extraordinary profits earned in stage five are thereby eventually evened out by in part being distributed on to other stages, which in turn experience similar dynamics as workers continue to migrate (though of lesser intensity). One stage's increased profitability, therefore, has ripple effects through the market and the increased wealth is in this sense 'shared' with all who contribute to the production. This is the case since these changes occur within a production process, which is aimed at producing a specific final good – and therefore the benefit of increased overall productivity is to some extent shared by all taking part in this effort in 'social cooperation'. Even though we assumed that only one product is produced and that production takes place in redundant production processes (ten identical processes producing side by side), the production apparatus constitutes an interdependent web both horizontally and vertically.

Even though profits tend to 'leak' into other stages, the increased productivity of stage five will still make it relatively more productive and it can therefore 'afford' to employ more workers than other stages. But it will, due to its increased productivity, in fact 'need' *fewer* workers to produce a certain quantity. This brings about a reversal of the inflow of workers as their higher productivity will, despite the initial increase in productivity-based profitability, greatly increase competition between them. In the short term, the available quantity of inputs for this stage, as produced in stage four, is fixed (more cannot be produced instantaneously) as well as in shortage (lower quantity than demanded by the increased number of workers in stage five). Performers of stage five must thus outbid their competitors to secure necessary inputs to earn a profit, which suggests that they, to paraphrase Mises, appear as bidders at an auction in which the owners of stage four output put up for sale their intermediate goods.[3] As this increases prices and thus profitability of stage four, as we saw above, it will attract more workers and thereby increase the stage's future output. Since stage five can produce more with less (due to their achieved higher productivity), the evening out of returns across production stages will continue past the previous scale – until profitability and output is approximately the same across the production process. The increased productivity in one stage in this sense first creates an inflow of workers (if profitability increases with sufficient magnitude) to then cause an outflow of potentially greater numbers due to their increased productive efficiency, and this increases the worker population in all other stages to support an overall increase in production. The previous worker population of nineteen in stage five is thereby likely to decrease to well below the original ten, while the worker populations of all other stages increase beyond the original in order to keep up with the absolute production capability of the more productive stage five.

The total output of this ten-process production structure has therefore increased through the productive capital innovation and the resulting reallocation of workers. The reason for this is in part the interdependency of stages within a production process. Each of the stages, and therefore the full 'length' of the production process, is dependent on inputs being carried through *all* stages. This is what effectively allocates resources to the less productive stages as productivity of some other stage is increased. Throughout the production process, the productive capability is evened out so that production can be carried on at the best possible overall volume. As a result, the returns to production within the process increase uniformly alongside the increased production volume.

There is also interdependence through competition for profit between the parallel production processes, which serves to reallocate resources and diffuse capital innovations. While we assumed a production structure that produces a single consumer good – a pin – competition works similarly between dissimilar production processes of different number of stages producing different consumer goods. Cross-process competition in such complex market settings arise for the same reasons: because producers anticipate improvement of their situation by gaining control of and using productive resources in general – and highly productive labour and capital in particular. The diffusion and reallocation process is similar to that above, but is much more complex due to the fact that productive capital has multiple but still a limited number of specificities (the same applies, though limitedly, to skilled labour). As the value of production processes ultimately depends on the value consumers place on the final or consumer good, a variety of consumer goods, of different and varying value and produced using processes of differing lengths, significantly complicates the analysis.

Nevertheless, what is at play here is that, within a decentralised but specialised production process, the individual labour workers must act as capitalist-entrepreneurs. In the face of change, whether of exogenous or endogenous origin, they must rely on their judgment and ultimately bear the uncertainty of their actions and decisions. Any worker is able to sell their output only because a capitalist-entrepreneur-worker in the subsequent stage is willing to procure the unfinished good, and this worker in turn will carry out a number of tasks or operations to add further to its completion, then sell to a worker specialised to producing the next stage, and so on. The whole chain of serially dependent stages is ultimately dependent on its eventual *completion* and the sale of the completed product; without a consumers' market in which there is an anticipated demand for the completed product, the production chain fails and workers in all stages are affected by the losses. In fact, at the time of failure any worker who is not idle (which means he or she is in possession of intermediate products) loses all funds invested in intermediate goods that have yet to be transferred to the following stage. Each worker thereby bears the uncertainty inherent in the production process and risks losses.

The issue of incompleteness

Production is technically a serial process from the top to bottom, but the market valuation of the production stages as well as their financing runs in the opposite direction. It is an obvious point if we consider how goods, including intermediate goods, change hands *for money*, but it is a point with important implications for the working of the production apparatus and so the capital structure and divisions of labour and capital in an economy. Indeed, from a temporal perspective a new production process must be completed before the first payment can be received and then transferred step by step upstream through the stages. If we follow the process from start to finish, a worker producing in the first stage must bear the uncertainty until the output is transferred to a worker producing the second stage, who then must invest funds to gain ownership of the former's output, add value to it through production efforts and sell the more complete intermediate good to a producer of the next stage, and so on through the full length of the production process. And at each stage, the assumed value of the unfinished or intermediate good increases as it gets closer to its final and consumable form. The point of the stages in a production process, after all, is to add value. Consequently, the capital funding necessary for each stage increases and therefore the burden of uncertainty escalates as production moves closer to the consumer good.

Whereas the uncertainty due to direct capital investment increases with value-added in the production process, the weight of the borne uncertainty diminishes as the uncertainty of predicting a given event in the future diminishes as the event draws nearer. There are therefore opposing forces on the burden of uncertainty as it affects labour workers in the production process: uncertainty increases downstream with the increased capital investment, but also decreases as the outcome of the process appears as less uncertain. The former can be conceived of as the loss suffered should the production process fail to be completed, whereas the latter is the probability for it to fail. We will here focus on the impact of the uncertain outcome (loss or gain) on the actions within and coordination of the production process. We assume there is some probability of failure throughout the process and that it is of sufficient magnitude not to be disregarded.

The dynamic within the production process, and the problem to be discussed below, becomes clear if we assume that each worker initially lacks funds to invest and so pays for his/her stage's input with an IOU and sells the output for another IOU. For the sake of simplicity, we also assume that each stage in the ten-stage process adds an estimated tenth of the anticipated market value of the final good and that the value of the IOU also reflects each worker's time preference. The IOU that purchases the first stage's output for the worker in the second stage is consequently worth one-tenth of the final good; the IOU that purchases the second stage's output for the worker in the third stage is worth two-tenths; and so on. The completion of the first final good has therefore generated a situation where each worker owes the producer of the previous stage a sum corresponding to the estimated value of the inputs used. Each worker is then in net debt a total of one-tenth of the final good price. As the worker of the tenth step sells the final product to a consumer and is paid in full, the worker honours his/her issued IOU and consequently pays the worker in the ninth step a sum equal to 90 per cent of the price of the good (assuming the received price is equal to the anticipated price, which of course may not be the case). The worker of the ninth step, now with the 90 per cent cash on hand, can then honour his/her IOU issued to the worker in the eighth by paying a sum equal to 80 per cent. And so on backwards through the production chain until all IOUs are honoured and each worker has one full tenth of the price of the final good in cash.

The nature of specialised production processes, as implied by this example, increases the need for investment beyond the capital goods used in production (both goods aiding production and goods in process). Labour workers are not only investing capital funds into production, but necessarily wait for payment. The labour worker producing the first stage must wait nine full periods (plus the time it takes to redeem the IOUs) before payment for invested capital and effort. At the time production commences, this person must therefore have consumer goods in store to draw from during this period of waiting or anticipate income from other sources. In other words, a specialised production process requires both capital funding to support production and a wages fund to draw from before receiving payment in the future.

Should this production process at any point fail, including if the final product turns out to be altogether unmarketable, all workers generate losses of both kinds: the capital invested in the production process and the funds consumed during the time lapsed. As there is no 'double coincidence' for redeeming the issued IOUs, the workers end up debtors *and* creditors if there is no working money capital market. As none of the workers has earned an income from this particular production endeavour, they probably lack the funds to pay outstanding debt. Consequently, the worker specialised in producing the eighth stage will owe the worker in the seventh stage a sum equal to 70 per cent of the anticipated but unrealised market value of the final product while also having an irredeemable IOU from the ninth stage worker corresponding to 80 per cent of the value. The consequent situation is, financially speaking, highly problematic for the worker.

It is of course possible that workers are able to initially finance their production (and anticipated consumption) with savings instead of IOUs, but this is unlikely to lessen the risk involved for workers since our implicit assumption that only one product is produced is unrealistic and should appear overly cautious (and, to the extent the production process is successful, it is a very costly approach since it relies on all but one worker waiting for the end result). If the workers believe strongly that there is a market for the end product, which of course must be the case since they are investing in its production, there is no reason for the worker in the initial stage to be idle while awaiting the completion of the product. Rather, it may be reasonable to expect this worker to continue to produce the first stage and thereby supply the second stage worker with continuous inputs; and the same for the second stage worker, who can continue working and thereby supply the third stage worker with inputs. But this greatly increases the risk involved. If we assume that each stage takes one standard time period to produce, which means the completed product will be available for the market ten full time periods after initiating production in the first stage, the worker in the first stage will have completed inputs for the second stage at the end of *each* time period. The outstanding 'value' is therefore equal to ten times the first stage's contribution to the complete product. Likewise, the producer of the second stage will have completed nine intermediate products to be used in the third stage (the first time period is spent waiting for the completion of the first inputs); the producer of the third stage will have completed eight intermediate products to be used in the fourth stage; and so on. We then see that each worker in this production process, at the time of completion of the first product, has invested substantial capital assets in the process. It should also be clear that, to the degree workers invest their own funds (rather than IOUs), the money trickles up to pay for inputs. But it also means the risk of the endeavour is distributed and compounded downstream before it is known if there is a market for the final product.

Just like in our discussion above, holding inventories in each of the stages is neither feasible nor would change the situation. Inventories will have to be accumulated before they can be used, which only compounds the problem of waiting by adding periods before the final good is sold to consumers.

As the production of intermediate goods in each of the stages of the process is well underway and a market for the final product has been found, the aforementioned problem shrinks to a much lesser magnitude. The reason for this is that payment has been received for the final product and therefore started flowing in the direction opposite to the production process; the workers are then relieved of the uncertainty borne through the debt incurred by investing in the process. Due to the division of labour in the specialised production process, all workers participating in and thus contributing to the process depend on the completion of the final product for payment as well as on each other to bring the final product to the consumer market. The 'social cooperation' through the division of labour is therefore a necessity, since workers cannot afford not to cooperate – they are completely dependent on each stage being carried out at sufficient productivity and in a timely manner. Problems occurring somewhere in the process may affect all of them. This is due to the problem of *incompleteness*, which is a pervasive problem where there is not redundancy. As we saw in the discussion above, the market has ways of dealing with changes where there are redundant production processes and therefore market bidding within each production stage. This mitigates the scope of the problem by increasing the number of individuals sharing the cost of incompleteness. It provides an important extension of production that lessens the effect of uncertainty and relieves producers of its cost.

As soon as one successful pin-production process consisting of the previously discussed ten stages is created and proven profitable, other workers eager to increase the return on their labour may seek to compete for a share of the profits.

Note that it is not necessary for new entrants to produce a whole new process to be able to compete; rather, they only need to specialise to providing the same production services as are already established in the complete ten-stage process. In other words, a worker who has identified the greater return to labour made possible through the new pin-making process can step in and compete head to head with any of the workers in the process. All that is necessary is that the entrant worker adopts the existing end points of an established stage so that, in the case of the sixth production stage, the outputs from stage five can be used and inputs for stage seven are produced. In other words, the services offered (sixth stage production) must be fundamentally compatible with the newly established division of labour. Where this is not the case, an entrant worker forces incompleteness, and the costs thereof, on their own production undertaking. These costs cannot in any important respect be distributed to (and will thus not be shared by) workers in the established production process, since the entrant worker has failed to compete competently with and therefore been unable to become part of the process.

To get a share of the proceeds of the established production process, the entrant worker aims to supplant the existing worker producing stage six. To do this successfully, the stage must be carried out at lower cost so that the entrant worker can offer a higher price for the stage's inputs and offer its standard output at a lower price. In a situation where the pin-production process is so recently established that production is carried out at a low volume, it may be necessary only to be able to do the former. But to remain competitive and take the incumbent worker's place (at least in part), the new entrant should be able to match and outdo the prices relied on by the incumbent for both inputs and outputs.

The effect of the new entrant is the creation of a horizontal market within the production process for the specific stage (here, stage six). Entry thereby sets in motion the dynamics discussed above; it also undermines the monopoly-like situation of the incumbent worker and thereby relieves workers carrying out the adjacent stages five and seven of their interdependence on the single worker carrying out stage six. In other words, the worker producing stage five can, after the entrant worker's entry, choose the buyer of its outputs. Similarly, the worker producing stage seven can choose the seller of its inputs. This means the worker in stage five will have a chance to increase its revenue from sales while the worker in stage seven may be able to reduce costs of input, both thereby increasing their rates of return. All else equal, the increased rates of return increase the risk of attracting new entrants that specialise in producing stages five and seven. As the competitive forces play out, we may well end up with the market assumed at the beginning of the chapter with ten workers producing each of the ten stages.

As we saw above, the horizontal competition within any single stage moderates the productivity of workers, and the potential repositioning or movement of workers from one stage to another bring about an overall tendency to even out rates of return throughout the production apparatus. This does not mean that the number of workers must (or tend to) be evenly spread out across stages; the input and output markets for the stages may therefore differ. We can have a situation where workers have chosen positions such that the production process has the shape of an hourglass in terms of the allocation of workers. In our pin-producing market this may mean, for example, that stage five is carried out by only two workers whereas stages four and six are carried out by seven or eight workers, and other stages by even more. This suggests that the two workers in this stage must be highly productive, since they are able to produce sufficiently to demand adequately the supply of inputs and supply adequately the demand of outputs from the seven or eight workers in each of the adjacent stages; they are able to keep up with the preferred production volume of the full production process.

The specialisation deadlock

So far in this discussion we have elaborated on the dynamic within the production process, as well as the supply-side pin-making market overall, and we have briefly touched on how competition can create markets across processes within production stages. However, we have only briefly touched on the initial *creation* of specialised production processes. The reason for keeping this discussion until now is that it is important to understand how the market's production side dynamically responds to changes and adjusts to changes in incentives in order to produce the best possible outcome. The productive apparatus as a whole necessarily responds to and is subject to real consumer demand, which follows from the problem of financing production that is yet to be completed. This is central to how the structure of the process can change.

Incompleteness emerges as a very real problem in our highly decentralised market model due to the interdependence of workers throughout the production process. Where there are existent markets within stages, and thus redundant (which does not imply underutilised) production capacity, the production apparatus is overall more resistant to abrupt or unanticipated changes such as the introduction of new production technology or declining demand. The creation of a new production process is different, however, since it breaks new ground and for this reason necessarily takes place outside the established market (see Chapter 2). There can here be no redundancy or market dynamics to rely on, and therefore those involved – even if successful – are necessarily more vulnerable to changes. Even more so than in the discussion above, incompleteness is a necessary consequence of innovating in production, whether this relates to implementing a new and previously unseen process (to replace production processes or to introduce a new final good) or changing the structure of an existing production process (by dividing work differently, in different stages, even if this only affects a part of the existing process). The effect in both cases is the same, as we shall now see.

If we again assume the ten-stage pin-making production process with 100 workers evenly distributed across the production stages, we can trace the steps and forces involved in the creation of a limited new process through (1) the creation of new capital goods to aid production and (2) dividing work in a new way, respectively. The creation of new capital that we are here interested in entails a much greater change than the case discussed above, in which E found a more productive way of utilising the tools and other capital readily available. Instead of reorganising the utilisation of existing capital and thereby simply changing the way in which it is used, the creation of capital entails the design of a new type of tool that could more effectively assist in the production of the stage. The implementation of this design is much more complex than simple reconfiguring or recombining existing components: it must be produced. The innovator, E, is therefore presented with the choice of (at least temporarily) ceasing production in order to produce the tool, or give up the income of current production to contract with someone else to produce the tool. Both alternatives entail a capitalistic investment. To the degree that this new tool is fully compatible with the existent production process and therefore can simply replace existing tools, such as introducing a new and more efficient type of hammer to carpenters, this innovation may not change the existing production process in a significant way. However, the production of this capital good itself would likely require a new production process, the implementation of which then takes place outside the market, which only shifts the incompleteness logic one step out from the pin-making production process.[4] What matters here is therefore the creation of a new production structure that, via producing a tool, aids a stage in the existing production process.

Consider first the example of creating a complete alternative production structure to compete with and, if successful, supplant the existing ten-stage structure for pin production. As we have already seen, the status quo utilises an intensive division of labour through ten distinct yet interdependent specialisations in production, and includes a dynamic that adjusts to changing circumstances and adopts minor innovations to the degree they increase productivity and, consequently, the rate of return. To compete successfully with this process, the new structure must provide a real advantage in this specific setting, such as better resource utilisation, and so rely on comparatively more intensive specialisation. Minor reconfigurations or reorganisations constitute no real challenge since such differences are easily adopted by labour workers in the existing process. Competitive efforts must therefore implement a new type of production structure that divides work into a greater number of stages. This can be done either through a greater division of labour that splits work into a greater number of stages or through extending the production structure by adding production of new, improved capital to assist in production.

Yet in order to establish the complete novel production structure, a total of at least eleven specialised workers need to be involved and sufficiently specialised towards carrying out all the new stages. As per our description, the competing process utilises more intensive specialisation through taking advantage of more stages: a more fine-grained splitting of the process into more intensively specialised stages or by adding one or more capital-producing stages. The new process must employ specialised labour workers to carry out each of the new stages.

Even if this new division of labour does not necessitate extensive, time-consuming re-training of workers to assume their respective positions in the production structure and carry out the necessary tasks, the new process must be fully populated in order to be economically viable. For this reason, the creation of a new production process cannot be an individual endeavour (in contrast to the bottom-up adjustment dynamics above), but suffers from being a collective endeavour subject to incompleteness. It must therefore be coordinated. At a minimum, the new production structure requires as many workers, appropriately specialised, as there are stages in order to be completed.

Add to this picture the fact that several if not most (or all) of the stages in the anticipated new structure do yet not exist, which suggests the workers who are to carry out those stages need first be properly trained. While such an undertaking takes time and may necessitate the use of specific (and sometimes new) resources, it is likely that the required information is neither accessible nor even in existence. As the novel production process has not yet been created, it is impossible to know whether there is sufficient knowledge of specifics available to realise the new structure or, if the knowledge indeed exists, whether this knowledge has been properly collected and understood. To some extent, the necessary knowledge is purely technological and in this respect the production stages could conceivably be calculated and specified in advance. However, even where this is the case there is still uncertainty in what routines and standards in production are technologically efficient and effective as well as unknowable specifics about deliverables of intermediate goods between stages. As is the case in the already established production process, the stages are necessarily interdependent and must consequently be fully compatible in order for the process not to suffer incompleteness.

Individual workers involved in specifying and implementing the new production process must not only rely on the information at hand, but must place their trust in the hands of all other involved workers without which the project fails. There must also be means to solve problems that may arise as well as for troubleshooting across the new process' stage boundaries and adapt designs. All of these tasks are theoretically possible under a decentralised structure where each worker acts in his or her own interest, but it is a costly process that may suffer from actors engaging in opportunistic or otherwise cost-avoiding behaviour. Even if workers are able 'spontaneously' to coordinate their endeavour, problems can arise due to decentralised financing and decision-making as well as conflicting interests: what is supposedly a low-cost or highly effective solution to one particular production stage (assuming this can be known) may turn out to increase costs in 'downstream' stages. A decentralised production structure without market prices lacks the means to optimise the overall process. In many cases the specific knowledge necessary for proper decision-making for the overall process or at the stage level may not exist but will be generated through the implementation process. Even considering only the engineering aspects of putting together a novel production structure, the costs of coordination are significant.

These problems still fade in comparison with the economic calculation problem existent in the new structure. Even if we assume that the structure produces an already existing final good using already existing inputs, which means it consists solely of a new production structure and therefore a different division of labour and capital, it is impossible to calculate which of the many stages are efficient and which are not. The reason for this is that the process is valued as a whole when the final product is sold. As we saw above, there is no value of incomplete products unless there is a market for intermediate goods. But a new process, using a new kind of division of labour and capital, does not produce standard intermediate goods to be used in competing production processes. Therefore, the contributions of the individual stages in the new process remains unknown until there are markets for each of their outputs or value-added. But this requires capital markets for exchanging standard capital in process, which cannot be the case for a novel and recently implemented production process. The existing production process offers little guidance, since the new process has a different structure.

Even if the structure as a whole generates a profit, the workers are still blind as to who of them are contributing (and how much) to the end result of the final good: who are profitable and who are, in contrast, consuming capital through inefficient resource utilisation. Without markets for the intermediate goods, and therefore no reliable economic valuation and no market prices, the process as a whole suffers from what Murray N. Rothbard describes as an island of noncalculable chaos.[5] The process can be improved technologically, but as there is no guidance for the economic utilisation of resources, there is no way of optimising or even improving its value creating properties. This requires markets for the individual stages.

We should note that there's an additional problem that faces the implementation of a new production process. Our limited production economy enjoys full resource utilisation, so all workers occupy a profitable space in the market's production apparatus. This means the new process must promise significantly greater returns to attract already fully employed labour workers. It is conceivably easier to attract a number of unemployed workers to new specialisations (though they would likely lack the funds to make such an investment) than it is to lure those who are already employed (and hence profit-earning) to the new structure with uncertain outcome. Financing therefore becomes an important aspect of, as well as a potentially significant problem for, putting together a new production structure. This issue will be discussed in Chapter 7.

It is not necessary to establish a new process to supplant *completely* the existing ten-stage pin-production process. A much more limited (and realistic) example could establish production to compete with an existing stage rather than the whole process. With the productive powers of specialisation in mind, such an endeavour could entail the simple splitting of an existing production stage into two (or more) more intensively specialised production stages.[6] Yet such comparatively limited innovation faces the same problems as above: the interdependent tasks to replace the market-traded stage suffer from costs of noncalculable chaos, coordination, uncertain outcome, and inexistent information. These costs can potentially be surmountable where the number of workers involved is very limited and there is a very high degree of trust between them – and the outcome of the innovation is relatively known. For instance, two innovative workers may figure out a novel way of collaborating in producing a standard stage traded in the market by splitting it into two distinct parts (thereby extending the division of labour and consequently the production process) – perhaps by having one of them produce a tool used by the other – and they may be successful in implementing it. While this scenario would be more costly and potentially involve slower full-scale market adoption since it is not simply an adjustment but an effectual 'splitting' of a stage, it bears resemblance to the dynamic process discussed above. The major difference is how the innovation requires upfront financing and collaborative coordination, without which it suffers from incompleteness – all parts of a production process must be carried out for it to be viable.

The simple adoption of a slightly more intensive division of labour and capital constitutes innovative low-hanging fruits, since they are comparatively easily implementable – and therefore also easily emulated. With a much more advanced splitting of tasks, whether or not it entails the production of supporting capital, it is a different story – the lack of market for stages' services and intermediate goods here constitutes a real barrier to productive development as decentralised, sovereign workers suffer the immense coordination and discovery needed in order to escape incompleteness. The implication is that while the overall market aims for and engages in specialisation through the divisions of labour and capital to the extent possible in the existing production structure, there is an upper limit to what is possible through the adoption of relatively simple innovation. The market, while unbeatable in efficient resource allocation, is unable to extend past its extent; the only developments possible are comparatively minor adjustments and simple innovations such as task-splitting that does not require extensive coordination and information generation. Seen from the point of view of the specialised exchange market, Adam Smith's comment that the division of labour is increased through the *gradual* simplifying of labour workers' operations is necessary. The splitting of a standard production stage into many, which the type of innovation we have focused on here implies, is unsupported by the market. This type of innovation cannot take place within the limits of the extent of the market since there is no market for novel means of production, whether they are specialised labour or capital.

This is a problem that is not simply of theoretical import, but that indicates a real limitation as specialisation makes possible increased productivity, but leads to a situation in which the production stages are highly interdependent. Productivity increases achieved through specialising under the divisions of labour and capital produces a relative abundance and therefore generates wealth, but it also points to a vulnerability and problem: decentralised and bottom-up efforts to specialise is a one-way street that increases productivity but that is limited to simple and gradual steps rather than collaborative leaps forward. The market faces a 'specialisation deadlock', as it were, in which the divisions of labour and capital engender a path-dependent development that is limited to gradual changes and adaptive responses to exogenous change. Yet this is neither what we have seen historically in terms of economic development nor what characterises a capitalist market order. Such incremental change as is supported and indeed embraced by the decentralised market does not account for radical productive innovations in the production of existing consumer goods or intermediate products; it also does not support the development and production of new goods and services that necessitate novel production processes or previously unseen intermediate goods. Only goods produced using exclusively (or at least primarily) existing production processes and skills can be created within the market.

Whereas the specialisation deadlock in an 'atomistic market', as we have here assumed, should be a real problem in terms of both development and vulnerability, the empirical market is differently organised. As Coase identified, a large part of production in the market takes place within firms. This is a major and important difference between our assumed decentralised market and the empirical market. We also see a great many innovations, new and fascinating products, and novel production processes being tried in the market surprisingly frequently. Indeed, the production possibility frontier is constantly pushed outward, by leaps forward as well as gradual changes, and we see continuous improvements in our standard of living and general prosperity. Thus, the specialisation deadlock is in some manner overcome, and the next chapter elaborates on how the market deals with and overcomes its own limitations in this respect.

Summing up

Before turning to the discussion in the next chapter, let us first recapitulate the main points in the discussion above. We started the discussion by elaborating on the implications of specialisation in production and the market's adjustment processes. Specialised production under the division of labour creates interdependence between stages in production processes, which are loosened through redundant production and the availability of substitutes. We looked at the boundaries of production processes and how adjustments are effectuated within and across production stages. This discussion emanated in identifying the problem of incompleteness as production processes must be carried out in full in order to earn an income. Whereas this is not a problem within the extent of the exchange market, it restricts further development of the market through adopting more intensive specialisation. Indeed, we found that the exchange market is in a 'specialisation deadlock' because it lacks the means to deal with incompleteness unless there is already market exchange. This, of course, cannot be the case with productive innovations or production of previously unseen products. These must be implemented outside the extent of the existing exchange market.

Notes

1 A. Smith, *An Inquiry into the Nature and Causes of the Wealth of Nations* (1776) (Chicago, IL: University of Chicago Press, 1976), p. 8.
2 In order to motivate E, the price reduction of the 85 per cent finished intermediate good would have to exceed E's cost of production plus their expected rate of return on producing according to stage five standard. As D_9 or D_{10} by assumption are less productive than E, the latter should have overall higher profitability and D_9 or D_{10} will therefore need to, at least initially, use their profitability to incentivise E to produce the remaining 15 per cent of stage four. This does not, of course, mean that D_9 or D_{10} are victimised, only that they must offer E sufficient remuneration to redirect part of their productive ability to the 15 per cent.
3 L. v. Mises, *Human Action: A Treatise on Economics. The Scholar's Edition* (1949) (Auburn, AL: Ludwig von Mises Institute, 1998), p. 335.
4 It is possible, though should be very rare, that the production of new and specific tools can be carried out without innovation in processes used for their production. As such cases are uncommon and do not entail the type of problem here discussed, they are excluded from this analysis.
5 See M. N. Rothbard, *Man, Economy, and State with Power and Market. Scholar's Edition* (1962) (Auburn, AL: Ludwig von Mises Institute, 2004), pp. 613–615.
6 Intuitively, this comparatively simple productive innovation must treat operations as finite and discrete, though potentially revolutionisable, but not continuous. The productive situation is therefore distinct from both Adam Smith's view of how 'the operations of each workman are *gradually* reduced to a greater degree of simplicity' (quoted above, emphasis added) and modern neoclassical economists' mathematical treatment of infinitely small, continuous marginal units.

4   Entrepreneurship and integration

In the previous chapter, we discussed the ramifications of changes to and within a specialised production process. The division of labour into separated operations, tasks, and stages that constitute a production process entails serial interdependence between the tasks as well as between the labour workers who carry out those tasks. As the market allocates resources and productive endeavours vertically throughout processes, as well as horizontally between them, the problem emerges as a 'specialisation deadlock' because the decentralised market is not equipped to deal with change that is more than gradual. This is not a matter of market frictions such as transaction costs, which apply to the process of resource allocation within and between already existing production processes, but about *incompleteness*.

This chapter follows up on that discussion and discusses what means are available for actors in the market to avoid the risk of incompleteness and thereby overcome the 'specialisation deadlock'. To do this, we discuss the problem in greater detail as well as how it applies to market production and focus on the issue of task-splitting in production and in a market setting. This captures the essence of the problem when a productive innovation makes use of an increase in the division of labour through adopting a more intensive specialisation. The purpose of the discussion is to trace the implications of establishing production processes that by definition are not and cannot be located within the extent of the market for the simple reason that there is no market for the capital used in novel processes. We also attempt to formulate a possible solution that addresses the need for coordination in the face of incompleteness where no market for used capital exists. To facilitate this discussion, we first elaborate on the theoretical construct of the specialisation deadlock and its implications for production.

The specialisation deadlock and production

The previous chapter implied that we must see production tasks (stages) as finite and discrete rather than continuous, which has important implications for the structuring of a production process. It means, for instance, that there can be no (or at least only marginal) gradual intensification of specialisation under the division of labour. The scope of a workman's production task cannot be continuously narrowed – it can only be reduced by removing discrete operations. Even so, productivity gains are not achieved primarily by populating a production with a constantly greater number of workers who carry out the same tasks, whether they all do the exact same operations or divide them between themselves. Such gains as those we have seen in history and in contemporary society are achieved through productive innovations in capital and by establishing more roundabout production processes.[1] But such revolutionising leaps forward, in contrast to gradual improvements, must be fully established to be viable; if they are not, they will suffer incompleteness and consequently fail.

Incompleteness is not a problem in production processes where there are already markets for the intermediate goods produced, which means there is redundancy in the production structure. In market production, as we saw in the previous chapter, the outcome of any production stage is standardised to such a degree that it can be sold to a market price. This is not the case for a productive innovation, since its operations effectively take place outside the limit of the present market, whether or not it is within the production possibilities frontier. The novelty or originality of such actions place them outside the limit of the market; frictions, in contrast, affect exchange taking place within the extent of the market.

It is important to note that incompleteness arises only where there is some form of uniqueness through specialisation and therefore a lack of markets. It becomes a problem in the market process because incompleteness faces any innovation that does not fully or primarily consist of already saleable capital goods, both in process and production-aiding. As this is the case, innovation requires coordination to overcome this specialisation deadlock. While it implies limits to the workings of the market process throughout, the problem is non-trivial where comparatively intensive coordination is required in a highly decentralised setting. That is, where more intensive specialisation through the division of labour cannot be established without significant coordination. This is the reason we assumed a highly specialised but thoroughly decentralised – even atomistic – market-based production process above, since it both raises the question and highlights the problem. The existence of this specialised but decentralised production process could not have emerged, since the process of establishing it is itself subject to the 'deadlock'. Consequently, the actors must have already overcome the problem somehow. This is also the case with the advanced and specialised exchange market we all partake in and can observe around us in modern society.

We have noted that the 'deadlock' is more persistent in a highly specialised market, especially if it is also highly decentralised, but it should be prevalent also in a relatively unspecialised market. The latter holds true if the market's production includes and relies on advanced capital. Consider the self-sufficient life of Robinson Crusoe, who must take any and all productive action himself. While he will learn from experience and may figure out better methods for producing the necessary foodstuffs, shelter, and clothing, and therefore can increase his standard of living somewhat, it is not until he meets Friday that he may engage in specialisation under the division of labour. This presents no great problem, however, since Robinson and Friday can agree simply to divide tasks between themselves and thereby focus their efforts on certain chores and then share the fruits of their labour. For instance, Robinson may focus on producing clothing and build and maintain his and Friday's shelter(s). Because this means Friday won't have to do these same tasks, he is able to spend his days securing their sustenance. Both of them can increase their productivity by focusing on fewer tasks and saving on transitioning between them, just as Adam Smith teaches. And through David Ricardo's law of comparative advantage we can see that this simple focusing on particular tasks, when Robinson and Friday do what they are relatively better at (they have no reason to do otherwise), will increase their total output. But such division of labour between separate productive chores will not give rise to the specialisation deadlock, just as a traditionally wedlocked couple are not deadlocked only because the husband focuses on labouring to earn an income while the housewife cares for their home and children. Similarly, the owner of a farm with employees can without much problem assign his labourers different tasks and responsibilities rather than employ each of them to carry out all tasks in parallel.

These examples have in common that they rely on a simple division of labour in to already specific, separate tasks or processes. There is no economic or coordination problem involved with having labourer *A* focus on working the field to yield crops while *B* focuses on caring for the farm animals and *C* repairs the buildings on the farm. These are already 'naturally' separate chores that any individual and self-sufficient farmer would carry out separately but as part of the total work necessary to run the farm. Ploughing, sowing, and harvesting the fields are activities that do not interfere with or depend on other farm activities such as milking cows, feeding goats, or fixing the roof of the farmhouse. The type of coordination problems we are here interested in emerge only when we introduce specialisation through the division of labour *into* a 'naturally' separate task where there is no market for the individual specialised subtasks or their required capital. The problem therefore arises only when a production apparatus espouses a certain minimum specialisation intensity: when there is a market for production and, consequently, market prices for the means of production. Indeed, the problem exists because non-marketable action is taken as though it was within the realm of the existing market – when a productive innovation that in its implementation falls *outside* the extent of the market is introduced to production carried out *within* this limit. In other words, the specialisation deadlock occurs where action is taken that expands the market. Some level of originality is thus required.

As is commonly the case in a modern market, the division of labour refers to splitting up a task into a number of processes and sub-processes with each part being carried out separately. Specialisation is not in itself problematic unless this type of division of labour is implied. One might also argue, without much error, that this kind of specialisation, to be effective, needs specific supportive capital to be feasible. Advanced production necessitates the development of capital to increase the productivity of labour, and it is reasonable to assume that split tasks, the 'creation' of several more narrowly defined and thus more specific tasks to replace a previous one, require or would benefit from new capital. This is what Mises referred to in the quote in Chapter 2, when saying that the division of labour had brought about 'amazing improvements in technical methods of production'. Rothbard makes a similar point, stating that capital is 'a way station along the road to the enjoyment of consumers' goods' and that it functions 'to advance men in time toward their objective in producing consumers' goods'.[2] Specialisation under the division of labour facilitates the production and use of capital, since capital aids in production by either making labour more effective or by replacing simple operations. Capital is itself the outcome of a production process, which mixes the original factors land, labour, and time with the purpose of bringing the state of the market closer to the satisfaction of specific wants, and is therefore specific in a sense that labour never is: it is developed for a single or several purposes, and therefore has a limited number of specificities.[3]

For the example of Robinson and Friday, the division of their labour in to the tasks necessary for their survival can be taken quite far as a number of separate tasks are needed to secure their survival. But it is bounded by the lack of density in their two-man economy, which constitutes a very narrow limit to their production endeavour. Even if they are joined by two more people, say a Saturday and a Sunday, they would have no need for task-*splitting* and they would not automatically constitute a market. Rather, the group could work together in the same way a family would, and perhaps share the yield of their labours brotherly as in an idealised socialist society. In this situation, Smith's observation that the division of labour is limited both by the group's accumulated stock and the number of labourers available seems to hold because these individuals' first priority must be survival.[4] As they are already a group, their everyday and constant struggle amounts to dealing with all but the first of the Hobbesian description of life in the state of nature as 'solitary, poor, nasty, brutish and short'. Unless they, despite being in this precarious situation, can accumulate a stock of goods or, conversely, have labour hours to spare, they cannot afford to develop advanced capital. The situation seems to validate the Smithian paradox.

Smith's argument does not hold, however, if our group is joined by more shipwrecked people or other natives like Friday, Saturday, and Sunday. With a comparatively large population, the division of labour can be taken much further through engaging in intensive specialisation. Simply due to the increase in manpower, distinct lines of production will emerge as separate specialisations for labourers: fishermen, hunters, farmers, tailors, and so on. This division increases overall output, but also brings about decentralisation of the coordination of production for the satisfaction of wants and needs through exchange – and therefore the inception of a simple market. This type of specialisation through the division of labour upon already separate tasks does not depend on a stock of goods overall in the little society, but decentralises the decision-making and thus management of production in separate processes. With decentralised management, and with it private ownership or at least de facto control of the means of production, the incentives to invest in the development of capital for greater yield are strengthened and so a rationale for saving and investment is manifested. It also becomes easier to identify opportunities for productive innovation. It is with this limited type of entrepreneurship, in the sense of individual uncertainty-bearing and innovation for increased yield and therefore better opportunities for barter, that advanced specialisation through capital development and task-splitting can begin.

Note that this is not an argument about population size, but the relative availability of labour to carry out necessary tasks. As labour workers adopt distinct specialisations and trades, they thereby discover, develop, and strengthen their comparative advantages. This leads to an increase in their limited society's overall output, which can facilitate investments into the production of production-aiding capital and the adoption of more roundabout, specialised production processes. When the market develops sufficient density, labourers will find reason to split production processes *vertically* within their specialisations, which necessitates cooperation and coordination among those specialised towards the same trade. This specialisation process is distinct from the division of chores that previously took place only horizontally. As processes are split vertically, they produce the type of serial interdependence we discussed above, which is of an entirely different kind and requires advanced coordination or standardised intermediate goods or both to function. Standardisation here relates to the interfaces between interdependent production tasks, and the specifications of intermediate deliverables: the goods in process that change hands within the production process. We briefly touched on this in the previous discussion on the adaptation within production processes and will return to it later, as it facilitates but is also the product of market trade, especially in advanced economies. At this point, as our island-based production lacks a developed exchange market, and standardisation hence is not yet a problem, we will focus on the immediately relevant issue of coordination as production processes continue to be split vertically and therefore become more roundabout. As the island's labourers are specialised towards specific production processes horizontally, or even specific tasks vertically within processes, but there are no directly competing production processes, there is consequently no market-based allocation of resources between them. This type of simplistic production economy without redundancy and competition should be rather inefficient and lacking of investments in capital. As it is relatively simple, there is no basis for strict interdependencies, and so a 'specialisation deadlock' could not occur. In this situation of primitive production, structuring the islanders' productive activities in ways akin to a socialist planned economy may be feasible or even desirable in the short term. However, centralising decision-making and resource allocation at this point also retards the economy's development towards more intensive specialisation through the division of labour and could for this reason stifle productive progress. Centralised decision-making, as Hayek[5] noted, is unable to take advantage of specific local and dispersed knowledge, and also reduces or fully abrogates incentives for innovation and experimenting in productive processes. It therefore deters economic progress beyond the scope of what is possible for the central planner or planners to experience personally.

Intensity of specialisation in an underdeveloped economy, first horizontally and then vertically, tends to be proportional to the increase in its productive density and, therefore, as Smith notes, to the supply of labour. As production processes are streamlined, specialised, and separated along with the intensification of this division of labour, productivity increases progressively with its economic density as producers develop their specialisations and discover and strengthen their comparative advantages. Even without innovation and capital investments, while increases in density and specialisation would tend to be approximately commensurate, the result of specialisation is overall increased productivity and therefore increasing output quantities. This suggests a solution to Smith's paradox.

In the higher-density island economy, multiple labourers specialise to each production process and can therefore discover their within-process comparative advantages and specialise accordingly. Redundancy in labour factors thereby facilitates vertical division of the process into its specific tasks and operations. This division is simple enough for specialised labourers seeking to maximise their production at minimum expense. Any production process consists of at least a few identifiable separate operations specific to the process, and simple division of labour between these known operations and the advantages of doing so are easily conceivable. It is indeed a fact, as Mises notes, that 'work performed under the division of labor is more productive than isolated work and that man's reason is capable of recognizing this truth'.[6] As far as is supported by and thus compatible with the overall production process, or can be agreed on by all involved, experimentation and minor improvements to the process will be carried out. However, specialisation through the vertical division of labour causes serial interdependence that could result in incompleteness should either labourer fall short in his productive efforts. As a rudimentary economy cannot sustain idle redundancy in its production processes, this is a real problem that our islanders face and that ultimately limits the feasibility of specialisation.

The division of labour within each production process will eventually come to a point where operations are so specialised that all of them can no longer be effectively performed by everybody involved in the process. In the least, as they specialise and improve on and develop their respective skills, the labourers are no longer fully substitutable but become experts. Just like the horizontal division of labour allowed the islanders to specialise in separate trades (fishing, hunting, etc.) and thereby develop specific skills, the vertical division of labour produces specialists with unique productive abilities. The labour factors are thus heterogenised through the development of their respective expertise. This type of division of labour is, writes Mises,

> a factor bringing about differentiation. It assigns to the various geographic areas specific functions in the complex of the processes of production. It makes some areas urban, others rural; it locates the various branches of

manufacturing, mining, and agriculture in different places. Still more important, however, is the fact that it intensifies the innate inequality of men. Exercise and practice of specific tasks adjust individuals better to the requirements of their performance; men develop some of their inborn faculties and stunt the development of others. Vocational types emerge, people become specialists.[7]

This development is augmented with advanced specialisation through the 'splitting' of tasks within the production apparatus of a market.

Advanced task-splitting

The very limited economy we have so far analysed in this chapter included no productive redundancy and each production process was in this sense a monopoly. As the population grows and economic density deepens, the new labour factors would likely be assigned tasks in this little undeveloped economy based on the population's most urgent needs. While there are productivity gains from populating a specific production process with labourers to specialise to its separate operations, there are very limited returns to over-populating a process. For hunting, for instance, different strategies may be used depending on the number of hunters available: from the lone hunter setting traps or waiting in hiding for his prey, to the hunting team with specific roles or positions relative their preferred game. But at some point the production process suffers from being overcrowded; the diminishing returns to the number of labour factors included in the process incentivises workers to adopt other lines of production or establish parallel production structures. For instance, the hunting team may split into two and concentrate on different areas, different types of game, or different hunting methods. We have still to see, however, how labourers in a production process adopt task-splitting rather than the comparatively simple division of labour on to already separate operations.

Intuitively, the first 'splitting' of a task includes the production of capital. While a hunter at the beginning may simply rely on his ability to kill game with his hands or throw rocks to assist in the hunt, he will eventually benefit from producing more elaborate capital such as a bow and arrows, a net, or elaborate traps. The single hunter can produce simple capital since it requires little specific skill and since the production and consequent usage of this capital increases productivity sufficiently to constitute an immediate gain. For instance, the act of sharpening a pointless stick to produce an effective spear will take time from hunting but could make the hunt so much more productive that the time and effort needed for the combined activities sharpening and hunting fall short of what is needed when hunting with a blunt spear. If it usually takes the hunter ten hours to find and kill a certain type of game when using rocks and sticks, and if spending two hours to find the perfect stick and sharpen it to produce a spear shortens the time necessary to find and kill similar game by at least two hours, then there is no problem as long as the hunter realises this or is willing to chance it. The act of hunting may be delayed and the time available for it shortened, but this has no negative effect on the outcome as the production process is shortened by no less than it takes to produce the better tools and the expected outcome is the same. To the extent that time and effort invested in production of capital does not affect the general flow of goods, production of simple tools used in rudimentary production processes generally constitutes no economic problem.

If we let the same production process become more densely populated, it would allow for labour to specialise in the two separate tasks of simple tool-making and hunting with the produced tools, respectively. While this situation is different in the sense that hunting now consists of a more roundabout production process including the production of capital, it is not essentially different from specialising in separate operations in the process. Even if two hunters divide the tasks of spear-producing and hunting between them, failure of the one to produce a spear does not mean the other cannot hunt – only that hunting will be a little less productive as it is no longer aided by the simple produced tool. The problem arises with innovation of advanced capital and a revolutionising *restructuring of the production process* – a new *kind* of division of labour rather than a simple acknowledgement of comparative advantages in workers' specialisations – that most likely requires investment of present resources for potential future gain.

Fast forward to when there are sufficient islanders to populate a particular production process so that at least one individual specialises to carry out each necessary operation. At this point, even though there are no competing production structures and thus no independent redundancy in production or market prices, we may see innovation of sufficient originality to cause a limited problem akin to the specialisation deadlock. The consequences are however of limited effect as there is no redundancy in production, and therefore no cross-process standardisation through factor markets. But they are still of economic significance and this limited case provides insights that are applicable also on the more advanced market situation.

Consider a generic production process consisting of three successive operations or production stages, o_{1-3}, including production of capital needed to assist labourers in carrying out production. These three stages are carried out by four labourers, l_{1-4}, with the more labour intensive stage o_2 being carried out by two labourers. As per our assumption, the middle production stage requires approximately twice the labour power to produce as much output as the other stages, and this is the reason two labourers work side by side: l_2 and l_3 both perform the operation o_2. Also assume that this situation is the result of the process described above, which means it has undergone a vertical division of labour to such degree that the separate operations have become distinct specialisations. Whatever naturally occurring inputs used in this process must undergo each of the three productive operations in the specified order to produce the expected outcome, which means the process is serially interdependent such that the output of operation o_1 is the input for o_2, and the output of o_2 is the input of o_3. Only the outcome of the full process is in itself a product and therefore the output of o_1 and o_2 are not serviceable for consumption. In other words, if operation o_3 is not performed the process is incomplete as the intermediate good, the output of o_2, remains unusable (or usable only at very high cost) unless it first undergoes o_3. The four labour factors l_{1-4} are therefore ultimately dependent on each other, since if either of them fails or neglects to perform his stage, all work done to that point is without value unless the remaining stages are performed at some point and the intermediate capital good does not perish while waiting in process. The value realised through production requires the full process to be carried out from beginning to end.

Imagine that, after another hard day's work, l_2 and l_3 walk together back to their shelter as usual and discuss the day's arduous experience. But today l_3 says that he has been thinking about how to improve the production process, and presents to l_2 an idea for how to make their performed stage more productive. His idea includes a new structure with two separate operations previously neither seen nor imagined. In essence, he suggests that there may be much to gain to carry out these two operations, which we will refer to as o_{21} and o_{22}, in place of the presently performed o_2. After l_3 explains more specifically what this innovation entails and how he expects it can be implemented, l_2 is thrilled by the idea. If it goes well, l_3 anticipates, it would lessen their burden and increase production or, alternatively, free up time for other activities. But it would require the workers to learn new types of operations. The innovation, in short, introduces the sub-process o_{21}-o_{22} to replace the operation o_2, which produces a new process that is comparatively more roundabout: o_1-o_{21}-o_{22}-o_3 instead of o_1-o_2-o_3. As the innovation has not been tried, they will need to invest time and labour to implement it and test if it will function as expected.

Whether or not specific capital investment is necessary, l_2 and l_3 will need to invest their precious labour time and effort into this experiment. To the degree this affects their performance of o_2, it will bring about a loss to all those involved in as well as dependent on the production process. If l_4 has accumulated inventory of inputs to use in production of o_3, which would be unlikely in this rudimentary production process, the production of outputs may continue even without production of o_2 but only until l_4's inventory is depleted. Whatever is produced by l_1 during this time will still be incomplete, and at the same time there will be no inputs produced to use by l_4 in performing o_3 and he is therefore kept, or will soon be, idle. This can amount to a significant loss of output, which a relatively undeveloped, rudimentary production economy may not be able to afford since there would not be sufficient stock of consumer goods to draw from during the time of implementation. In the face of incompleteness and therefore loss, innovation affects all of those involved in production (and those dependent on its outcome) and in this sense becomes a collective effort. Indeed, the cost of failure is immense and is borne by everyone, and for this reason l_2 and l_3 have little incentive to experiment with the production process. Only if they can reliably predict that their efforts have minimal effect on the existent production process or that the innovation comes with great benefit and has a great chance of success would they be inclined to go through with it. Even so, they may face resistance by the other workers unless they are able to convince them that the effort does not jeopardise production. Rudimentary societies that rely for their survival on limitedly specialised production should thus tend to be highly sceptical towards innovative entrepreneurship since the cost of implementation is comparatively very high. They may even develop institutional means, whether formal or informal, to resist such change effectively.

What matters for our analysis here, however, is not the specific social structure of this type of basic society, but the fact that innovation to an existent and vertically specialised production process can upset the whole process due to its serial interdependence. Production is therefore exceedingly vulnerable to unpredictable, uncontrolled changes to the inclusive stages as well as the process as a whole and any disturbances can have disastrous consequences. This vulnerability can only be mitigated in a decentralised productive system that includes productive redundancy or that accumulates and holds inventory of intermediate goods, which a rudimentary society cannot initially afford but that market coordination depends on. While redundancy, as we saw in Chapter 3, lessens the cost of change by reducing direct dependence and thereby limiting the impact of incompleteness, it in no way abrogates the problem.

Advanced task-splitting with redundant production

We saw in the previous example that the innovation introduced by l_2 and l_3 affects the whole production process because it is serially interdependent: the third and final stage depends on the input produced by the second and middle stage, which in turn depends on the input produced by the first stage. As failure of any of the stages means the whole process fails, those specialised to the individual stages all ultimately bear the uncertainty of innovation. This is a theoretically important limiting aspect of specialised production, but is not necessarily of prohibitive magnitude under rudimentary production. In the used example, it may not be an insurmountable obstacle for the four islanders. Indeed, they are already both collectively and individually incentivised to ensure the production process is complete. In the simplest case, the problem may be limited to the ability of l_2 and l_3 to communicate the potential gains to l_1 and l_4, and their ability to come to an agreement with respect to the chance of success, the strategy for implementation, and the costs involved.

As we saw in the previous chapter, however, the strict interdependence in a solitary production process under the vertical division of labour can be partly alleviated through redundancy. The effect of failure in one stage is of much lesser impact if production takes place in two or more production processes with their respective stages performed in parallel. Part of the reason for this is that competing, redundant processes constitute standardisation of stages. There is therefore redundancy not in production of a specific good, but also in production of the intermediate goods in each of the stages. For this reason, production as a whole will not fail with one of the operations but can continue, and failure of one stage does not cause failure to that separate process. The interdependence between stages is weakened by redundancy as there is a market for intermediate goods, and this allows producers of stages in all processes to adjust their production to the new situation. Another part of the reason is the effect of prices in redundant production processes. If the second stage of process four fails, the previous stage of process four can sell its output and the subsequent stage of this process can equally procure inputs in the open market. While production can continue due to redundancy, though with lesser completed volume, market prices will adjust to the new situation (as we saw previously): prices of outputs in the stage preceding the affected stage will fall and prices for the latter's output will rise, thereby incentivising producers to seek alternative means to complete the process (or shift their production activities to different types of production).

As the density of the economy and the availability of labour factors increase, redundancy can emerge. Indeed, it was the increase in density that made the initial horizontal division of labour possible, the further increase that facilitated the vertical division of labour, and it is this development that provides the required resources for establishing parallel production processes of similar function. We already noted this above, but as labour factors become available they are likely to be put to use in production to increase society's overall standard of living. As production processes have been established relying on operations-based specialisation through the vertical division of labour, adding labourers to individual stages increases the potential output of these stages due to the effectuated redundancy.

We immediately recognise two outcomes of unevenly populated production stages in our economy with rudimentary specialisation. First, the burden of production decreases as this stage has access to more productive resources and therefore can produce greater quantities. If the number of islanders specialised to performing the first stage in the three-stage process above is doubled, the production potential is also approximately doubled. Yet as the second stage cannot produce more than was previously the case, the effect of this increased production capacity in the first stage is to release labour. Those carrying out this particular operation can therefore find time for other chores and efforts that can contribute to increase further the islanders' standard of living. Alternatively, it affords them the opportunity for leisure.

Second, as these labour factors are freed from the burden of producing, they are also freed from some of the cost of interdependence. Say l_5, newly arrived to our island society, joins l_1 to produce o_1, and that him doing so (assuming the cost of capital in this first stage is negligible) approximately doubles the production capacity of this stage whereas the production capacity of o_2 and o_3 remain unchanged. While l_2 and l_3 in stage two and l_4 in the third stage continue to work long hours, the redundancy in stage one causes some of the productive factors to be idle since the other stages simply cannot handle more input. These slack resources can be used to produce savings that can support productive investments. In contrast to the example of innovation above, the addition of l_5 means the first stage can in one day produce sufficient inputs to be used for two full days in the second stage. So l_1 and l_5 can take every other day off – or produce today and use tomorrow to implement and try out a productive innovation. This innovation could potentially save even more resources, and thereby allow for investments in the other two stages and possibly increase overall production. Do not forget, however, that the resources used in the initial investment for increased productivity may be misplaced or the implementation poorly executed such that the resources are lost. But as the example does not at this point include credit and borrowing, which means production always must precede consumption and saving, the impact of such entrepreneurial failures is limited to affect only the first stage. As the inputs needed for the second stage (the savings) are produced in the previous time period, innovation failure does not affect the totality of the production process.

Similarly, in a situation with redundant production throughout the process organised in parallel processes without a single point of failure, any effect on a single operation is primarily limited to that operation. This holds true for any direct effects on the operation such as failure, since failure of one operation does not automatically cause the whole process to fail. But the indirect consequence of any change will affect the whole process as well as parallel processes, and cause ripple effects throughout the economy. We saw this in the previous chapter as resources were reallocated across processes as well as between stages, as a response to more productive uses being revealed.

Advanced task-splitting in a market

Let us revisit the example used throughout this chapter, but instead of the previously discussed productive innovations, the little island society experiences a large increase in population. More people need to be fed, but there are also more hands to exploit in production. It just so happens that the inflow of people are sufficient to populate triply the already fully vertically specialised production processes. The previously discussed production process o_1-o_2-o_3 can therefore triple its output and the processes are split into three separate production processes, each of them structured like the original and with four labour workers performing the three stages. The new workers contribute new perspectives and have ideas for how to improve the process further, but the resultant three parallel processes are nevertheless similar to the original process and as the labourers learn from each other the processes become close to carbon copies of each other. They are fully substitutable as processes as well as in the separate operations carried out.

These processes are subject to the dynamics discussed in the previous chapter. As there is redundancy, the cost of direct productive interdependency is averted somewhat and can also be dealt with to some extent through adjustments of production across processes and pooling of resources. What remains of the interdependence constraint is in the form of standardised deliverables: the intermediate goods changing hands between stages are sufficiently similar to be considered substitutes. The production process is standardised and modular in the sense that it can be reorganised through any combination of stages from the three separate processes. A process consisting of the first stage from the first process, the second stage from the second process, and the third stage from the third process functions as well as any other combination as long as each stage is carried out in order. What holds a process together is the serial interdependence between stages, but as all stages are redundantly performed there is no dependence on a particular labourer with this specialisation. The deliverables are standardised and can be used interchangeably. In other words, the output of the first stage in the second process can be used by the second stage in either process.

While this situation is more similar to the modern market than a single unique production process, its division in specialised stages that are produced redundantly also provides means to introduce productive innovations into the existing processes as long as it shares interfaces – the intermediate goods changing hands to connect the stages – with existing stages and there is capital available to support the investment. This means that the second stage, in its present shape, can be fully replaced by a new operation or set of operations as long as it (1) uses the same inputs and (2) produces the same output. How production within a stage is carried out, the technologies or methods or even materials used, is from the point of view of the production process as a whole and the production of the final good irrelevant. What matters is that the production stages are carried out in the correct order and that their interfaces match, no matter how a production stage accomplishes the standardised outputs using the standardised inputs. Market production is agnostic as to the execution of any particular stage, but depends on the intermediate goods, the stages' outputs, to be compatible through adhering to the established standard. This state of the production apparatus as specialised and standardised facilitates innovation since revolutionising production innovations can be adopted within a specific stage without affecting other stages (unless there is failure). Production doesn't suffer incompleteness and can continue 'like before' despite any and all of its parts having been replaced.

If we again consider the example above, in which l_2 and l_3 in stage two decide to try implementing a new way of carrying out o_2, it becomes obvious that them doing so has only marginal effect on the overall production process. Even if they need to take full days off in order to attempt to realise the perceived improvement, doing so will not cause the whole production process (and therefore the supply of the end product) to come to a halt. It will not suffer incompleteness, but will only suffer partial loss of output. Production is still completed through redundant production processes and the limited production market will be able to reallocate intermediate goods to maximise production as circumstances change.

What is of import here is not the adjustments taking place in the remaining and standardised production process, but what the innovative efforts of l_2 and l_3 imply from the point of view of the productive system. Implementing the innovation is practicable only because it completely replaces the existing stage of production o_2 and therefore does not suffer from incompleteness. This means that the innovative production sub-process o_{21}-o_{22} also is internally strictly interdependent: the extent of the market for the producer of o_{21} consists solely of the single producer of o_{22}, who in turn is fully dependent on the output of o_{21} to commence production of o_{22}. The effect of implementing this innovative sub-process, which implies an outright splitting of a task and therefore intensified division of labour, is that l_2 and l_3 become strictly interdependent in carrying out this process, or, as I discuss elsewhere,[8] *mutually specialised.*

A limited and very specific case of this is discussed by Oliver E. Williamson in terms of costs of misalignment due to opportunistic behaviour following relationship-specific investments.[9] To Williamson, the risk of incurring such costs is a powerful driver for integrating existing transactions within organisational hierarchies, which makes possible the use of selective intervention. The general problem, however, is another. Regardless of whether l_2 and l_3 trust or mistrust each other, the risk of opportunistic behaviour (as is Williamson's focus) is miniscule. Our previous discussion shows why this is the case: opportunistic behaviour by either or both parties causes incompleteness for the process, and is therefore prohibitively costly for their mutual specialisation. It is indeed true that l_3, specialised to carrying out the downstream sub-task o_{22}, can 'hold up' the producer of o_{21} l_2 by refusing to use or purchase his output, as Williamson assumes. But it is difficult to think of specific cases where this would be a real concern for l_2 and l_3, unless we also assume that they are motivated to engage in self-destructive behaviour. The problem identified by Williamson, it turns out, is applicable only in very specific cases: where there already exists a market for the given transaction *and* where it requires an investment specific to the relationship such that it makes one party dependent on the other but not vice versa. The former is necessary because without an existing market for the intermediate products produced in the individual stages carried out as part of the transaction, both parties would suffer incompleteness and therefore loss in the case of holdup. The latter is necessary to make opportunism a real and credible threat, as without specific investments creating a bilateral monopoly the threat of holdup is inconsequential. For both to hold, we must assume that the productive transaction itself and the transactional relationship are on different analytical levels and therefore distinct. Alternatively, we can assume that the transaction as carried out by the parties as facilitated the specific investment is not sufficiently innovative to constitute a real and significant productive gain, but that it is sufficiently different from the market to make resorting back to previous market positions costly to the point of deterrence.

The case considered here is much more general in the sense that we consider the implementation of a productive innovation into an existent market situation. There is a market of sorts for each of the stages of production in the established production process, but not for the individual tasks carried out in the innovative sub-process. So neither of the parties l_2 or l_3 has an incentive to act opportunistically with regard to the other party or the sub-process itself, since it entails incompleteness and therefore failure. Williamson disregards incompleteness as the result of holdup in highly specialised production processes, yet assumes mutual specialisation of transactional parties around relationship-specific investments. The sub-process o_{21}-o_{22}, as we have seen here, is an all-or-nothing production solution as it is a unique alternative to existing and workable production stages. It is therefore either successful in its entirety or it fails, which leaves no room for self-interested opportunistic behaviour. Whether o_{21}-o_{22} is successful, which will be recognised by earning profit in an advanced money economy, or by measurably lower resource usage or higher output in our rudimentary production economy example, requires completing the whole sub-process and supplying subsequent production stages with inputs. Opportunism therefore cannot be a factor.

As is indicated by the completeness criterion for estimating the relative success of the productive innovation, the implementation of the sub-process takes place outside the limits of the market. The labourers l_2 or l_3 are fully and mutually dependent on each other *because* there is neither market supply for the individual sub-tasks carried out in the new sub-process nor market demand for the intermediate outputs. There are no fall-back options, and this is what produces the strict interdependence between the parties and gives rise to the completeness criterion. In the simplest case as considered here, where one task is split in two, each new task is compatible with the market at one end while dependent on the other new task at the other. There is ample market supply of compatible inputs for o_{21} and ample market demand for o_{22}'s outputs, but there is no external market at all for their intermediate product, that is, o_{21}'s output and o_{22}'s input. Each of the two parties is completely dependent on the other party doing his part. They are therefore at each other's mercy and equally dependent on each other's success, so their incentives are aligned rather than opposed. This is the opposite of Williamson's prediction, since he would have the parties take advantage of each other. We see here that neither of them has anything to gain from doing so, however, since they will both lose due to incompleteness. However, their mutual specialisation effectively creates an 'island' outside the extent of the existing market that utilises a different kind of division of labour since it does things differently, and this entails a form of necessary integration of productive tasks that would be of no value within the extent of the market. Whereas the tasks may be observable as separate, everything else about them is integrated: the result is joint and inseparable; the operations are interdependent; and any failure or shortcoming is suffered by and threatens the whole enterprise. But this 'island' is not subject to opportunistic behaviour triggered by guileful self-interest seeking.

It is true that the operations share interfaces with the existing market structure and the new sub-process therefore is compatible with established market production. But the innovated process itself is ultimately insulated, or auto-insulated, as it were, from market influence and is structured in ways not possible in the market. The process is therefore productively decomposable into specific tasks, but not decomposable into the surrounding market since there is no market and thus very limited saleability for the individual tasks.[10] Those carrying out the tasks in this sub-process are for this reason blind with respect to improvements of specific tasks as there is no feedback mechanism available other than for the complete process. For production processes established within the extent of the market, each production stage has a market and is therefore appraised separately. This promotes discovery of opportunities for improvement through competition and eliminates comparatively inefficient or ineffective production tasks and structures. These forces are not available for tasks carried out within the new production sub-process. This means that the implementation of innovative production necessitates the uncertainty-bearing for the complete process rather than individual parts, which is akin to Robinson Crusoe's primitive production discussed at the beginning of this chapter.

Entrepreneurship

As we have seen, the newly implemented production process is, for all practical purposes, placed squarely outside the extent of the market. This follows directly from the nature of innovating, which must include novelty and implies an action that, at least to some not insignificant extent, breaks new ground where the market is inapplicable and impossible. If this were not the case, the innovation would not be novel. We have also connected this novelty to the market's production structure, showing that an innovation is by definition distinct from production within the extent of the market and therefore of a different kind. This, we argued, gives rise to mutual specialisation so the process requires coordination not to suffer incompleteness. We will now see how entrepreneurial imagination offers a solution to the problem highlighted.

The previous discussion suggested that changes to a production structure that are innovative to the point of being disruptive, and therefore of greater impact than simple arbitrage, fall outside established market production. The decentralised market adjusts well to both endogenous and exogenous changes by reallocating resources, but is impotent with regard to creation of novelty. The reason for this is that the market requires substitutability for goods to be saleable and appropriately priced: the novel productive innovation cannot be allocated towards uses of different value if productive stages are uniquely interdependent, as in the case of mutual specialisation. In the case of the novel sub-production process o_{21}-o_{22} there is compatibility with the outside market, but no basis for interaction with that market for the 'internally' coordinated operations. The sub-process is therefore practically encapsulated and protected, as it were, from market influence: there is no proper pricing and no decentralised reallocation of resources *within* the o_{21}-o_{22} process. But this also means that the process cannot benefit from these market forces, and that it consequently is subject to a severe calculation problem: whereas the return to the full sub-process is realised through profits, the value contribution of each individual part cannot be observed, identified, or calculated. The result is that the process overall cannot be properly improved because the economic efficiency of its parts is unknown and unknowable. The uncertainty of the enterprise is for this reason irreducible and borne centrally.

The lacking interconnectedness between the novel production structure and the market effectively separates it from the market and in effect makes it a separate phenomenon. It is unaffected and therefore unaided by market competition in its parts simply because they are unique, interdependent, and for this reason cannot find substitutes in the market. But this does not imply that it is completely free from market conditions. The market has through competition established a minimum required level of efficiency in resource use and allocation, below which no alternatives are viable. This applies to the innovation as well as to actors producing competitively within the extent of the market. We therefore expect to see such innovations only where they outperform the regular market. In this sense, innovation may serve as a productive catalyst that functions to establish new technology or organisation of productive efforts. Innovation constitutes a challenge to the present market order by offering an alternative that, to the extent it is successful and therefore makes lasting rather than transient impression, can revolutionise production. Productive innovation is the task of the entrepreneur, whose function is limited by the market's existing production structure yet reforms and improves upon it. Joseph A. Schumpeter summarises the role of the entrepreneur in specialised production under the division of labour thusly: 'the function of entrepreneurs is to reform or revolutionize the pattern of production by exploiting an invention or, more generally, an untried technological possibility for producing a new commodity or producing an old one in a new way'.[11]

Following Schumpeter, we find that the entrepreneurial function is disequilibrating in the sense that implemented innovation constitutes a challenge to the status quo. The productive innovation upsets the established market order and its standard processes by introducing new tasks and specialisations, new intermediate goods – and threatens to outdo the market. It is a disruptive force that breaks with the accepted order and defies assumed truths and conventional production. The entrepreneur leaps into the productive unknown where technological and economic knowledge are unknowable and will become accessible only through the implementation process. By deliberately acting outside the realm of the market, the outcome is fundamentally open-ended and at best imaginable. The uncertainty of the entrepreneurial enterprise is for these reasons irreducible and incalculable, and must be borne in its entirety until the implementation is complete and proven to satisfy consumer wants by earning profit.

The entrepreneurial implementation process is a very different undertaking from partaking in or organising production processes coordinated through market prices. Whereas we can acknowledge entrepreneurial elements in market arbitrage, resource reallocation and adjustments to production processes within the extent of the market, the entrepreneur as here perceived is of a very different type. Entrepreneurship establishes innovative production processes outside the extent of the market. We also hold that it is by recognising the conditions for and characteristics of this extra-market development that we can best understand the business firm, which can be defined as the productive endeavour undertaken in an extra-market setting. The firm can most easily be characterised as an 'island' of integrated productivity that implements and utilises intensive specialisation of a degree and kind that is different from and aims to outperform the present market order. It is a market-based phenomenon that serves the entrepreneur in his attempt to establish a new type of production process.

Note that this view of the firm is neither subject to the 'legal fiction' nor of formal character. We see the firm simply as an economic phenomenon that arises around entrepreneurial pursuits placed firmly outside the realm of, but that ultimately become part of and transform, the market. It has a pure economic function that appears to be of transient nature but is frequently occurring (see Chapters 6 and 8). As a generalised economic function, it is unrelated to any formal identification of firm entities and therefore unaffected by legal concerns. The firm, then, is simply what emerges when more specialised production processes are implemented through entrepreneurial action. It is an economic phenomenon that overcomes the inertia of the interrelated market order, and that constitutes a productive challenge by introducing change and in the end disrupting the status quo. This function appears to be a necessary component in the progression of the market process not only for technological reasons and due to specialisation deadlocks in physical capital, but for social reasons as well. For as Schumpeter points out,

> the environment resists in many ways that vary, according to social conditions, from simple refusal either to finance or to buy a new thing, to physical attack on the man who tries to produce it. To act with confidence beyond the range of familiar beacons and to overcome that resistance requires aptitudes that are present in only a small fraction of the population and that define the entrepreneurial type as well as the entrepreneurial function.[12]

Summing up

The market indeed resists novelty, and this is why the entrepreneur is able to and must implement the imagined production process outside the extent of the market – through the economic firm. This has been the aim of this chapter: to show how a firm as an 'island of specialisation' can provide a solution to the specialisation deadlock. It started by discussing wherein the specialisation deadlock applies, and we noted that this is not a problem when Robinson Crusoe and Friday divide tasks between them. The problem emerges not because already separate tasks are performed by different people, but when tasks are actively split and thereby necessitate new and previously unseen specialisations that are unsupported by the existing production structure and, consequently, the market. Those new tasks comprise a novel sub-process in which each of the tasks carried out are mutually specialised. This is where the problem of incompleteness comes in – because of strict interdependence. We further looked at the effects of advanced task-splitting when there is redundant production and when it is carried out within (or, more accurately, outside the extent of) an existing market. We then concluded the chapter by looking at entrepreneurship as the implementation of innovative production, which we found to be very different from production coordinated through existing market prices. Indeed, this type of endeavour that establishes production as an island of specialisation outside the extent of the market, is how we would conceive of the firm.

Notes

1 See E. v. Böhm-Bawerk, *Positive Theory of Capital* (1889) (South Holland, IL: Libertarian Press, 1959).
2 M. N. Rothbard, *Man, Economy, and State with Power and Market. Scholar's Edition* (1962) (Auburn, AL: Ludwig von Mises Institute, 2004), p. 52.
3 With regard to labour, the stronger claim that it 'is almost always nonspecific' can be made; 'very rare indeed is the person who could conceivably perform only one type of task', Rothbard, *Man, Economy, and State with Power and Market. Scholar's Edition*, p. 523. Mises similarly states that 'human labor is both suitable and indispensable for the performance of all thinkable processes and modes of production' and that it 'is the most scarce of all primary means of production because it is in this restricted sense nonspecific and because every variety of production requires the expenditure of labor', L. v. Mises, *Human Action: A Treatise on Economics. The Scholar's Edition* (1949) (Auburn, AL: Ludwig von Mises Institute, 1998), pp. 133, 135.
4 Quoted in Chapter 2, above.
5 See e.g. F. A. v. Hayek, 'The Use of Knowledge in Society', *American Economic Review*, 35:4 (1945), pp. 519–530; F. A. v. Hayek, 'Economics and Knowledge', *Economica*, 4:13 (1937), pp. 33–54.
6 Mises, *Human Action: A Treatise on Economics. The Scholar's Edition*, p. 144.
7 Mises, *Human Action: A Treatise on Economics. The Scholar's Edition*, pp. 163–164.
8 See P. L. Bylund, 'Explaining Firm Emergence: Specialization, Transaction Costs, and the Integration Process', *Managerial and Decision Economics*, 36:4 (2015), pp. 221–238.
9 See e.g. O. E. Williamson, 'The Logic of Economic Organization', *Journal of Law, Economics, and Organization*, 4:1 (1988), pp. 65–93; O. E. Williamson, 'Comparative Economic Organization: The Analysis of Discrete Structural Alternatives', *Administrative Science Quarterly*, 36:2 (1991), pp. 269–296.
10 H. A. Simon, 'The Architecture of Complexity', *Proceedings of the American Philosophical Society*, 106:6 (1962), pp. 467–482.
11 J. A. Schumpeter, *Socialism, Capitalism and Democracy* (New York: Harper & Bros., 1942), p. 132.
12 Schumpeter, *Socialism, Capitalism and Democracy*, p. 132.

5   Authority and hierarchy

The previous chapter showed that there is a productivity rationale for integrated production within a market setting based on specialisation through the division of labour. This structure of argument is in line with the extant literature on the firm, from Ronald Coase's 'The Nature of the Firm' and on, in which the firm is seen as a means to overcome specific shortcomings in the market. However, our discussion indicated that innovative production processes are distinct and integrated *by default* as there is initially no market support for the new production structure. As the specific 'internal' allocation of resources that makes up the productive innovation constitutes a novel use of specialisation, broadly perceived, those involved in the implementation cannot rely on the market for core functions. This means that integration is not something the actor chooses to overcome a specific problem in the market (such as transaction costs, control of valuable resources, or knowledge, and so on), but is an unchosen effect of implementing a new production structure. The firm is here not a means but an effect, and is not directly subject to a choice of organisational form. Productive innovation through the introduction of intensive specialisation always takes place outside the present extent of the market.

This conclusion turns the conventional logic of economic organising as a means for market actors to deal with and ultimately overcome market imperfections or failures on its head. The literature on organisational economics and the theory of the firm tends to begin with the market and hypothesises that integration is a special phenomenon in it. It is an assumed deviation from standard price mechanism coordination that is intended to solve a specific problem or shortcoming inherent in the market. The argument, then, is that market actors choose to form a firm because of its specific problem-solving property, such as transaction cost avoidance. Stating this type of rationale for the firm does not, however, explain how it, in contrast to the market, is able to produce this exploitable property. As this problem-overcoming property is core to how we recognise and can understand the firm, this missing piece of the puzzle – how it accomplishes what it is perceived to do – ties into what the firm in reality is and therefore also how it can be explained. This may be a reason why individual Coasean questions, and foremost among them the one about the firm's boundaries, or where firm ends and market begins, have received much scholarly attention. Yet, despite this vast literature, we do not seem to be much closer to answering the questions than when they were first posed.

Part of the reason is the tautological nature of the argument for the firm as a choice of governance. In the case of Coase's transaction cost explanation, the firm is simply defined as the type of production organising that supersedes the costly price mechanism by relying on the directional authority of a manager. But defining the firm as the transaction cost saving device it is sought out to be does not escape the fundamental problem in finding satisfying answers to the Coasean questions of the firm's rationale, boundaries, and internal organisation. Coase himself was able to answer the question about the firm's boundaries by simply asserting the firm's rationale and by assuming its internal organisation is very similar, if not identical, to the market's allocation of resources (which is presumed efficient). The Coasean firm integrates individual transactions until the marginal net saving on transaction costs (the firm's asserted rationale) is zero. The boundary is therefore set and then continuously adjusted by the manager dealing at the transactional margin through integrating more or fewer transactions when the cost structure fluctuates. Indeed, it is 'always possible to revert to the open market', writes Coase, if the cost of management becomes higher than the cost of transacting in the market.

The logic of the Coasean transaction cost story is internally consistent, but has ambiguous implications because of its reliance on assertions about the institutional structure of production and definitions formulated to support the wanted outcome. Coase's assumption of an efficient market allocation of resources subject to costs of transacting that can be avoided through integration in firms, which aim to 'reproduce' market allocation internally by non-market means, is puzzling and raises quite a few questions that are still to be answered in the literature. Treating the firm as an outcome or result, as we do here, rather than a means avoids the ambiguity inherent in the literature by not begging the question. This also has implications for how we perceive the firm's internal structure.

This chapter looks at the widely held assumption that the firm is organised around or makes up a type of 'authority' that does not exist in the open market. We will look at the presumed bases for authority, and discuss whether authority arises in our conception of the firm as an 'island of specialisation'.

The firm as an authority relation

The literature since Coase asserts and depends on what Herbert A. Simon called the 'authority relation', a hierarchical power relationship that allows for low-cost direction of resources within the firm. This assumption has been subject to heavy criticism, notably in a 1972 article by Armen A. Alchian and Harold Demsetz,[1] but remains core to the definition of the firm in the literature. Alchian and Demsetz argued that the firm 'has no power of fiat, no authority, no disciplinary action any different in the slightest degree from ordinary market contracting between any two people'. There is no real difference between a manager firing an employee and a consumer firing his grocer. In both cases, the parties have only two means to 'punish' an exchange partner, either 'by withholding future business or by seeking redress in the courts for any failure to honor our exchange agreement'. Their conclusion, which I have substantiated elsewhere,[2] is that 'To speak of managing, directing, or assigning workers to various tasks is a deceptive way of noting that the employer continually is involved in renegotiation of contracts on terms that must be acceptable to both parties.'[3]

Alchian and Demsetz's view is that, economically speaking, a contract is a contract. Whether we prefer to call a specific type of contractual relationship 'market exchange' or 'employment' is of no relevance to the economic implications of that contract: its function is to equally bind parties to what was voluntarily agreed, presumably for their mutual expected benefit, when the contract was set up. A manager has no power to force a future employee that the consumer does not have vis-à-vis a grocer. This may seem unintuitive considering how we commonly perceive of the firm as a hierarchy and that we as employees 'follow orders' from higher-ups in the workplace. But this perception is unfounded. An employer (purchaser of labour) has no other means of punishment than the employee (seller of labour), as Alchian and Demsetz point out. This is easily illustrated by considering as example a specific long-term contract establishing the terms for exchange of services for payment. Whether we call the buyer of these services a customer or employer, and whether the seller is called supplier or employee, does not change the contract or its implications. The effect is the same as the contract is the same: it sets the terms for the exchange. What may differ depending on what we call the contract is the legally instituted obligations of the parties by decree of government, which indeed have economic implications. But this does not amount to an economic argument since it does not address how and whether the nature of the firm as an economic phenomenon, as opposed to the legal firm, provides a basis for internal authority. Calling exchange contracts between buyers and sellers of services within the firm 'employment' contracts, while similar or identical contracts with external parties are 'market' contracts, does not change the economic reality of these contracts or their implications.

The organisational economics literature remains vague on the causes of hierarchical authority within firms but relies on the conception of the firm as hierarchy to separate theoretically within-firm transactions from undirected market exchange. As in Coase's original analysis of the nature of the firm, the authority relation establishes the market–firm boundary that in turn makes possible the comparative institutional analysis of organisations contra markets. The argument changes, however, if we see the firm as the result of implementing an innovative, specialised production process outside the limits of the market. The boundary question is of little concern here, since the firm is naturally separated from the market it is embedded 'in' by utilising a different degree and kind of division of labour. The firm consists of the coordinated production process that is established outside the reach of the regular market's price mechanism and thus is unaffected by its high-powered incentives. It is recognised as an 'island of specialisation', an intensification of specialisation beyond the productive powers of the division of labour already established and exploited in the market. This means there is indeed a contrast between firm and market, but also that they are interdependent. Karl Marx perspicaciously made this point, building on Adam Smith's insight about the division of labour, that specialisation in the market and the firm 'differ not only in degree, but also in kind'.[4] He further noted that the firm's comparatively intensive division of labour depends on the market's:

> division of labour in manufacture demands, that a division of labour in society at large should previously have attained a certain degree of development. Inversely, the former division reacts upon and developes and multiplies the latter. Simultaneously, with the differentiation of the instruments of labour, the industries that produce these instruments, become more and more differentiated.[5]

This is very similar to what we established in the previous chapter, where productive innovations are implemented within the institutional structure of production of the market and challenge the status quo. The question here, however, is whether this implies authority and formal hierarchy, as is maintained by both Marx and contemporary theories of the firm. To Marx, the intensive kind of specialisation established within the firm by increasing the division of labour ultimately serves both to increase the productivity of and to alienate labour workers involved in the production process by separating them from the fruits of their labour. This alienation and the resulting lack of knowledge of the true worth of their exerted labour makes it possible for capital owners to extract the labourers' produced surplus value. Herein lies the Marxian exploitation dimension of capitalist production and the oppression of the working class.

To the contemporary theory of the firm, the cause of a within-firm authority relation is identified as one or a combination of several factors: the particular nature of the employment contract as open-ended and long term,[6] that courts of law rely on forbearance with respect to firms' 'internal' affairs,[7] or a rejection of the reciprocal nature of contracting. But these factors provide no real answers; they raise new questions. The first factor seems to provide a basis for 'authority' through open-endedness. The contract specifies payment for the buyer but lacks specific terms for what the seller is to supply for this payment. It thereby establishes the buyer's right to request specific services at will, though within established limits. This is how Coase originally identified the employment contract, but was unable to distinguish it fully from the long-term market contract. Indeed, open-endedness is not a property specifically of the employment contract, but exists in varying degrees also for market contracts. Examples of open-ended non-employment contracts include the sale of services like consulting, talent resourcing, staffing solutions, and all-inclusive hotels and spa resorts. The 'authority' of the buyer of consulting or a weekend stay at a spa resort is never considered an economic problem with governance implications. What makes the employment contract distinct is the legal implications.

The first two factors, the employment contract and the forbearance doctrine, therefore have in common their reliance on the legal system. They both depend on the legal aspect of firm organising, which makes the firm identifiable as primarily a 'legal fiction' – not an economic phenomenon. The object of study is therefore seen as in an empirical phenomenon, an outcome that has primarily legal causes, much like the effects of regulation are indeed economic whereas the regulations themselves are not economic or of market origin.

The third factor asserts that there is an underlying power dimension in all types of relationships, including voluntary market exchange, that skews the outcome of negotiation (primarily between employer and employee). Contracts only establish this pre-existing power in a formal and therefore enforceable authority relation, which serves to strengthen the stronger party. Jeffrey Pfeffer makes this point using remarkably Marxian language, stating that 'power is, first of all, a structural phenomenon, created by the division of labor and departmentation that characterize the specific organization'.[8]

Legal matters are of no concern in our treatment, since we attempt to explain and understand the economic function of integrating production in a firm. Involving legal matters can only confuse the economic analysis, and thereby direct our attention to factors that may be economically insignificant. But the Marxian argument needs to be taken seriously, since it addresses the division of labour in a sense that is similar to the discussion above. Indeed, Marx identifies firms as islands of specialisation that through artificially increased density allow for a more intensive division of labour and therefore improved productivity. His argument is made more explicit in recent literature adopting the resource dependence view, which holds that resource heterogeneity and specificity produce dependence that gives rise to or increases social power. To use Marxist-inspired terminology, the social power of the capitalists is derived from their capital ownership combined with capital-deficient workers' need to sell their labour for income; the latter is dependent on the former's willingness to buy for their survival, and this translates to capitalists' social power over workers. This argument appears valid when adopting a static view of the economy and a situation where productive innovation has already been implemented and proven successful. But if we instead consider our dynamic model of the market, as we developed in previous chapters, the logic fails.

Consider again the example from Chapter 4, in which production of some consumption good is carried out in parallel processes with similar if not fully standardised stages. The implementation of specialisation-based innovation can only take place outside the limits of the market, as we have already seen, and those involved are therefore separated from the market in a real sense: the intermediate goods they produce within the new sub-process are not saleable. Their mutual specialisation creates a chain of interdependent relationships, which is the strongest possible form of resource dependence. The success of the innovated sub-process depends on being compatible with the market setting and therefore the previously established market production processes, without which it would suffer incompleteness and fail. As the incompleteness argument is equally applicable to the new tasks carried out within the sub-process as it is for the entire sub-process's placement within the larger context of market production, any dependence and therefore authority relation is reciprocal. The threat of holdup from any party acting within the newly established sub-process is not credible, since the result is that the whole process suffers incompleteness and all investments made are therefore lost. There are no rents to extract for any individual participant in a production process where the parts are serially interdependent and the compensation of each is dependent on completion.

If this is a non-repeated production process that produces, and presumably was intended to produce, only one final good, then there would be potential for opportunistic behaviour. For instance, the producer of the last stage could threaten to withhold their contribution to production and, by leaving the good unfinished and therefore the production process without income, thereby extract quasi rents. In a production process with repeated production, perhaps in a constant flow of goods in process, reciprocity is prevalent: should the producer of one task attempt extraction of quasi rents, the producers of the other tasks can easily reciprocate as the next good is produced. Because of this, there is no way for any of the actors involved in the specialisation-based productive innovation to establish a lasting advantage; the outcome of opportunistic behaviour is much more likely the failure and dissolution of the process.

Failure is a cost on all of those involved in the new production process. This is not simply a result of losing any capital invested in the process, which is certainly the case, but also a cost due to loss of expected income. Profits are generated and earned only when the entire process is completed. For an implemented productive innovation, consequently, losses are primarily losses of expected income. They are incurred at any type of failure at any point in the sub-process – and are borne by all involved. We should remember that the very reason the process is established is that it promises to raise each worker's return on labour as compared to his or her previous market position and standard income. Those involved expect some level of profit in addition to normal income from partaking in the new production process. Failure takes away all expected profit, so engaging in holdup is a very costly endeavour.

The argument changes if there is a limited market, and therefore some substitutability, for the intermediate goods (and stages) of the new process. In this situation, opportunism can be a credible threat, and therefore may occur, because actors have choices and are therefore not dependent on a specific party. This is not the case for the innovative production process discussed here, which consists of strictly interdependent tasks. But even if there is some substitutability in its parts, the reciprocal nature of contracts limits the potential for holdup because the production process is expected to be repeated. The resource dependence argument for authority applies only in non-repeated situations. This is implicitly the case in Williamson's conjecture of opportunistic behaviour by guileful parties to a transaction that is facilitated by a significant and rarely repeated relationship-specific investment. The case here, in contrast, is one of production being organised through the division of labour and splitting of tasks, where all parties are dependent on the continuous completion of the entire process.

Implementation as discovery of the process

We must also consider the situation where production within a novel 'island of specialisation' is established top-down and therefore implemented vertically (as a hierarchy). Resource dependence can here emerge in the Marxian form of the capital owner's initial investment to realise the production process (ownership issues will be discussed at length in Chapter 7) or through the access to and control of knowledge. Both cases suggest that a central authority, perhaps the innovator, enjoys initial control of the project and its implementation, and then invites labourers to take part in the new production process. It is likely that the idea from which the innovation springs is formulated by one or a few individuals, who may not constitute the entire team needed to implement it and therefore they assume a leadership position. The founders are in this sense the initial owners of the enterprise, who employ others for carrying out specific tasks. The question is if this type of leadership, whether based on ownership or superior knowledge, suggests organisational hierarchy with authoritative or directional power.

Let us revisit the example from Chapter 4 where the innovative sub-process o_{21}-o_{22} is implemented to replace the standard market stage o_2. But rather than l_3 introducing the idea to l_2 and then collaborating on the implementation effort, l_3 secretly develops blueprints of the process and intends to keep it hidden from all others to reap the benefits for as long as possible. The situation is different from previously discussed because l_3's control of knowledge of the process suggests a potential advantage over l_2, who will be invited to contribute specific labour services to complete the sub-process, as well as others. By controlling the knowledge and only sharing necessary bits of it to l_2, it is conceivable that l_3 could maintain this informational advantage for some extended period of time and, therefore, possibly, benefit from this position of 'power'. But this conclusion overlooks the fact that the sub-process does not yet exist.

No matter the technical expertise of an innovator, a novel production process is unlikely to be properly optimised until it is fully implemented. It is theoretically possible to approximate technical (but not economic) efficiency in the production of capital goods to support an imagined innovative production process, but in reality any productive innovation is still subject to unknown parameters and the implementation and operation to unforeseen events. Knowledge of this type is unknowable as it does not yet exist – it is generated through the implementation process. This is even more so where the innovation, as in this case, depends on intensive specialisation under the division of labour, which means first implementation and then completion of the process depends on the craftsmanship of those involved. Lacking perfect foresight and perfect information, it is impossible to determine accurately all details required to carry out the yet to be implemented process. The more advanced the imagined process is, the less likely it is that everything can be foreseen and considered. As what we are dealing with here is innovation that uses intensive specialisation through the division of labour, the imagined production structure is always more advanced than what already exists in the market in the sense that it includes more distinct stages (is more *roundabout*). Only in very rudimentary production can technical efficiency in a productive innovation be accurately approximated, and then only where its originality is so limited that the innovator can rely fully on production experience that has already been established through trial and error in the market. That is, on specific knowledge that has already been generated and is fully available.

For any productive innovation with some degree of originality, which is suggested by the very term innovation, its implementation constitutes a discovery process. Kinks and errors need to be worked out, and some of the problems may not be discoverable until the process is tried empirically through scaled production. Many innovative production processes look promising, but turn out to be failures when tried practically. In addition to trying out the innovation technology, the process also needs to be aligned with the specific expertise and craftsmanship of those invited or hired to carry out the specific tasks. In our example, l_2 is employed to carry out a single task in the innovative sub-process o_{21}-o_{22} originally imagined and controlled by l_3. Whereas implementing the sub-process will allow for the discovery of possible errors, the introduction of l_2 to the specific task will reveal new knowledge about how it could be carried out. It is likely that this knowledge is revealed specifically to the factor carrying out the task, which provides l_2 with specific knowledge necessary for improving the process. This knowledge is not available to l_3 unless l_2 chooses to share it, which reverses the assumed dependence of the employee on the employer.

Also, where the task has not been designed specifically with (full knowledge of the expertise of) l_2 in mind, the task itself may need to be adjusted in order to take full advantage of l_2's specific experience and skill set. This, in turn, could effectuate changes to the intermediate good between the tasks o_{21} and o_{22} or shift the boundary between the tasks altogether. If we hypothesise that l_3 intends eventually to hire a second labourer to carry out the other task, the process may again change as new knowledge is revealed in the intersection of the task and the new labourer's skills. Due to strict interdependence, any change to a part of the process can cause changes to intermediate goods and therefore other tasks. Implementation entails discovery both at the process level and for the individual tasks (and the intermediate products between them).

This is highly problematic for an innovative entrepreneur l_3 seeking to control specific knowledge about the process, since the risk of errors, incompatibilities, and inefficiency increases as the specific information available to labourers becomes more limited and fragmented. Implementing a new degree and kind of division of labour in which those carrying out the specific tasks are provided only fragmented knowledge suggests the necessary adjustments, optimisations, and solutions to cross-task errors – including the detailed monitoring necessary to identify them – falls on l_3. This suggests the process is burdened with significant costs that could easily be avoided under full disclosure and that may put the whole project at risk. Attempts to control knowledge should in any case eventually fail, and will thus be ephemeral, since improvements, adjustments, problem-solving, and other changes to the tasks themselves reveal knowledge about the overall process. Observant workers should soon be able to figure out specific information about adjacent stages in the process that has been kept from them. They even have an incentive to learn about the process as this helps them carry out their specific tasks more effectively. If workers in the process interact, which at a minimum should take place through the delivery and receipt of inter-mediate goods, information about the entire process would soon be revealed in its entirety. Or, at any event, to a sufficient degree to undermine the entrepreneur's attempt to control knowledge of the process.

Even if technical efficiency could be approximated, we saw in the previous chapter that the implementation of a new production process takes place outside the extent of the existing market. This means the process, even after having been implemented, can suffer from allocative inefficiency. Regardless of whether this is the case, there is no way of finding out until market prices for the individual stages are available. But this will only be the case when the 'island' is located *within* the extent of the market and therefore can no longer be considered an island.

These problems can be mitigated through full disclosure within the innovative enterprise, which would make implementation a coordinative endeavour and thereby take advantage of the experiences, skills, and knowledge of all involved. This would also minimize the chance of failure, which should be a strong incentive for the innovator to share information.

We should also consider the means by which the innovator entices workers to join the enterprise. To attract the type of skills and experience necessary to support the novel process, wages would have to be offered that exceed those already offered in the labour market. The process has not been implemented and is therefore uncertain, and l_2 cannot easily be convinced about its success since l_3 keeps information about the process secret. Consequently, l_2 is in the position to demand substantial payment, since undertaking a new job and skill set is an investment for a labourer (and his employer). The higher wage forces l_3 to dedicate even more capital to the project, which further increases the cost burden on the enterprise and therefore escalates the risk of failure. Also, since any returns will be available only upon the completion of the process, assuming it turns out to be a profitable undertaking, there may be significant delay before invested funds generate return. This too is a cost that falls on the original innovator as sole principal whereas those employed in the process are paid from the principal's funds in the present.

Yet even ownership of the process does not imply authority in a meaningful sense. Implementation requires training and the development of specific skills by those instructed to carry out the tasks. As there is no labour market for these skills, they are difficult if not impossible to replace. This makes them highly valuable specifically for the innovative process, especially considering how the failure of any task implies incompleteness and failure to earn returns. It is therefore as likely that employed workers can hold up their employer as the other way around. Interdependence and the threat of incompleteness keeps opportunism at bay both horizontally and vertically; all involved parties suffer if the process is not completed and repeated, including the party acting opportunistically. So there are no grounds for real authority, at least not unidirectional and hierarchical, since costly threats can be made both ways.

Summing up

To summarise the message of this chapter, there is no reason to perceive of the firm as a hierarchy. Indeed, we find no basis for authority in an 'island of specialisation' other than the right to make claims as instituted through contracts. But such rights are reciprocal as both (or all) parties are bound by the terms previously agreed on. Instead of a top-down hierarchy, we found that the nature of the production process that makes up the firm is discovered and established as part of the implementation process. Indeed, the production process cannot be fully known in advance, and therefore the innovator is in as vulnerable a position as the individual worker – if not more so. As the whole process is subject to the problem of incompleteness, none of the parties to it can make a credible threat and we are therefore unlikely to see opportunistic behaviour. It would therefore be a mistake to view the firm as an authority relation.

Notes

1 A. A. Alchian and H. Demsetz, 'Production, Information Costs and Economic Organization', *American Economic Review*, 62:5 (1972), pp. 777–795.
2 P. L. Bylund, 'The Firm and the Authority Relation: Hierarchy vs. Organization', in G. L. Nell (ed.) *Austrian Theory and Economic Organization: Reaching Beyond Free Market Boundaries* (New York: Palgrave Macmillan, 2014), pp. 97–120.
3 Alchian and Demsetz, 'Production, Information Costs and Economic Organization', p. 777.
4 K. Marx, *Capital: A Critique of Political Economy* (1867) (New York: Charles H. Kerr & Company, 1906), p. 389.
5 Marx, *Capital: A Critique of Political Economy*, pp. 387–388.
6 H. A. Simon, 'A Formal Theory of the Employment Relationship', *Econometrica: Journal of the Econometric Society*, 19:3 (1951), pp. 293–305.
7 O. E. Williamson, 'Comparative Economic Organization: The Analysis of Discrete Structural Alternatives', *Administrative Science Quarterly*, 36:2 (1991), pp. 269–296.
8 J. Pfeffer, *Power in Organizations* (Boston, MA: Pitman, 1981), p. 4.

6   The volatile character of the firm

We have seen that the firm can be viewed as an 'island of specialisation' that establishes production outside the limits of the existing market. Production that utilises a more intensive division of labour, one that is 'different in degree and kind' than that already employed in the market, is from an economic point of view necessarily located outside the extent of the market for productive capital, which makes it observable as a separate entity of sorts and thereby has clearly defined boundaries. There is therefore a real and observable difference between market production and the type of highly intensive, specialised production that is established outside the market's extent. This type of 'island' is defined by its distinct internal organisation, which is what separates it from the market as well as determines its boundaries. This provides a single answer to two of the Coasean questions, while making the remaining question about rationale irrelevant: there is no specific rationale for integrating production *in a firm* for the simple reason that the firm is not the intended purpose or even the means – it is instead the result of implementing a novel production process, which falls outside the extent of the market.

Note that this explanation of the firm is not dependent on a specific legal apparatus or institutional context. It is not a 'legal fiction', but is a purely economic explanation: the firm, as it here emerges, is an implemented production process that utilises extra-market specialisation and is thereby distinct from the existing market. It is defined by the fact that its internal organisation is not and cannot be coordinated through a market – it supersedes the market specifically by establishing productive innovation outside the market's scope. The theory of the firm is hence not a separate theory of organisation per se, but an explanation of how productive innovation is implemented within the larger context of market production, though not integrated into the market, to satisfy consumer wants better. The firm is a 'formal organisation' in the sense that it is naturally and observably separate from the market's price coordination due to the strict inter-dependence between tasks that compose its production process. The identification of the firm as 'an entity' arises due to the fact that it necessarily is a unit: all parts of the innovative production process are necessary as it would otherwise suffer incompleteness and therefore fail. It indeed relies on a non-price means for coordinating production, just like Coase and others have asserted, but it is not formed with the intention to replace it. In fact, this central point is much more general than that: the firm is not a means chosen in order to avoid the market or to minimise costs or to control information, but the outcome of implementing innovative production through intensive specialisation. The firm is the necessary outcome of implementing productive innovation that cannot be realised through means available in the market.

But the question is whether we can conceive of the firm as anything but an intentional construction, a means to attain some specific end. The actual firm that we observe in the empirical market appears to be real in a different way from an intensively specialised production process consisting of interdependent (due to uniqueness and therefore insubstitutability) parts. The usual way we think of a firm is as a formal, concrete organisation that exists in a very real sense. The concept of the firm that arises from our discussion of the distinction between market-based and extra-market production – as an 'island of specialisation' – seems much more fluid and volatile. There are two ways of approaching this question about the 'nature' of the firm and attempting to answer it. One becomes available by decomposing and, as a consequence, criticising the common understanding of the firm by realising that the substantive nature of the firm is in many respects an illusion. The other is to elaborate on our previous discussion of specialised production in order to show that the type of firm that arises from it in fact significantly (or even perfectly) overlaps with the empirical firm's economic being. We will attempt to do both in the discussion in this chapter.

The elusive nature of the actual firm

The contemporary theory of the firm tends to begin with an implicit assumption of what a firm entails based on empirical observation, and then theorise on its meaning. To again refer to Coase's ground-breaking article, his starting point is the identification that the market is not a pure market as assumed in economic theory's model of perfect competition. In contrast, he notes that in 'a large sphere in our modern economic system' production is coordinated within firms in a way that 'is akin to what is normally called economic planning'.[1] Coase asserts that the firm is a formal organisation that is based on the concept of authority, which supersedes the market's price mechanism and therefore is distinct from market coordination. This view, he maintains, suggests a definition of the firm that 'corresponds to what is meant by a firm in the real world'[2] and should therefore be both useful and relevant from a theoretical point of view.

It is worth nothing, however, that Coase here avoids much of the complexity of the world by uncritically accepting the common perception of the empirical phenomenon as definition. By asserting that the firm is constituted by economic planning through authority, Coase's theory can only reiterate and reinforce this assertion – his theory follows from an inadequate definition, which should raise doubt about the conclusions drawn from his theorising. His identification that production within the firm is hierarchical and 'directed', in contrast to market production as only passively coordinated through prices, emanates from his definition but is ultimately questioned by his later work. The reciprocal nature of economic action and its implications, a major contribution in Coase's other seminal article,[3] suggests that authority cannot be established through market contracting. The very nature of contract is to specify rights and duties for all the parties involved, and unless there is some other basis than economic incentives for the contract (such as legal mandates or decrees) it is difficult, as we saw in Chapter 5, to think of how any authority can be established that does not also imply reciprocal authority for the counterparty.

As discussed in previous chapters, there is reason to question the relevance and validity of much of what is commonly thought of as characteristics or qualities of the firm. The basis for authority within the firm, especially when assumed to be different from any authority arising in the rest of the market, is at best unclear. The assumption that unidirectional authority is established through voluntary contract, employment contract, or other types, does not hold water unless we also consider extra-economic aspects such as legal implications of contracting. The identification of the firm as a formal hierarchy that is thereby distinguishable from the horizontal and undirected market exchange also appears to be an assertion without much basis.

It is very difficult to find the definitive explanation for why we consider a corporation such as IBM an organisational entity. The exercise of finding a purely economic definition of a business organisation amounts to peeling an onion in search of its core. Much of our 'real world' understanding of what the firm is appears to hinge on identifications that are primarily of legal origin. It is therefore problematic to rely on empirical observations to discover inductively the function that the firm may play in a market process, that is, its specifically *economic* function. To explain the economic function of the firm, which is our purpose here (as it was Coase's), we must decompose the empirical conception and rid it of legal aspects. This is not to say that the firm's legal status is without import, but only that an economic theory of the firm cannot rely on extra-economic explanations. Legal aspects of course have consequences and implications that are of economic character and that may be worthy of analysis, but the task here is to find the firm's economic function from which we can study the impact of legal interventions (see Chapter 10).

In separating the economic firm from the legal firm, we must also consider the social implications, as the formal legal entity of IBM and its thereby assumed legal authority provides a basis for identifying 'it' as a concrete presence. The fact that we believe there is a corporation called IBM that is involved in certain types of production undoubtedly affects our actions, but this does not in itself suggest that IBM exists independently of our perceptions or that it is a specific economic phenomenon in itself. It also does not provide a basis for an economic function provided by the presumed identity IBM independently of the market actors presumed to be 'inside' the firm. In other words, the function of the firm remains to be discovered despite the vast literature intended to solve this exact problem.

The fact is that unless the firm, however we conceive of the phenomenon, solves a problem or in some other way provides a real value that is not possible through non-firm market action, it has neither a function nor a rationale. It is not sufficient to assert that the firm is different from the market and then uphold this difference as a reason for firm organising. Coase ultimately asserts that the firm is defined by the supersession of the price mechanism through reliance on authority, itself without explanation, and that there is value to firm organising because authority escapes the costs of non-authority (in Coase's case marketing costs, later termed transaction costs). This type of circular reasoning based on a seemingly realistic but essentially unargued-for assertion (such as the unique implications of the employment contract) gave rise to the extensive and important discussion on the legal fiction of the firm in the 1970s. Despite this discussion, this type of reasoning is still commonplace in the theory of the firm literature.

It is the purpose and contribution of this book to shift the focus in the literature towards the economic function provided by the firm. Rather than starting with some conception of the firm, the discussion here starts with the market and looks specifically to the limits of production due to the extent of the market. The assumption is that firms play a role in production, and that it is in some distinct value provided to the market's productive apparatus that we find the economic function of the firm. We elaborated on this in previous chapters in terms of a 'specialisation deadlock' that limits the market's ability to implement innovative production processes of certain originality. This discussion suggested that production processes implemented outside the extent of the existing market are integrated by default, if not encapsulated, by being subject to strict interdependence and therefore devoid of market as there is no redundancy. It is not a supersession of the price mechanism in the Coasean sense, since it is not a means to avoid costs of the market. Rather, it is impossible to establish this type of production outside the extent of the market using market means, and therefore the firm is necessarily non-market. But this suggests that it comes at great cost, since the nature of production relying on extra-market specialisation is subject to excessive uncertainty due to strict interdependence and deferred returns on investment. It is for these reasons, and not as a preferred or chosen course of action, that it is necessary in order to realise the type of productive innovation imagined. Whenever the costs of uncertainty can be avoided through adopting market means, doing so should be preferred by those involved in the endeavour.

The cost of uncertainty

It is possible to 'break free' from the market's specialisation deadlock, but doing so is fraught with uncertainty due to implementational unknowability and incompleteness in case of failure. The costliness of this uncertainty suggests that projects to realise innovations would not be undertaken unless there was significant potential for gain through improved productivity. Innovator entrepreneurs should therefore find that innovations of lacking originality, which may not be sufficiently novel and productive to make up for the uncertainty, have very limited appeal. As we saw in Chapters 2 and 3, the decentralised structure of the market fully supports adjustments and adaptation to changing circumstances, and can also sufficiently support the implementation and adoption of innovations of limited originality. Such 'minor' innovations are analogous to the gradual increase of specialisation that we find in Adam Smith's treatment of the division of labour, but do not have a major impact on the market's structure. Such continuous progress that makes up the market process is the result of resourceful, self-interested market actors aiming to improve their situations and they commonly entail limited coordination. What we focus on here is the type of innovations that Schumpeter referred to as revolutionising the pattern of production.

Innovations of limited originality can be expected to increase productivity merely to a limited extent. This is no problem to the degree that they can be implemented within the extent of the market, since any improvement is a gain and the cost of achieving it through exchange-based reallocation of resources is comparatively small. Innovations that are sufficiently original to make their implementation impossible within the market can from the perspective of the imaginative entrepreneur be unrealisable unless they significantly increase productivity. There is an 'infeasibility zone' between the market's present and supported specialisation intensity, that is, market production, and the intensively specialised productive innovations that increase productivity sufficiently to cover the cost of uncertainty, or what we refer to as the firm. This 'zone' arises due to the fact that all productive innovations that are impossible to realise through market means suffer from unknowability and that their internal strict interdependence suggests incompleteness even from failure in one of their parts. Implementation of these innovations should therefore primarily take place for those that constitute radical rather than marginal change in the structure of production.

Whereas this fact is limiting in terms of the scope of what can and will be realised, it also indicates that only the most promising productive innovations will be undertaken. In this sense, the productive innovations that see the light of day will be the ones that can potentially disrupt the present state of market production. The effect of a successful endeavour should therefore be noticeable on a market level since existing production becomes relatively unproductive by comparison. We will return to this issue from a market process perspective in Chapter 8. The discussion here is limited to the effects and implications on the actor or firm level.

As indicated by the nature of a productive innovation, conceived here in terms of intensified specialisation through implementing a novel and more far-reaching division of labour, the undertaking is uncertain, costly, and likely transient. It is uncertain because it is fundamentally unknowable prior to being implemented, and it is costly because of this uncertainty as well as because the process itself – due to being firmly placed outside the extent of the market – is subject to incompleteness. Whereas a process that has been implemented, completed, and shown its worth through profitability should be subject to lesser costs of uncertainty, it may still be subject to severe inefficiencies. The only feedback available to the entrepreneur is in terms of the process as a whole, as we saw in previous chapters, since it either makes a profit or fails the market test by generating a loss or suffering incompleteness. But the value of the individual parts is necessarily unknowable, and this state of affairs translates into strong reasons for the firm as an island of specialisation to be a transient phenomenon – a 'temporary' solution, as it were.

The first reason is the expected competitive pressures from imitating entrepreneurs that will see the opportunity to implement similar production structures and thereby capture part of the profits. This in fact provides the firm with a function in the macro-level discovery process of the market and the development and evolution of society through productivity and economic growth that we will discuss in Chapters 8 and 9.

The second reason applies on the micro level and relates to the internal organisation of the firm irrespective of external competitive pressures. Whether or not the new process is implemented by an original entrepreneur with contractually employed labourers or as a collaborative effort by a team, there is no figuring out whether any single part of the process contributes to or subtracts from the bottom line. The reason for this is that each part is unique and previously untested, and therefore there can be no market valuation. This state of affairs, at least to some limited extent, suggests that there may be an incentive for those involved to shirk somewhat in their specific duties (to the degree effort is not measurable). As shirking could cause incompleteness and therefore failure, workers would generally refrain from doing so (as we discussed in Chapter 5). But in an established production process that already generates a stream of profits, some may choose to hold back on effort not needed to uphold the achieved production level. We can explain such labour 'savings' by referring to the infeasibility zone, which suggests that the firm should be sufficiently productive to generate returns in excess of existing market production. If these profits are already sufficient to satisfy those involved in the established firm, they may see no intrinsic reason to improve the production process further. If they are not, and especially if the anticipated relative cost of improvement is low, there is incentive to minimise waste and effort as well as to maximise output – to increase profitability further.

Improvements to the process are necessarily carried out as tweaks to the structure of the production process and/or its parts. But such improvements are limited to technological advances since only this type of information is available through limited trial-and-error and by simple observation. As workers gain experience carrying out their specific tasks, they will identify better ways of carrying out the tasks (as we discussed above). However, the *economic* efficiency of the process remains both unknown and unknowable, since there is no competition to determine market prices of individual parts. It may therefore be the case that a certain task is carried out in the wrong way, by the wrong person, or for the wrong reasons. More importantly, some tasks and features of the output may be economically unnecessary, and some that would greatly increase its value may remain undiscovered. Whether the output of this productive innovation is in its most valuable form (both in terms of quantity and quality) cannot be known and should therefore never be optimal or maximised.

As the 'island' of intensive, extra-market specialisation is located outside the extent of the market, its internal economic efficiency cannot be discovered or learned.[4] It is in this sense similar to a purely socialist economy, but not because it is centrally planned or directed (as Coase's firm) but because it functions without market input. This in itself is a cost to the entrepreneur(s), which is avoidable only through the making of markets for the individual tasks of the innovated process. As there are no market data to guide efficiency within the firm, it will typically be less efficient than had the production process been coordinated using the price mechanism. Its relative inefficiency is a burden on the venture whether or not it is already profitable in absolute terms. This becomes all too clear when imitating entrepreneurs establish competing production processes that capture part of the potential profits, and aim to outcompete the original implementation.

The initiating entrepreneur or entrepreneurial team must bear the uncertainty of the new process, and the cost thereof (at least part of which is in the form of unrealised profits) is a reason to seek and engage in market-making. Without an established market, the parts of the process cannot be evaluated separately and therefore the output cannot be properly positioned. The only way economically to improve the process is to test changes blindly and then wait for real market feedback through effected changes in profitability levels. This is a costly and onerous process that could ultimately lead to failure; even tweaks and changes that are imagined to have little or no effect on the output may have important implications on the innovation's ability to meet real demand. In a dynamic market situation with changing customer preferences even seeming improvements to a product (or the production process) can lead to losses.

Without market signals, the firm is blind whether or not it is profitable. It is therefore an easy target for imitating entrepreneurs, who – with different knowledge or understanding of market needs and different technological capabilities – could find ways to undercut the original firm and improve on its design technically, organisationally, or economically. There is no means of protection against such threats, since the economic imperfections and inefficiencies of the implemented process are undiscoverable. This uncertainty is a burden on the shoulders of those involved in the project. The burden is further increased as the whole process is subject to failure due to incompleteness – which would mean losses across the board – if any task or worker should fail. For these reasons, the original entrepreneur and workers would welcome the introduction of market signals as guidance and to relieve them of the cost of uncertainty.

Market-making and the firm

Even if a competitor emerges with the purpose of, and is successful in, capturing part of the profits made available by the innovation, this may be a welcome development for the original entrepreneur(s). The reason for this is that even a single competitor means there is potential for bidding to acquire resources throughout the production process and therefore introduction of money prices that to a limited extent facilitate economic appraisement. The original implementation of the productive innovation took place outside the limits of the market, but the introduction of competition in this production space effectively expands the extent of the market to encompass the new innovation. This change therefore relieves the original entrepreneur(s) of the burden of economic uncertainty. It makes it possible to discover and implement improvements to the process, to continue to develop the production process, improve or even replace individual tasks, and adjust the quality of the output to fit real demand better.

From our perspective, this development also indicates a beginning of the end of the firm. Whether or not the individuals involved continue to work together and be co-located, the economic function of the firm ceases to exist. With the entrant competitor, market prices – even though they are initially of limited reliability, in the sense that they may not properly reflect opportunity costs in production or real consumer demand, as there are only two bidders – are approximated for intermediate goods. These emergent prices lead to market appraisals of the separate tasks that compose the (formerly) productive innovation, and therefore the extent of the market expands to include the innovation in its production structure. If cross-process bidding for resources takes place through the limited redundancy of only two parallel processes, a process towards pushing competition down from the process to the task level begins. Less efficient workers as well as tasks now become more easily identifiable and therefore avoidable, and this makes all the difference. Errors and failures must no longer affect the totality of the process, but can be limited to the task where the error is made; it is possible for all other tasks to remain profitable even should one task fail, since it may be possible to sell intermediate goods to the competing process. The strict interdependence between tasks is then relaxed and this limits the uncertainty assumed by those involved in the productive endeavour. This solves the knowledge problem within the process.

We will discuss the details of the market-making process in Chapters 8 and 9. It should here be sufficient to note what was stated above, namely that the firm, as we have here identified it, is necessarily a transient phenomenon. The firm exists only as far and as long as there is no market. Any other conclusion would be counterintuitive, since we found the firm to be the implementation of a productive innovation outside the market's extent and thereby unaffected by the existing market's limited reach. The firm's production process is then integrated in terms of the firm's internal strict interdependence and its parts united through the shared responsibility and uncertainty due to incompleteness. Its function from the perspective of the market is to 'break free' from the specialisation deadlock, and thereby break new ground and achieve production unattainable strictly through market means. If this undertaking is successful and profitable, which implies that others may attempt to imitate it for a share in the revealed profits, it leads to market-making and therefore an expansion of the extent of the market by including the new type of productive innovation.

It should be noted that expanding the extent of the market is not the aim of those involved in the original undertaking, but it is the possible end result. Implementing productive innovation through extra-market specialisation does not itself create a market, and in this sense it is possible for a firm to be long-lived – all it takes is that nobody else competes for the same profits. Market-making does not happen until competitors enter and compete with the original productive innovation and therefore determine market prices for intermediate goods and effectively dissolve the firm. Market valuation is formed between competing processes not because there is explicit bidding for every intermediate good, resource, or task, but because there is the potential for bidding and therefore market prices that estimate social opportunity cost. It is sufficient that there are potential other buyers to bid up payment, just like the potential for other sellers is sufficient to bring about lower prices. The original entrepreneur may attempt to bid up the price for resources used in the firm for the purpose of keeping other entrepreneurs from entering this production space. This is in itself market feedback that signals real valuation, since insufficiently high prices invite competitors and too high prices cause losses – even though the exact origin of those losses on a task level cannot be identified. This facilitates indirect appraisement of resources and thereby economic efficiency through allocation of resources towards real wants.

Competing entrepreneurs help the original innovator-entrepreneur identify the proper scope of the firm as their bidding for resources provide benchmarks for individual parts of the process, and therefore introduce a limited form of market pricing. Even if the competing production process is different from the original innovation, the extent to which they compete for resources to use in production, as well as for buyers of the end product, provides guidance in improving the process. Competition also reveals to the entrepreneur what parts of the established process may be less valuable or efficient, thereby facilitating further improvements and a change of scope. It may very well be that what the entrepreneur was convinced was the proper scope of process, quality of product, and so forth, is improper given the demand. This information is revealed as competitors do better or worse by choosing different approaches and as they make tweaks and adjustments to the processes to serve customers better.

This market-making as competitors enter the same production space and compete directly with the original innovating entrepreneur ultimately leads to the dissolution of the firm. It no longer serves a function as competing entrepreneurs bid for the same resources and competencies and thereby determine real market prices for the individual parts of the production process. The market in this sense expands to include the firm, and for this reason the process can and will be broken up into its parts as they are no longer interdependent. Yet this ultimate effect is not established immediately as a competitor emerges. The first result is that better information about the proper scope of the process is made available. This allows for the entrepreneur to tweak and make improvements to the process economically, which means that it better satisfies the wants and needs of those buying the product or service.

In addition to tweaks and changes to quality, quantity, and composition of the output of the process, the information that is revealed and made available through competition guides the entrepreneur in terms of what tasks should or shouldn't be carried out. It is possible that competition reveals that more tasks should be part of the production process. In other words, the entrepreneur can realise that the firm should expand through insourcing tasks that were previously thought to be separate or unrelated to the process. More likely, especially in the longer run, the firm will engage in outsourcing of specific tasks that are no longer necessary to include 'internally' and that are better carried out by others. Whereas this may be the case for parts of the core production process, this should not often be the case since this is the unique contribution of the firm. But supporting services, which are originally part of the firm but not core to the productive innovation, could more easily become spinoffs as competitors would likely rely on those services also. For example, a novel production process could necessitate innovation in accounting, marketing, logistics, or skills development processes that are necessary to support the core production process but are in fact separate to it. This is a possible opportunity for breaking out such services if competitors who attempt to establish similar production processes, or form unique production structures that recreate similar benefits only in the end result, could also benefit from such services. The original entrepreneur can choose to keep such services internally, but it is likely that they are spin off and let go. The reason for this is that they are not core to but established to support the production process, and therefore not essential to keep within the firm. Even if separating the core process from supportive processes would make them available for competitors, it means the entrepreneur benefits from being able to purchase the service at the market price. With competition in such services, the cost is likely to go down. But it also releases resources, at a minimum in terms of the entrepreneur's own time and attention, by allowing him or her to focus on the core contribution: the productive innovation. For these reasons, it can often be beneficial to let go of direct control of such services. This narrows the firm's scope and makes it, as an entity, more specialised and therefore potentially much more effective and profitable. It thereby relieves the entrepreneur of uncertainty by both allowing market forces to regulate the supporting services and by being able to focus fully on the core innovation. We will return to the interplay between the firm and the competitive market process in Chapter 8.

Summing up

The purpose of this chapter has been to show how the firm satisfies a market function and that this leads to a lifecycle of firms. They are, in other words, volatile and temporary in their core function as the novel production structure is either a failure, which means it will suffer losses, or a success, which means it will earn profits that attract competitors. The former eventually means exit from the market, whereas the latter means the firm will dissolve into market contracting as the market expands. Indeed, the firm as we here see it is a means to implement a productive innovation that is unsupported by the market, but as the original firm together with competitors effectively produce a market for the internally coordinated tasks, the firm has fulfilled its function and is replaced by market transactions.

Notes

1 R. H. Coase, 'The Nature of the Firm', *Economica*, 4:16 (1937), pp. 386–405, p. 388.
2 Coase, 'The Nature of the Firm', p. 386.
3 R. H. Coase, 'The Problem of Social Cost', *Journal of Law and Economics*, 3:1 (1960), pp. 1–44.
4 The reader may recognise this argument about economic (as opposed to technological) efficiency as an application of Mises's argument against socialist planning. See L. v. Mises, 'Economic Calculation in the Socialist Commonwealth', in F. A. v. Hayek (ed.) *Collectivist Economic Planning* (London: George Routledge & Sons, 1935), pp. 87–130, L. v. Mises, *Socialism: An Economic and Sociological Analysis* (1936) (New Haven, CT: Yale University Press, 1951).

7   Financing, ownership, and boundaries of the firm

Previous chapters established how the firm, conceived of as an 'island of specialisation', emerges as a result of establishing innovative production processes that fall outside the extent of the existing market. Focus was on the practical aspects of technical production – how to overcome the 'specialisation deadlock' that inhibits further specialising and division of labour through innovation. Market exchange cannot support novelty that goes beyond recombination or reconfiguration of already existing and traded resources. New types of production processes must therefore be established outside the extent of the market, which makes the novel production structure stand out as a separate, non-market phenomenon: a firm. This type of production structure suffers from strict interdependence between its 'internal' parts due to the lack of compatibility with production in the existing market, which is akin to integrated production. It also causes another impediment to realisation: a need for comparatively substantial upfront investment of financial capital.

For a new production structure to be established outside the extent of the market, it is not sufficient to populate each imagined task with specialised labour (possibly supported by novel capital goods). As we saw in the previous chapter, the outcome of the new process is unknown until it is completed and it therefore has to be figured out as part of the implementation process. Should any part of the process fail, the outcome is incomplete and therefore incompatible with production taking place in the market. For this reason, the whole process fails. Even if the process is successful, income and thus return on investment will not be available until the full process is completed and the outcome sold in the market. Yet costs of production are incurred whether or not revenue will accrue to the firm upon completion. Consequently, the firm will always have a lag between costs and revenue – which can be substantial where the process is highly roundabout and the time lag therefore substantial. In contrast to decentralised market-price coordinated production processes, which may require investment in both capital aiding production and goods in process, an 'island of specialisation' requires a comparatively substantial initial investment.

As the 'firm' cannot sell intermediate goods, because they are not saleable in a market, it requires a substantial upfront investment: costs in the present, both for implementing the process and carrying out production tasks, must be covered for the promise of future earnings. Or, in other words, goods in the present are traded for goods in a comparatively distant and uncertain future. This is not different from market production in principle: market production also requires upfront investment to cover costs, even though this relates to a single production stage or task. Also, sales of any intermediate good within a stage may be uncertain. The difference is one of magnitude and structure, since a firm requires upfront investment to cover costs of its whole production process across all tasks and stages – including its potentially lengthy and open-ended implementation and production of necessary capital. We therefore see that whoever makes the initial investment to cover the immediate costs, as well as costs that arise when implementing and carrying out the production process, bears the burden of uncertainty for the whole process. The capitalist function of supplying temporal investments is therefore at the inception of the 'firm' largely inseparable from the entrepreneurial function of bearing uncertainty: whoever makes the initial investment also bears the uncertainty of the enterprise, since any returns to the novel production structure are fundamentally unknown and unknowable (though not unimaginable) prior to its completion.

The risk of loss amounts to a cost of capital invested in the firm that extends over greater time than investments in the open market. As the productive innovation includes a period of uncertain implementation and then, during regular production, waiting over several time periods for the outcome of the entire process, the cost of capital increases. The 'firm' is therefore more capital intensive than market production, and the realisation of productive innovation requires substantial and risky financial investment as a result. The productive innovations that are successful in attracting capital investments should therefore fall outside of the infeasibility zone discussed in the previous chapter. While uncertainty increases with originality, we have already seen that revolutionising productive innovations should be expected to yield higher returns than comparatively minor adjustments or additions to existing production. As the 'firm' emerges around the former, it requires comparatively large upfront investment but also promises greater rates of return when successful. Only firms promising expected returns that exceed the cost of capital will be able to attract capital in the market for financing.

As productive innovations necessarily see a lag between investment and returns, possibly a lag of several time periods, any implementation is impossible without capitalist investment. This follows from the fact that sufficient funds must be made available in the present to cover costs of implementing as well as carrying out the production process before revenue is generated. This does not mean that the capitalist function must be undertaken by a single party – it can be a cooperative endeavour, perhaps by those called upon to carry out the tasks that make up the new production process. Yet it requires that funds are made available through investment in the present, which can neither be repaid nor earn returns until some time period in the future. It also requires bearing of uncertainty as the outcome of the untried and unrealised productive innovation is unknown; investment made in a standard saleable production stage in the market, in contrast, does not risk internal incompleteness or uncertainty of implementation to nearly the same degree as such production is tried and proven and likely performed through a standard task. The undertaking to establish novel production (create a firm) outside the extent of the market faces uncertainty of a different degree and kind; it is a fundamentally entrepreneurial undertaking in a sense that does not apply to within-market production and exchange.

We may wish to think of the entrepreneur in Schumpeterian fashion, as the genius who comes up with the idea and drafts the novel process, and then sets the implementation process in motion. It is unnecessary to assume that the imaginative entrepreneur has this role, however. Whoever invests in the project must bear the uncertainty of the undertaking through this investment, whether it is in the form of capital or time, and is in this sense both capitalist and entrepreneur. Unless we assume centralised financing of and full upfront payment of factors used in the endeavour, a discussion we save for later in this chapter, entrepreneurship includes those carrying out the production tasks as they bear the uncertainty of the enterprise. The strict task interdependence within the firm and the all-or-nothing nature of production in the face of incompleteness make all parties dependent on the end result.

Those partaking in production within the firm have likely abandoned prior market positions that earned them the going market rate of return on labour services in their specialisation. This is their opportunity cost for entering the firm. To the degree they are not paid by someone else in the firm, they have thereby already made an indirect investment by giving up income in the present for the promise of future returns in their new roles within the firm. So they bear part of the uncertainty of the firm until it has generated revenue through sales and thus passed the market test, by taking part in the process. This can be easily understood when considering the time period between the initial investment and the first sale, since the whole enterprise incurs costs and therefore faces failure due to incompleteness with a negative capital balance unless completed. The uncertainty is borne by the capitalist-entrepreneurs who invest funds to cover outlays during implementation and initial production.

Investing and divesting in the 'firm'

A major part of the uncertainty borne by the capitalist-entrepreneur arises due to the strict interdependence within the production process and therefore the threat of incompleteness. We touched on the cost of uncertainty in the previous chapter, and noted that there is both technical and economic uncertainty. The former relates to whether the totality of the imagined production process can be completed without errors and without causing incompleteness due to failures in materials or practical production tasks. Economic uncertainty relates to the issue of whether the outcome of the process will find sufficient effective demand to generate revenue that covers its costs, and whether the process is an efficient use of resources. It also relates to the issue of economic efficiency in allocation and use of resources within the separate tasks – without market prices an entrepreneur is essentially 'blind' to what would be the socially most highly valued use of resources (or even what uses should be considered destruction of capital). The opportunity costs within specific tasks in a productive innovation are unknown and unidentifiable as there are no existing alternative procedures to compare with or even alternative uses for the intermediate goods generated within the firm's production process. Indeed, assuming a firm emerges around a productive innovation that constitutes a 'splitting' of a market production stage into many mutually specialised tasks, the opportunity cost of the firm's entire process is the market stage it replaces. Profit for the entire firm can therefore be calculated, but we cannot from this derive the economic contribution of each separate, interdependent task carried out within the firm. Market prices do not exist for the unique tasks that compose the production process that is implemented through a firm.

This suggests that the cost of uncertainty within production that takes place outside the extent of the market is of significant magnitude and can even be prohibitive. The question then is whether or not this cost is avoidable, the answer to which depends on the time horizon considered. The cost of uncertainty should be initially unavoidable for the reason discussed above: the novel production structure suffers from the incompleteness problem, strict interdependence between its parts, and lack of knowledge: the effectiveness, efficiency, and realised structure of the yet to be implemented production process is unknown and unknowable, but entrepreneurially imagined. As none of the tasks within a production process that is established through 'splitting' a market production task exists prior to the firm's forming, there should be no question that the full uncertainty must be borne throughout the implementation, improvement, and completion of the process. Either an individual investor supplies the funds necessary to realise the productive innovation, or savings of those partaking in the enterprise are used to cover expenses. Whoever invests in the undertaking risks losing the principal investment unless the firm is successful and at least breaks even. These investors or capitalist-entrepreneurs should wish to limit this cost of uncertainty, but lack means to do so as there is no social valuation of the novel production process or its parts, and consequently no market pricing.

The lack of economic means to guide improvements to a process does not mean it cannot be improved technologically. Labour workers in the firm can improve the process through adopting existing technological standards, choosing materials that are harder or more flexible, and so on. In terms of economic uncertainty, however, the only basis for making decisions and attempting to identify room for improvement is entrepreneurial judgment: there are no market prices to guide the entrepreneur. This situation is unfavourable and costly but inescapable, which means entrepreneurs have a strong incentive to seek all means possible to reduce the economic uncertainty of the enterprise. This can be achieved by shifting tasks from being coordinated internally to market-based and priced production. By relying to the greatest degree possible on market-tradable inputs and services, a firm can limit the extent of uncertainty suffered in the internal production process.

As we saw in the previous chapter, the successful firm would soon be emulated by entrepreneurs seeking to capture part of the earned and thus revealed profits. This may have a negative effect on profits for the original firm, but could also relieve the entrepreneur of some of the burden of uncertainty. When other entrepreneurs enter the new production space and markets for factors emerge between the firms, the formation of approximate market prices through bidding helps the entrepreneurs estimate the economic value of each task. The cost of uncertainty that is due to the lack of reliable market prices therefore decreases as competition for profits emerges and intensifies. The approximate prices of internal stages provides the entrepreneur with real market data that reduce the uncertainty of the undertaking's economic use of resources. The inflow of competitors also potentially increases the availability of capital as investors become aware of the profit opportunity in this production space. Whereas competition will put downward pressure on prices of outputs and may force input prices up, it should typically result in lower production costs and lower financing costs. If production tasks can be outsourced, the uncertainty borne by those in the firm diminishes.

As competition further intensifies, more opportunities to escape uncertainty may surface through the innovative actions of other entrepreneurs. Not only will the new markets for factors used specifically in the novel production process lead to increased quality and lower prices, competition also increases the chance for improving the tasks themselves through allowing cross-firm discovery of improvements. But as competition intensifies and factor markets stabilise and mature, it is reasonable to expect innovative entrepreneurs to imagine productive innovations that can replace tasks that were previously necessary to coordinate within the original firm. Such innovations would take advantage of the specific knowledge and judgment of innovative entrepreneurs to further 'split' tasks by producing sub-processes utilising even more intensive divisions of labour. The original firm, which disrupted standard market production, is then at first subjected to uncertainty-reducing and profit-seeking competition through the entry of emulating and imitating entrepreneurs in the new production space, and then subject to disruptive innovation through the formation of new firms outside the new extent of the market.

This process may in fact be to the original entrepreneur's advantage, depending on which tasks are disrupted, since it could improve his or her ability to focus on the greatest value added and therefore competitive advantage. It is probable that the productive innovation that caused the original firm includes tasks that are both core and supportive, since the process had to replace completely an existing market-traded production task. In other words, there may be tasks or functions that were part of the original composition of the new firm's production process that were neither core to the innovation nor of great value to it. These tasks, which may include coordinating functions across production tasks, tools maintenance, marketing, human resources, and other administrative functions, were necessary for the firm to avoid incompleteness – at the time the firm was formed, and as imagined by the entrepreneur. Without this type of function, the original firm could not have been successfully implemented. But as a limited factor market forms and innovative entrepreneurs follow suit and attempt to replace specific tasks carried out within firms in this market, these non-core supportive functions would be an easy target for innovation and new firm formation. The market-making as competitors enter the production space created by the original entrepreneur both reduces uncertainty and allows entrepreneurs to choose between internal production of a specific stage and procurement of the production service in the market.

It is possible that several competing firms carrying out similar processes may need similar types of administrative functions that are necessary but not core to the production process. As they are not core to their productive innovation but supportive to the core process, it would be advantageous to these firms not to produce these services in-house but to procure them in the market as stand-alone services. Indeed, we might even hypothesise that if entrepreneurs could outsource these functions or purchase them at competitive prices they would be happy to do so if only for the reason that it allows them to focus on their primary contribution: the core innovation. The supportive functions would therefore be low-hanging fruit for further extensions of the division of labour. There is then already potential, but perhaps latent, market demand for these services within existing firms, and in this sense these services are opportunities for other entrepreneurs seeking to earn profit. While offering of these services does not immediately bring about a market valuation reflecting the social opportunity cost, it provides entrepreneurs with the choice to continue producing them in-house or purchase them from an outside 'expert'. This may be important enough for non-core services, since entrepreneurs can refocus their efforts by outsourcing peripheral tasks. And it offers a choice for how best to organise the tasks that were originally part of the firm.

Consequently, outsourcing of these functions does not only allow the entrepreneur to focus on and streamline the firm's processes around core tasks, but also relieves him or her of part of the uncertainty borne in the enterprise. When supportive or other services can be purchased in the market, the choice to 'make or buy' makes it easier to estimate their worth and contribution to the firm's bottom line. The entrepreneurs focusing on supplying that specific service engage in firm-forming and market-making of their own by first innovating and then contributing to competitive discovery, which would push down costs, lower prices, incentivise innovation, and standardise service offerings. And, as the services are provided by another party in the market through contract, they will be procured at prices that eventually (with the advent of competition for this business) converge to the true market price. They are also no longer part of the coordination problem inside the firm, and, consequently the entrepreneur's uncertainty is reduced by the extent of outsourced services. Outsourcing is therefore a means to lessen the burden of uncertainty, not only a means to increase emphasis on core production activities that allows the entrepreneur to focus on improving the core innovation. Improvements in effectiveness, in turn, can free up resources – time used for coordination and comparatively inefficient production, at a minimum – for further development and improvements.

Of course, as other entrepreneurs enter the production space to offer competing production processes, or specific tasks carried out within the original process, the firm may begin to dissolve. The tasks within the firm are no longer strictly interdependent if they are offered for procurement or potentially can be offered by other market actors. While there may be gains from trade between firms, the initial price determined between pairs of entrepreneurs does not determine the true and final market price, however. Only as competition intensifies and the task offered emerges as a standard economic good is a market price that reflects the social opportunity cost in production determined. At this point, the market has fully subsumed the original entrepreneur's innovation and there is consequently no firm; its unique and innovative production process has become the market standard, and so this type of production is no longer located outside the extent of the market.

This process of firm formation followed by the emergence of factor markets and then outsourcing reinforces the argument we made in Chapter 6: that the firm is a volatile, transient construct that provides a specific economic function in the progression of the market process. This conclusion is seldom drawn in the literature on the firm, perhaps due to the empirical observation that legal firms last for very long periods of time and have no legal time limits, but follows logically from the argument presented here. As the firm is not an end in itself, but a structure that is observable due to the distinct nature of implemented productive innovation, it serves only to overcome the attendant problem of production that we discussed in Chapter 3.

As the firm is subjected to competition and the competitive discovery process reveals more efficient configurations and better production structures, the rationale for and indeed the basis on which we identify the firm is undermined, and the firm therefore eventually ceases to exist. From our perspective, it makes sense that the firm, as an integrated production structure, because it is firmly located outside the extent of the market, eventually becomes part of the market – the firm is a starting point for market-making, not an escape from the market. As the firm dissolves into the expanded market, the specific tasks originally carried out within the firm may be better provided by specialised parties in a competitive market – and traded at a market price.

Note that this was also the starting point for our investigation: the firmless market. But as the decentralised market lacks means to surpass the extent of the market, a productive innovation cannot be implemented within it. Instead, the implementation of a production process consisting of a highly intensive division of labour that is not supported within the existing market falls outside the market's extent and therefore suffers from strict interdependence and so risks incompleteness. The innovation around which the firm is formed is no longer novel or even a contribution to productivity as its ingenuity is copied and improved on by others. The market, in a sense, 'catches up' with the entrepreneur's innovation as competitors adopt the new specialisation intensity and thereby expand the market to incorporate the new degree and kind of division of labour. There is no longer a role for a firm (see further Chapters 8 and 9).

This suggests a lifecycle of the transient firm that begins with the implementation of a revolutionising productive innovation outside the extent of the existing market, and ends with the dissolution of the firm into the market. This reaffirms what we discussed above: that the endeavour requires an initial investment, likely one of significant magnitude. But with time, as tasks can be outsourced, the range of tasks part of the innovative production process integrated within the firm diminishes. The firm should consequently be as extensive (in number of tasks within the scope of the process) as needs be at its founding, including supportive tasks and production of specific capital goods to be used in production.

It is of course possible that the entrepreneur or those employed to carry out specific tasks within the new process as time progresses identify better ways of achieving the imagined end, and such changes will be implemented to improve the outcome of the process. This suggests that the process is not navigated by a fixed blueprint, as was discussed in previous chapters, but a process that facilitates discovery through implementation and experimentation. While the originally imagined scope of the production process remains, it includes too many tasks in a competitive setting. The emergence of competition and therefore markets for factors allows for tweaks and improvements of the process that may include downsizing or even the termination of certain tasks that were originally believed to be necessary but proved to be superfluous. Necessary but non-core supportive, administrative, or coordinative tasks can then be outsourced as new entrepreneurs enter the market to offer these services efficiently at a market price. The firm, as a result, is then further reduced in size as individual tasks are being outsourced to external parties. For as long as the firm coordinates the one production process, therefore, it should always be of the greatest size, in terms of the number of tasks integrated, in the beginning. The size should then diminish over time as competitors enter the production space.

This does not mean that actual firms can never grow, only that the original scope is necessary to attain the original end. As should have been clear in the examples discussed in previous chapters, replacing a market-tradable production task with a new process has a specified scope: it must maintain compatibility with inputs as well as outputs, and so has fixed starting point and end. The roundaboutness of the process – the number of tasks that are carried out – depends on the entrepreneur's imagined innovation, but the scope of what is achieved is fixed: it still produces the same market-saleable outputs using the same market-procurable inputs. This is not to say that there are no benefits attainable through increased resource utilisation. It may be the case that the tasks identified as part of the productive innovation are underutilised within the production process, but that they can favourably be used in other types of production. They can consequently be shared between processes, and depending on the anticipated cost and availability of slack resources, it is conceivable that it is advantageous to increase the size of the firm so that it coordinates several production processes simultaneously. This appears to vindicate Coase's view that the profitability of the marginal transaction (process) determines the boundary of the firm. Yet note the difference: Coase's firm typically coordinates several transactions, whereas our emphasis on innovative production processes would make this a rare occurrence. In contrast, a firm should typically be formed around one productive innovation, not many. Opportunities to increase resource utilisation by coordinating additional processes may be perceived at the outset, prior to implementing the process, revealed during the implementation phase, or identified during production. However, as the tasks comprising the productive innovation are highly specialised, if not unique, they would commonly require additional productive innovation that dovetails with the original innovation.

This means that the development of resources would typically precede expansion of the firm's size to include additional processes. This is partly a consequence of uncertainty, since the outcome of the original productive innovation is unknowable until it has been implemented and tested. The entrepreneur could believe that there are several uses for tasks to be performed within the production process, and therefore speculate about expanding the firm's scope from the inception, but this greatly increases the uncertainty of the endeavour. As the imagined task has not been implemented, details about its performance and conditions cannot be exactly known. It is possible that the task, when implemented, needs restructuring or even be replaced by some other task or function. Basing two or more production processes on the specific contribution imagined from one task the processes have in common creates a bottleneck and single point of failure that could turn out to be very costly over time. As the processes are already subject to incompleteness, the uncertainty of the endeavour should increase dramatically if it includes more than one process. This doesn't mean that entrepreneurs will not attempt to do this, only that the cost of uncertainty should in many cases be a reason to postpone expansion of scope until the first process has been fully and successfully implemented. The particular conditions of the situation in which the entrepreneur undertakes to implement the productive innovation are likely to provide guidance in specific cases.

The underutilisation of tasks within the newly implemented production process should be a reason to consider expansion for increased profitability. But expansion is also a means to deal with the risk of competitive entry, since evidence or perception of underutilisation or slack resources provide an incentive for other entrepreneurs to enter the new production space with somewhat altered processes that improve resource utilisation. The original firm could therefore choose to expand even before competitors emerge in order to get the full benefit of the developed and implemented productive tasks. In rare cases, overall profitability of the productive innovation may depend on finding ways to increase the use of highly specialised tasks through expanding the firm's scope. This would be the case if, for example, a task is so highly specialised and requires such upfront investment that it becomes prohibitively costly not to achieve a very high degree of utilisation. Where the anticipated production volume is insufficient to reach minimum utilisation, making the task part of more than one specialised process would solve the problem. Though it would be done at the cost of increased uncertainty and incompleteness problems.

As a process has been implemented, improved, and found workable, the real effectiveness and utilisation of its parts will be discovered. At this point, the entrepreneur may find it advantageous to expand the business into other types of production that could make use of one or more of these tasks (unchanged or with slight modifications). So while the scope of the productive innovation is fixed, though the structure could potentially be improved through inserting further innovations and thereby make the process even more specialised and round-about, the size of the business is not. The firm is a first implementation of a new specialisation intensity that relies on a new degree and kind of division of labour, and to the extent that it is successful (that is, effective and efficient) it will be able to replace existing production processes. A successful firm can in this sense take advantage of 'internal' innovations in specific tasks by expanding its size; that is, by going into other lines of business, other types of production, and other industries. The successful firm can thus grow in size and influence until the innovation is fully disseminated through competitive imitation or replaced by superior productive innovations.

The firm can also expand the range of tasks carried out within the existing production process by attempting to replace adjacent, market-based production stages to 'integrate' vertically. There may be synergies from co-locating the productive innovation or sharing its supportive resources with either upstream or downstream stages, which from the market's point of view could resemble vertical integration. But as we have pointed out in previous chapters, contracting specifics are insufficient for distinguishing between the market and the firm as different means of organising production. A firm, located outside the extent of the present market, can find value in owning or in other ways controlling a provider of a market-traded production stage (that is, production placed within the extent of the market), but this in itself doesn't move that provider to a location outside the market, i.e. inside the firm. Rather, the transaction establishing ownership between the firm and the provider of a marketable production stage is a simple market contract. Buying an existing producer outright will make it a subsidiary, but not an integrated part of the original firm. There is one exception to this, however, and that is if it is acquired in order to obtain a specific resource, competence, or experience that is to be modified, altered, or redirected towards a highly specialised task within the proper firm. The acquired producer would then be a component of an expanded productive innovation. This latter case may be an adequate response to identified weaknesses or other possibilities for improvement in the implemented process. This issue of insourcing and expansion of the firm's scope after its formation raises the question of what we mean by ownership of an 'island of specialisation' and how acquisition of market-based production stages affects its boundaries.

Ownership and boundaries of the firm

As the discussion above shows, the boundaries of the firm typically change over time. Absent additional innovation, the range of tasks performed within the firm should diminish as the production process is improved and supportive services are outsourced. Part of the reason for this is the cost of uncertainty, which can be avoided by adopting market-provided solutions instead of relying on in-house provision. Part of it is also that competition is expected to emerge and then intensify for as long as the firm is profitable, which will eventually bring division of labour in the market to par with the productive innovation and thereby subsume it. As increasing competition eats away the rationale and function of the firm, it will eventually dissolve into the market as the price mechanism is a more efficient means to coordinate production tasks. The interdependence of tasks within the firm is then loosened with the entry of the first competitor and more so as other entrepreneurs enter the production space until the tasks are fully or primarily traded and saleable in the market. This relieves the entrepreneurs within the firm from the uncertainty that it entails.

The firm can continue to exist beyond its 'natural' longevity only if there are specific barriers to entry for competitors or if it successfully engages in continued innovation. The former can emerge as a result of relatively far-reaching resource scarcity, which is in essence a limitation of, rather than to, the market. Scarcity is a precondition for trade and the existence of market, as abundant supply makes allocation of resources to their better uses completely unnecessary, but trade-deterring scarcity arises because the market has not provided the production apparatus with sufficient supply of a specific good or satisfactory substitutes. This may be a result of production's reliance on a (presumably natural) resource that either sees very little or prohibitively expensive substitutes – or if the resource is so little understood that no substitutes have been invented. These are all problems that could very well be solved with the passage of time and the continuation of economic and market progress through competitive discovery.

The changing boundaries of the firm are indicative of the problem of ownership that the firm as an 'island of specialisation' causes. Legal entities such as the actual firms in our modern economies can own and deal with resources, and whoever is the legal owner of the legal entity called the firm enjoys ownership of its resources. In our analysis, however, the firm is not an entity but the implementation of a productive innovation outside the extent of the market. This is done through establishing a more intensive specialisation within the overall production process, as compared to the market, through a different degree and kind of division of labour. Whereas it may be useful to assume that the originator of this innovation is a single person, this may not be the case. We have already found that the implementation process entails discovering necessary changes and tweaks to the imagined process, and that the exact nature of the individual tasks as well as the outcome of the process is unknown and unknowable. Whereas the original entrepreneur initiates the implementation process and has the basic idea, the nature of each task, their coordination, and thus the functioning of the full process will not be discovered until the tasks are performed. Those carrying out the work will likely be best positioned to identify problems and weaknesses, and also figure out how to solve or overcome them. In this sense, each person involved in implementing the productive innovation is an innovator, however within the realm of the original purpose. This process, as we saw above, is very costly and requires a substantial capital investment. We therefore have a number of parties that could potentially be denoted owners of the firm: innovators at different level of abstraction (primarily the original entrepreneur and those specialising to carry out specific tasks within the new process), and 'external' investors. All of them bear the uncertainty of the undertaking, but perhaps to differing degrees.

This discussion is however beside the point for the same reason as when we discussed authority in Chapter 5. Whereas we as observers can identify the firm as seemingly distinct from the wheeling and dealing in the market, where market actors actively bid for inputs and seek the highest possible bids for their outputs, it is not an entity in itself. It is but production located outside the limits of the extent of the market and its parts and totality are subject to strict interdependence that keep the parts together. There is no 'it' in the sense that there are only productive tasks carried out by labour factors specialised to those very tasks. What allows us to here distinguish the firm from the market theoretically is the fact that the tasks carried out within its boundaries are unique – they are, when implemented, completely without substitutes or redundancy. This is why there is no (and can be no) market for the individual tasks carried out within the firm, which translates to their strict interdependence and subjection to the incompleteness problem. And this is how we can recognise the firm as something distinct.

What the firm really boils down to is a contractually based attempt at producing outside the limits of what can be supported by the market. Within the firm, just as Coase originally identified, there is not a 'series of contracts' between any pair of parties. Instead, at least according to Coase, there is a single, long-term contract between the factor and the employer, who is awarded the authority to direct the resource. But we saw in Chapter 5 that this does not provide a basis for authority within the firm, and we based this conclusion on Coase's insight about the reciprocal nature of market action (including contracts). As for the numbers of contracts, it would be impossible to contract on details before the process has already been implemented, since the details are fundamentally unknown. Even so, upon implementation there is still no good reason for parties to contract on all details since there are no alternatives: due to the incompleteness problem and strict interdependence there is neither reason nor possibility to establish contracts that specify all possible details. All parties to the novel production process are at the mercy of all others: if any one fails (or even misunderstands expectations) the whole process is left incomplete and therefore will not earn returns. Also, as the exact nature of the tasks and how they relate to each other cannot be known, it is impossible to regulate contractually to such detail. All contracts within the firm should therefore at least during its formation and the improvement and implementation phase be open-ended. Contracts between parties 'within' the firm may be prudent, however, in response to emerging competitors, as a means to protect the 'firm' from incompleteness due to competitive bidding for individual tasks.

The implications of our theory for ownership of the firm are therefore not novel but reinforce previous findings. We hold that what matters in terms of ownership within the firm as an 'island of specialisation' is who owns the resources used: capital goods or tools, inputs, and so on. However, our perspective provides a potentially more fundamental understanding for why this is so. We can agree almost in full with Oliver D. Hart and John Moore, who

> identify a firm with the assets it possesses and take the position that ownership confers residual rights of control over the firm's assets: the right to decide how these assets are to be used except to the extent that particular usages have been specified in an initial contract.[1]

Whereas those involved in the implementation process, whether as labourers specialising to perform specific tasks or in some other capacity, may choose to contract with each other to minimise the risk of opportunistic behaviour at some future time, such contracts are not necessary to form a firm. What matters is the capital investment and thus ownership of the resources that are used within the firm. This can be easily seen if we again consider the process of firm formation. To implement the productive innovation, capital is needed to cover the outlays for development and purchase of tools, machinery, and inputs. To attract labour factors to partake in the undertaking and specialise to specific tasks in the process, payment or promise of payment or a share of the return must be made. The need for capital investment was discussed above.

As we briefly mentioned above, it is not obvious that a capital investment to implement the imagined production structure and thus form a firm must be made by one party. It could, and it may be likely that the entrepreneur has access to funds of his or her own or indirectly through a willing capitalist investor or by taking a loan. If this is the case, then the entrepreneur is the owner of the capital resources to the extent ownership has not been offered to the capitalist investor or lender and established contractually. To the degree these funds are used to pay labourers for their service, they are not owners of the firm (they are then essentially suppliers or subcontractors, but monopoly performers of production tasks that are located outside the extent of the existing market); to the degree labourers contract with the entrepreneur or investor about ownership, they are owners. As the firm itself is neither a real nor a legal entity, it cannot own resources. The resources used within the firm must be owned by someone. As the firm does not exist as a separate entity, no one can own 'it'; what remains is ownership of resources and contractual commitments between parties. Centralised ownership is not a requirement for there to be a firm.

Coase's point about the single contract is valid, however, since it would make sense for the entrepreneur or capitalist investor to regulate contractually the expectations of the parties to the firm. The firm is a contractual construct, but the nature of contracting doesn't change the fact that the firm, as an 'island of specialisation', is, in a sense, its resources and that ownership can exist only of those resources. The nature and coordination of production is outside the extent of the market, but this in itself does not require a particular form or nature of ownership.

Summing up

What we have seen in this chapter, then, is that while the firm requires upfront capital to cover the costs during implementation and until production generates revenue through sales, financing is not different from within the market. But the period of time between investment and return is longer than for investments within the market. There is also greater uncertainty due to the firm's internal interdependence and thus that its success is subject to the incompleteness problem. We also saw that the firm's boundaries are subject to change as competitors enter the production space and the entrepreneur therefore can be relieved of borne uncertainty through outsourcing functions previously carried out within the firm. This suggests, we noted, that the firm's size, in terms of number of internal tasks, is greatest at its forming, and should then typically diminish. This reinforces our finding in Chapter 6 about the lifecycle of the firm.

We also reiterated the point that the firm is not an entity in itself and therefore that 'it' is nothing but the capital goods used within its specific production process. Ownership of the firm is therefore the same thing as owning the resources in the firm. Whether these resources are centrally owned by a single party, owned in common by those working in the firm, or the capital used in each task owned separately, are of little if any relevance for our study of the firm.

Note

1 O. D. Hart and J. Moore, 'Property Rights and the Nature of the Firm', *Journal of Political Economy*, 98:6 (1990), pp. 1119–1158, p. 1120.

8 The firm as a market institution

We saw in previous chapters how we can view the firm as the manifestation of an implementation of a productive innovation brought about by an entrepreneur or entrepreneurial team. The nature of the innovation means the tasks and intermediate goods produced by those tasks are purely interdependent; there are no (and can be no) markets for them. For this reason, the implementation falls outside the reach of the price mechanism and therefore takes place outside the limits of the extent of the existing market. In this sense, the firm is a separate phenomenon that is related to, functions with, and depends on, yet is internally unique in the sense that its internal parts are not replaceable by the market. For an observer, the firm therefore appears as a separate organisation or entity that is created by the entrepreneur. The firm emerges as a means to solve the problem of implementing innovation that is not supported by the market.

However, it is important to remember that the firm is not in itself an economic end or a purposefully created occurrence, as is oftentimes hypothesised in the theory of the firm literature, but the observable result of implementing a productive innovation in the form of an 'island of specialisation'. It is separate from the market and utilises a division of labour that is different in kind and degree, but 'it' is not necessarily more than the implemented innovation: the 'organisation' is coordination of novel production but does not exist economically in addition to the specialised, coordinated production process. Chapter 7 indirectly addressed this issue in terms of financing and ownership, and we found that the firm is little if anything in addition to 'its' resources. An implication of that discussion is that the firm is not a distinct phenomenon and is not in essence distinguishable from other types of productive contracting in the market from an ownership point of view. Whether the firm is financed fully by one party, internal or external to the firm's production process, or if it is financed collectively by those taking part in it, is rather irrelevant for our identification of the firm as an economic phenomenon as well as for how it is implemented. It is the type of implementation itself, the fact that it is necessarily located outside the reach of (rather than supersedes, as Coase has it) the price mechanism that characterises and defines the firm.

The firm is thereby the result of entrepreneurship's endeavour to realise a type of production process that cannot be implemented through market-based exchange or contracting. But its function is not to provide a laboratory for entrepreneurs to engage in innovative experimentation, even though this may be a common type of activity taking place within the firm once it is formed. As the firm is the observable *result* of entrepreneurs implementing innovation outside the extent of the existing market, the economic function cannot reasonably be to provide a means for innovative entrepreneurs to implement the imagined production process. Rather, the economic function of the firm can be seen by assuming the perspective of the progression of the market process. This is the task for this chapter, in which we draft the place and role of the firm in the process of market expansion.

As we will see, the firm as the implementation of a productive innovation outside the extent of the market explains the continuous flux of the market process through adaptive change and, especially, its progression towards increased productivity and value creation. In fact, we find that 'the firm' is how the existing market structure is revolutionised by productive innovation and how production breaks free from the specialisation deadlock – and therefore how the extent of the market expands.

Competition as a discovery process

As the firm, as it is here conceived, necessarily is formed outside the extent of the market, there are and can be no market prices for the capital goods in their particular uses within the 'island of specialisation'. Therefore, there is no guidance offered to the entrepreneur in terms of the efficient social allocation of productive resources within the production process. The firm is consequently blind to whether resources are used to their fullest extent from the point of view of consumer wants satisfaction. It is in fact unlikely that the firm is economically efficient, since there are no market prices to indicate what is a better allocation of resources. This uncertainty of neither knowing nor being able to figure out the firm's efficiency, which was discussed in Chapter 7, is borne by the entrepreneur or entrepreneurs within the firm through their investments. But it does not mean that the firm cannot make a profit. To the contrary, the firm can be highly profitable despite being comparatively inefficient. Economic efficiency in the allocation of resources used is not necessary for profitability. Instead, what is needed is that the firm produces greater value than existing competing uses of similar resources. It is possible for the firm to outdo the market because of the productive innovation implemented through increased specialisation through the division of labour. The firm is successful because it finds a new and improved use for resources, but is inefficient compared to a conjectured market that has adopted the new division of labour as standard.

Even if the market would be fully arbitraged and all opportunities for profit within the extents of the market exploited, the market is in a *constrained* maximum: it uses only the knowledge and the production processes that are known and traded. In other words, the market, which does not include the productive innovations imagined by entrepreneurs, can only through exchange maximise outcome given its already adopted and supported division of labour. This is why the entrepreneur's productive innovation takes place outside the extent of, and thus potentially revolutionises the structure of, the existing market: it creates new knowledge of what can be achieved through production that was not previously considered in and even less was incorporated by the market. The market, as we discussed in Chapter 3, is subject to and continuously improved through profit-incentivised reallocations *within* the specialisation deadlock, a limitation that is effectively circumvented by the innovator-entrepreneur. Even a fairly inefficient allocation of resources within the new production structure in the firm can therefore potentially outdo a fully arbitraged market because the firm uses a more intensive specialisation. Indeed, the firm can outdo the existing market, and consequently replace market-traded production stages, while still being inefficient on its own terms.

The combination of the firm's highly intensive but almost decidedly underutilised, non-maximised specialisation combined with revealed profitability provides strong incentives for actors presently occupied in trading positions within the market to act as imitator-entrepreneurs in order to capture some of the new value created and revealed by the original firm. Not only will an imitator-entrepreneur have the chance to capture some of the profits that are generated by the original firm, but there are opportunities to increase the overall profitability of the productive innovation through improving the production process by adding specific knowledge or entrepreneurial judgment to how it is carried out. Imitator-entrepreneurs may see ways of emulating the original process while improving on it using their own specific skills, knowledge, and contacts. As the original firm provides a benchmark for potential entrants, there is an opportunity for second-movers and late-comers to compete with and possibly outdo the original firm. There should thus be a strong incentive to follow the original firm into the new production space and compete with it head on, especially for those who deem they have a good chance to capture part of the innovation's profit potential.

On the other hand, there are impediments directly to enter the new production space to compete with the original firm. The latter is automatically integrated through pure interdependence between its parts, so the knowledge revealed to potential competitors through its implementation is likely to be incomplete. Whereas the implementation itself is not maximised and therefore can be improved, the knowledge used within the production process is only partially available to anyone outside the firm. This suggests that imitator-entrepreneurs cannot simply copy the original structure but must engage in innovative entrepreneurship themselves in order to implement a competing production structure; the partial knowledge available or appropriable must be completed by the imitator-entrepreneur. There is therefore entrepreneurial uncertainty-bearing in production also in being a second-mover, since innovations are necessary to fill the gaps and also must be fitted with what is known about the process and can be imitated. The effectiveness of competitors to implement their competing structures may therefore be limited, but it also means competition will rarely arise between identical or very similar implementations of the original production structure. Rather, competition will initially emerge between production innovations that differ in various ways but that share one characteristic: they are designed to replace an existing market productions stage in full.

Even after the entry of competitors, there are no real market prices to guide the competing production processes. Neither the original nor the imitating entrepreneurs can be expected to discover immediately the efficient internal allocation of resources. Competition therefore takes place between imperfect implementations (as opposed to a hypothetical market situation) that differ in various ways, both in terms of how the overall production process is implemented and in the effectiveness of individual parts of it as well as their contribution to the value produced. These differences result from the entrepreneurs' different skill sets and knowledge, their idiosyncrasies, and the types of resources – human and otherwise – that are available to them. As they attempt to implement production processes similar to (and that therefore compete directly with) the original process, they attempt to fill in gaps in the available knowledge while also playing on their strengths in attempting improvements to the production process. There is no reason to expect them to produce identical solutions to perceived problems, so their implementations are likely different in certain respects. Even though they compete directly with each other, there is variety in their internal production processes: they consequently have different strengths and weaknesses.

This state of affairs suggests that entrepreneurs are collectively, through competition for profit, involved in a discovery process of which production processes are more effective and therefore produce a greater value or produce at a lower cost. It should be expected that the entrepreneurs, upon implementing their own versions of the production process, attempt to continue improving its effectiveness. This can be accomplished by tweaking the process and learning from as well as attempting to imitate competitors. As more entrepreneurs enter the production space, they add new skills, ideas, and knowledge to the type of production implemented by the original entrepreneur. The new production space should therefore, from an aggregate point of view, see continuous improvement in effectiveness and efficient use of resources as more entrepreneurs enter to compete for profits. We should see both increased competition to capture the revealed profits and increased profitability of the production space overall. Indeed, the former leads to the latter for as long as the production stage in the market has not been fully supplanted by the productive innovation. Increased competition between the firms will both lower their respective production costs (as well as force the least effective to exit) and increase the degree to which the firms displace the market-coordinated production stage. *Ceteris paribus*, therefore, the implemented processes are improved and perfected, and can thus be performed at lower cost, while the total profit available by production in this space increases (unless the market price falls).

Whereas we would initially see complete task-replacing implementations compete with each other, each at least at first suffering from pure interdependence of its internal parts, entrepreneurs are likely also to engage in competition for individual factors used within their individual 'islands of specialisation'. An imitator-entrepreneur has a different implementation of the original productive innovation, but tries to accomplish the same type of production. After all, they use the same inputs, procurable in the market, and produce the same output, saleable in the market. There is variety in how the firms implement their specific solutions, but not sufficient to make them completely incompatible. Even if there is not perfect substitutability between firms' processes, there are similarities. These similarities only increase as the entrepreneurs attempt to incorporate others' solutions in order to improve their own processes.

An imitator-entrepreneur can consequently find that it is potentially beneficial to attempt to outbid the original entrepreneur for workers or capital employed within the original firm. He may, for instance, find that a worker's particular competence is highly valuable and rare, and that it is very difficult to train someone to gain this important skill because this specific productive contribution falls outside the realm of his own entrepreneurial skill set. Or it may appear easier to lure a worker from the original firm than perceivable alternative courses of action. Similarly for capital, the original firm may use some type of production-aiding capital good that imitating entrepreneurs cannot reproduce or for other reasons are interested in acquiring.

Such competition for individual competences and resources that were specific to, and therefore purely interdependent within, the original firm loosens the grip of interdependence. Cross-firm bidding is made possible because the imitator-entrepreneurs produced competing production processes that implement a similar structure, potentially with similar interfaces between at least some of its internal tasks. As a result, the specific resource becomes complementary to a lesser degree while potentially more substitutable, since it can be used in two (or more) competing production processes. With the imitator-entrepreneur engaging in bidding for resources previously used exclusively within the original entrepreneur's productive innovation, an undeveloped market emerges between the two. As other entrepreneurs enter, the bidding generates a market price for the previously unpriced factors based on the entrepreneurs' joint appraisement of their productive value. This further strengthens competing entrepreneurs' ability to discover and implement improvements to the process and should therefore lead to rapid improvements in terms of both technical effectiveness and allocative efficiency. The original firm's ability to absorb revealed improvements – and to develop new ones – determines its continued profitability and therefore survival. It is by no means necessary that the original firm persists in the face of increasing competition; the original innovation leads the way and breaks the ground for a new kind of production, but whether it survives the competitive process depends on its entrepreneurial ability to make use of and implement improvements discovered by others.

Market-making and the dissolution of the firm

What follows from the original implementation of the productive innovation as the first imitator-entrepreneur enters the production space is a type of discovery process through productive competition between firms.[1] Each firm attempts to implement improvements in order to capture as large a share as possible of profits. These improvements are produced both internally to the individual firm, through continuous experimentation and innovation, and externally through copying from other firms. This is what also facilitates the bidding for competing firms' resources, since the overall effectiveness of an internal production process is revealed through profitability. Discovery of how to improve one's internal production process can therefore in part be brought about through bidding for and winning over other firms' core competencies (primarily labour workers, since capital is a more specific factor of production and thus is less likely to be fully compatible). The discovery process entails configuration of processes to find optimal overall structure and maximising quantities, but, more importantly, firms attempt to improve the effectiveness of each internal task and the capabilities of factors employed. The latter can be done through both reconfiguration and recombination of resources, and by replacing one task or resource with another. As the discovery process focuses on bidding for and improving specific tasks and factors within firms, market prices for these factors eventually emerge. Determined market prices facilitate more precise valuation of factor use and thereby, as the discovery process progresses, provides a means to estimate the firm's internal effectiveness and allocative efficiency through economic calculation. Competition therefore makes internal discovery possible by loosening and ultimately undoing the interdependence between factors within firms, which as a result makes further improvements possible.

It is conceivable that many firms at their founding, even though they may be profitable, incorporate tasks that are found to be either inefficiently implemented, are of little value, or even contribute no real value to the firm's output. Such tasks are promptly improved within or jettisoned from surviving firms under competitive pressure. As we saw when discussing the boundaries of the firm in the previous chapter, tasks that are not considered core to the firm's productive innovation may also be outsourced to competing firms or newly formed firms specialised to producing that particular task.

The bidding for firms' internal factors will determine their market value by establishing market prices, and this results in a market in the production space that was previously outside the extent of the market. A successful and imitated productive innovation – the implementation of a profitable firm outside the extent of the existing market – therefore sets in motion a change process in which the existing market structure is ultimately challenged. The more intensive specialisation that is used in, and indeed defines, the new production space, as originally created by the productive innovation and attempts to imitate it, constitutes an improvement over the existing market's division of labour, and will therefore require market actors to adjust their activities. Previously marketed production that the productive innovation effectively replaces is in other words outcompeted and the resources used in these marketed tasks released. As competing firms in the new production space engage in cross-process bidding for factors and, consequently, market-making for these factors, they effectively bring about an outward shift in the limits of the extent of the market.

The creation of market between firms ultimately exposes the existing market to the new and more intensive specialisation under the division of labour. This has repercussions for the existing allocation of resources as well as market prices for substitutes. The innovation causes ripple effects that will reallocate resources towards what are now revealed to be their better uses, in differently configured and specialised production processes, and prices change as a consequence. As the market adopts the new state of production, and consequently the new knowledge discovered by the original and imitating firms, the firms in this production space dissolve into market trade as the new extent of the market incorporates their kind and degree of specialisation. It is no longer necessary for this specialisation to be implemented outside the market in the productive innovation that we identified as a firm, and this concludes the lifecycle of the 'island of specialisation'.

This process from firm formation to dissolution may be anything but instantaneous. Before market prices are determined and accepted, the entrepreneur who decides to rely on the undeveloped market between firms still faces extensive uncertainty of the kind that necessitates the 'island of specialisation'. Reliance on external actors to supply factors in the very limited factor markets between competing entrepreneurial endeavours, means failure to procure them leads to incompleteness. It is easy to understand how entrepreneurs may resist the temptation to 'outsource' for this reason alone: if it is done too early, their productive innovation may face incompleteness. This does not preclude bidding for factors perceived of higher value currently located within competing firms, however. If they can be won over, it is to the winning firm's benefit and at the same time the competitor's loss. In the infancy of cross-firm factor markets the loss of any resource will greatly increase the risk of incompleteness. This fact may under certain circumstances be sufficient for entrepreneurs to start bidding wars for factors in the new production space.

Entrepreneurs are nevertheless incentivised to use the price mechanism when they can. As we saw in previous chapters, the uncertainty within the 'island of specialisation' is very costly, but necessary since the implementation of the productive innovation is impossible through market means. If entrepreneurs could rely on the price mechanism instead of bearing the full uncertainty of the enterprise, there is reason for them to do so. Indeed, they should always choose reliance on the price mechanism over other means of coordination wherever it is feasible.

One reason for this is the flexibility that comes with independence, since access to more than one supplier of a necessary input or service lessens the risk of incompleteness. Another reason is the calculability that market prices facilitate, since they offer a social appraisal of the means and factors used in production.

Furthermore, procuring necessary factors, inputs, and services in the market can reveal that imperfect substitutes are available as back-up solutions in the face of temporary incompleteness. It also suggests that the entrepreneur can limit the time between investment and payment, since inputs procurable in the market are their own, separate projects. Moreover, the firm avoids development costs as well as costs of controlling, monitoring, and managing the sub-production process, which is another entrepreneur's project. There may also be opportunities to lower input costs by letting suppliers compete for the order, which also suggests any costs of price discovery are effectively assigned to suppliers as they advertise their prices and qualities as part of the competitive process.

The entrepreneur, as we have already seen, does not make the choice to form a firm, but it is the inevitable result (whether or not it is intended or favourable) of implementing the productive innovation outside the extent of the market. There is for this reason, as well as the specific cost reasons noted above, little economic reason for the entrepreneur to maintain the firm as it was originally constituted beyond the emergence of factor markets between the firm and its competitors.[2] Indeed, the emergence of markets relieves the entrepreneur of the burden of uncertainty since time, effort, and other productive means can be focused on a limited set of the production process rather than distributed across the tasks in the production process. The boundaries of the firm should therefore always shift with the emergence of markets for the factors necessary to complete the production process. Consequently, the primary tendency should not be towards an expanding scope of the firm, but the very opposite: the entrepreneur – as well as labour workers employed in the firm – benefit from consistently transferring previously internal tasks to emerging and maturing markets.[3] We can see then that the lack of perfect knowledge (bounded rationality, as it were) of the entrepreneur or entrepreneurs in the firm, offset in part by their imagination and judgment, is an important factor for the effective and economic scope of the firm, but that it plays little role in determining the firm's boundaries. Indeed, the firm needs to be complete – at least in terms of its scope – at its formation, or it will fail due to incompleteness. The imperfect knowledge of those involved in the firm can be a reason *not* to form the firm, since the productive innovation will then seem very difficult or costly, if not impossible, to implement. Imperfect knowledge also affects the costs within the firm and thereby increases the incentive to outsource initially necessary internal tasks. But this cannot determine the boundaries of the firm, which are set by the existence of markets: the firm itself is non-market, and dissolves as markets form or expand to encompass tasks previously organised in the firm. The primary tendency of existing firms is consequently the reduction of their scope through increasing adoption of market means for coordinating production – outsourcing of tasks and functions supplied in the market.

The firm and the market

With the scope of the firm being reduced, more and more as time passes, the original entrepreneur is relieved of his or her initial responsibility and can therefore focus more intently on what is (to him or her) the firm's original and core contri-bution to society's overall production structure. Outsourcing, therefore, has the effect not only of expanding the market's reach by generating market prices of previously internal production tasks, but also facilitates continued improvement and, possibly, innovation within the original firm. In general, the firm can out-source tasks carried out within the productive innovation following one of two changes in the firm's production space. As competitors enter and bid for intra-firm factors, the task's market value is revealed and its originality undermined through the firms' competitive actions; it can therefore eventually, in a standard-ised form, be provided by independent producers in the market. Commodifica-tion of tasks makes it easily procurable through simple market trade, and there is consequently no reason for the firm to dedicate resources to organise the task in-house. For supportive tasks or tasks that are already partially compatible with the market, there should be comparatively limited costs involved with outsour-cing. Alternatively, entrepreneurs who enter the production space as the com-petitive discovery process is already well underway may identify that there is a profit opportunity in innovating to replace a recently priced task. These entre-preneurs provide the same function as the original firm by establishing a novel, innovative way of carrying out a function that can replace an existing production task – only they do so before the task has been fully overtaken by the market and commodified. As this new firm is formed, it offers to carry out and replace a task carried out within already existing firms.

The effect is in both cases a reduction of the outsourcing firm's scope and therefore increased possibility to focus on the remaining tasks. It is likely the entrepreneur most eagerly welcomes outsourcing of supportive functions and those tasks that are not core to the innovation, that is those tasks that were neces-sary at the inception to maintain the firm's productive completeness but are no longer so. The reduced scope accelerates possibilities for productive improve-ment and the firm's ability to identify and experiment with opportunities for further innovation. Such innovations can include the further splitting of an already implemented task (that is, a task that is the result of previous, firm-forming task-splitting), which, were this to take place in the market (when the firm has dissolved into the market's price mechanism), would constitute a new firm. While the entrepreneur can engage in productive innovation and task-splitting at any point within the firm, doing so before competitors relieve the entrepreneur of some of the uncertainty is risky. As the efficiency of tasks cannot be known and economic improvement of tasks does not take place until a com-petitive discovery process has begun, the entrepreneur is to a significant extent blind to whether the task to be further split is of sufficient quality to be viable in the market. Splitting such a task into a sub-process may therefore have the effect that existing errors or mistakes, primarily of economic rather than technical nature, are cemented or amplified. This can risk the profitability of the enter-prise, whereas awaiting competitive discovery can substantially lessen this risk.

The productive scope of the firm, by which we mean the internally coord-inated production stage, should therefore decrease over time, but the number of tasks, the resources and factors tied up in production, and 'size' of the organisation may increase through further innovation. The firm's scope will only increase by including more of the existent productive stages, which is of little use unless there are significant synergies in co-location or the added stage is split into a novel production process. Synergies should be available only under particular circumstances, including for example abnormal scarcity, or as a step towards innovation. For instance, the firm can offer employment to a factor engaged in the previous (upstream) or following (downstream) stage for the purpose of tweaking the task or otherwise changing the way this task works together with the intra-firm tasks. Without innovation, the addition of a production stage does not change the boundary of the firm as an 'island of specialisation' simply because it involves no specialisation; the firm's employment of upstream producers is akin to exclusive contracting with a supplier but not a merger.

We have until this point argued that the firm is integrated simply for the reason that it makes use of and constitutes a division of labour that is more intensive and therefore of a different kind and degree than that traded in the market. The market does not support the innovative splitting of standard tasks since they are not saleable, and neither does it support the coordination of those tasks through market contracting or pricing. The firm must therefore be established outside the extent of the market. As the firm is established and real profit opportunities are revealed through earned profits, other entrepreneurs will be incentivised to follow suit and compete with the original innovation, which leads to a competitive discovery and 'maximisation' of the innovation's economic value – and eventually the dissolution of the firm through explicit outsourcing of tasks to other entrepreneurs or shifting towards market procurement as the market adopts the new intensity of specialisation and therefore determines the market price of specific tasks. The emergence of competitors, competitive discovery, and the dissolution of the firm are part of the process towards re-equilibration of the market, but on a different level of utilisation of specialisation under the division of labour. Whether or not the market was in equilibrium prior to the original productive innovation, the establishment of the firm and competing firms constitute a disequilibration process, of sorts, from the point of view of the prevailing market structure. The original firm disrupts the prevailing market structure by implementing an imagined productive innovation, and the 'creative destruction' of the innovation is brought about through the competitive discovery process as entrepreneurs enter the production space and, inadvertently, generate markets for factors used within those firms. Imitating entrepreneurs amplify and bring to a close the change that was facilitated by the original entrepreneur's implementation. Differences are evened out, unnecessary tasks are abandoned, and inefficiencies are resolved as the productive arbitrage between firms that is the competitive discovery process proceeds; this process concludes with market standardisation of production where firms are neither necessary nor possible unless they introduce innovations that disrupt the new order. The competitive discovery process following the implementation of a successful and hence profitable productive innovation brings about the shift from a prior market state to the new state revealed by the entrepreneur's innovation. The firm in this sense explains what causes and brings about the shift from one particular market state to another that Schumpeter originally hypothesised. It is a story about production and value creation, and entrepreneurship, and not one of cost avoidance.

Summing up

The purpose of this chapter has been to tie together much of the discussion in previous chapters by pointing out that the firm is an institution with a specific economic function: it facilitates the expansion of the extent of the market, and therefore continued and intensified specialisation in the market. We therefore elaborated on the firm's lifecycle. A successful original firm induces its own competition through earning profit, which is an incentive for imitating entrepreneurs to establish competing production processes. Competition within the new production space amounts to a collective discovery process that leads to improvements, standardisation, and consequently market-making that ultimately dissolves the firms into market transactions. The firm has thereby fulfilled its economic function by providing a productive innovation that is eventually subsumed by the market.

Notes

1 See F. A. v. Hayek, 'Competition as a Discovery Process', *New Studies in Philosophy, Politics, Economics, and the History of Ideas*, (1978), pp. 179–190.
2 See P. L. Bylund and R. Wuebker, *Where Do Factor Markets Come From? Toward a Resource-Based Theory of the Entrepreneurial Firm* (Keystone, CO, Entrepreneurship exemplars conference, 2014).
3 This reinforces Stigler's point that integration precedes markets. See G. J. Stigler, 'The Division of Labor is Limited by the Extent of the Market', *Journal of Political Economy*, 59:3 (1951), pp. 185–193.

9 The nature of the market process

The previous chapter outlined the role of the firm in the micro setting of specific production processes. The firm with our definition emerges as a market institution that supplies the important function of implementing novel productive innovations that are not realisable through market exchange. Indeed, sufficiently original innovations fall outside the extent of the existing market since they cannot be realised within the existing production structure, and their implementation must therefore be separate from it. The firm is consequently recognised as the phenomenon that we observe as separate from, though its internal structure is unsupported by, yet in its entirety compatible with, market production. This is the reason we have referred to the firm as an 'island of specialisation' located outside the extent of the market.

In response to revealed profits in the original firm, imitative entrepreneurs establish competing production processes that are equally separate from the production structure that is coordinated through decentralised exchange in the market. This brings about a competitive discovery process. Through this process, the original and competing firms jointly discover the socially maximised use of resources and, by so doing, contribute to the expansion of the extent of the market through market-making for new factors. They thereby undermine the rationale for integrated production and, as a result, the firms dissolve as their distinct degree and kind of division of labour becomes supported in market exchange. Hence, coordination of production can be provided through the market's efficient price mechanism.

The market process can from this perspective be understood as consisting of two simultaneous processes that combined explain the progression of the market. Within the market there are exchange-based adjustments to resource allocations through arbitrage, and the extent of the market is expanded through disruptive productive innovation. The former can be thought of as similar to Israel Kirzner's conception of 'equilibrating' entrepreneurship as primarily arbitrage to deal with revealed misallocations within the extent of the market. This is an ongoing process that improves the overall production structure by continuous adjustments through market exchange that effectuate resource reallocations for improved efficiency.[1] These adjustments are made in response to exogenous changes that cause imbalances and misallocations in the market as well as to endogenous change and existing imperfections such as remaining inefficiencies where previous entrepreneurs have erred when acting to exploit perceived opportunities. While this type of Kirznerian entrepreneurship is an important part of the market process, it is limited to the arbitrage opportunities that exist and arise within the extent of the existing market. The entrepreneur is responsive to changes and alert to existing inefficiencies that amount to profit opportunities. As the entrepreneur is neither omniscient nor omnipotent, and is also subject to limited knowledge and bounded rationality, he or she is unlikely to exploit perfectly an arbitrage opportunity and will therefore leave errors for other entrepreneurs to exploit. Furthermore, as the market process is subject to continuous changing conditions, even optimal entrepreneurial actions will eventually become misaligned with the market structure. They should therefore be replaced by investments more properly adjusted to and consequently better aligned to present conditions, and the profit motive and free exchange in the open market incentivises entrepreneurs to continuously partake in these improvements. This type of entrepreneurship within the extent of the market was a part of the market model that we used as our point of departure for analysing the firm (see Chapter 2). It plays an important role in the gradual and seemingly automatic adjustments of market production processes that bring about the 'equilibration' tendency of the market process. But as this type of entrepreneurship is exchange based and therefore is in no need of a firm, a detailed discussion falls outside the scope of this book.

Arbitrage versus innovation

The actions of imitator-entrepreneurs discussed in previous chapters constitute a 'Kirznerian' function of sorts to the overall market by inadvertently arbitraging between the existing market structure and the productive innovation in the original firm. Upon the discovery and implementation of an evidently profitable, and therefore market-superior, productive innovation, imitator-entrepreneurs reallocate productive resources from their current and comparatively inefficient uses in the market towards their newly discovered and more profitable uses. They redirect their resource usage towards competing with the original entrepreneur, which results in a process of competitive discovery as entrepreneurs compete for the share of the profit. These attempts to capture profits revealed by the original productive innovation eventually lead to market-making for firms' productive tasks and the division of labour relied on.

This process that emerges as entrepreneurs attempt to emulate and outdo the original innovation constitutes a type of arbitrage between the present market state, the existing allocation of resources within the extent of the market, and a future market state that has absorbed the productive innovation of the firm and made the novel production tasks saleable in the market. As the market's total resource supply, and therefore its production structure, is reconfigured and reallocated in response to the new knowledge that is revealed through the implemented productive innovation, the boundaries of the market are moved outward to incorporate the innovation. Market-making around firms in a new production space consequently constitutes market expansion and establishes the firms' specialisation intensity as the market's division of labour. The extent of the market is therefore increased.

The process of arbitrage between the present and future states of the market, which brings about a reshuffling of the resources used in accordance with the former towards their preferred allocation in the latter, cannot exist without the innovating original entrepreneur. Kirznerian entrepreneurship without productive innovation is limited to arbitrage within the extent of the market and the entrepreneur is therefore, as Kirzner notes, a responsive agent acting within the market. For example, changing consumer preferences bring about changes in relative prices and therefore also in the profitability of specific resource uses. The alert arbitrageur-entrepreneur discovers profit opportunities brought about by and revealed through such changes, and exploits this new knowledge. Without productive innovations, however, the extent of the market remains essentially unchanged as only very limited innovations are realisable through producing new combinations or configurations of existing capital goods. The entrepreneur is therefore trapped, as it were, within the price mechanism's reach and thus the existing exchange market's boundaries.

Realigning the market's productive structure to changing conditions such as changing consumer preferences is a comparatively simple problem since it takes place within the existing boundaries of the market. Whereas the cause of the change can be exogenous, the extent of the market persists and market exchange incentivised and facilitated by the price mechanism is sufficient. This is not the case where a productive innovation is implemented outside the extent of the market and therefore, in essence, challenges the current market structure. Such productive innovations, as we have seen in previous chapters, cannot be established through arbitrage since they are not gradual or fully realisable through market means, but constitute radical change in the knowledge of how society's productive resources can be used. Innovation therefore requires a different kind of function from that of the arbitrageur-entrepreneur, whose actions are limited to reallocating, recombining, and reconfiguring existing resources. The breaking of new ground through implementing novel production structures, which likely requires also the production of new and highly specialised capital goods, changes not only the structure of the market and its resource utilisation, but also its extent by establishing a potentially imitable 'island of specialisation'. This implementation of a productive innovation is structurally distinct from and outside the extent of the existing the market, and thus composes a 'firm' of integrated production.

The type of arbitrage imitator-entrepreneurs engage in between the existing market and the 'island of production' is therefore categorically different from the arbitrage possible within the extent of the market. There is no price mechanism that spans both the existing market and the new production space, so production processes in the latter must be created and coordinated using a different means. Parties engaged in productive activities in the new production space in accordance with the productive innovation's 'internal' structure, can still acquire goods and services in the market. Indeed, we have seen that the production process that constitutes the firm needs to be compatible with the market such that it uses either inputs or outputs or both that are saleable in the market. (The only exception would be a completely integrated production process that stretches from virgin land through consumption goods and therefore is never in contact with market trade.) But the tasks carried out within the 'island of specialisation' are not saleable.

Imitator-entrepreneurs increase the outflow of resources from the market by establishing competing production processes that compete with the original firm. The outflow raises prices in the market as the supply decreases relative in-market demand, but increases competition in the new production space as the number of firms and their production volume increases.

Competition between firms entails collective discovery as the original innovation cannot (and likely should not) be perfectly imitated and there is consequently variation in the processes implemented by competitors. Imitator-entrepreneurs through their actions bid up market prices of the inputs used by firms and increase competitive pressure on firms to improve and further develop their internal production processes. As we saw in previous chapters, the original entrepreneur is blind as to the efficiency in the specific implementation of the production process, and therefore to the firm's economic allocation of resources. This leaves imitating entrepreneurs able to improve on the original innovation by exploiting their specific knowledge and skills, which is an opportunity to *create* profits in addition to capturing those profits revealed (and earned) by the original entrepreneur. Consequently, we should expect imitator-entrepreneurs to innovate in order to increase the effectiveness and efficiency of the original innovation and thereby increase their profitability. The discoveries that are ultimately made as a result of this process establish an efficient allocation of resources within this type of production. Competition thus brings about the structure of the future market following successful implementations of productive innovations. This suggests that imitator-entrepreneurs, while engaging in arbitrage between two states of the market, contribute a more significant economic function than simple market arbitrage: they create capital goods by forming firms of their own and, through the ensuing competition, cause the emergence of factor markets.

Imitator-entrepreneurs innovate but do so primarily within the bounds of the already implemented productive innovation and the profit opportunity it represents. They are in this sense knowledge brokers between the 'island of specialisation' and the existing market, who take inspiration from the original innovation and reconfigure its structure, recombine its parts and reuse the original thinking, introduce alternative solutions and new knowledge. Their experimenting improves on and perfects the innovator-entrepreneur's imagined production process and their competitive efforts expose the original firm's productive shortcomings. The bounds of the original innovation are thereby extended as new knowledge is introduced and used, but the fundamental purpose and aim remains intact. Its scope typically remains the same, since it relies on inputs procurable, and outputs saleable, in the existing market.

The original and innovative entrepreneur therefore has a distinct and important function in the progression of the market process. He or she imagines a novel way of producing, and by attempting to implement it pushes the production possibility frontier out. The original firm's production is initially located entirely outside the extent of the market, yet as imitator-entrepreneurs' competitive efforts refine the production space they also reunite the 'island of specialisation' with the market and make it the new standard. The innovator-entrepreneur does not, as do the Kirznerian and imitative entrepreneurs, engage in arbitrage. Rather, the innovator should here be conceived of as a revolutionary force in a Schumpeterian fashion that, assisted by the discoveries made by competing imitator-entrepreneurs, fundamentally disrupts the structure of the market.[2]

Direction of the market process

The three types of entrepreneurial functions we have here discussed – the arbitrageur-entrepreneur, the imitator-entrepreneur, and innovator-entrepreneurs – seem to support as many potential conclusions about the effects or implications of entrepreneurship in an economy. From the point of view of the market as it is presently structured, simple Kirznerian arbitrage provides equilibrating change through continuously improving the allocation of resources within the extent of the market. As entrepreneurs engage in exchange for profit through correcting errors and reallocating resources in response to changes, the overall effectiveness and functioning of the market is improved. Holding the boundaries or extent of the market constant, the market is equilibrated as alert entrepreneurs exploit discovered opportunities for profit. The direct effect of entrepreneurship of this type, which generates profits by exploiting and correcting apparent inefficiencies, is equilibrating, regardless of entrepreneurs' imperfection and their inability to solve recognised errors or misaligned resources fully. Entrepreneurship is therefore, as recognised by Kirzner, from this point of view necessarily an equilibrating force. However, whether the market tendency overall is equilibrating depends on the relative frequency of entrepreneurship as compared to exogenously effectuated change. The net effect of Kirznerian entrepreneurship and change is equilibrating only where the former exceeds the latter.

From the point of view of the existing market, the disruptive innovator-entrepreneur is, as was recognised by Schumpeter, a *dis*equilibrating force as this type of entrepreneurship reveals new opportunities and can make previously recognised opportunities void. But it would be jumping to a conclusion to claim that the innovator-entrepreneur disrupts *the market*. As we saw in the previous discussion, the innovator-entrepreneur has little effect on the market structure unless the implemented productive innovation is sufficiently profitable to attract imitator-entrepreneurs. A productive innovation that does not attract imitators could, if successful, offer profitable returns to the original entrepreneur, but this will only have minimal effect on the market's production structure through the direct influence on prices of inputs and outputs.

It is, as we discussed in the previous section, the imitator-entrepreneurs who bring about the innovation's potentially disruptive effect by extending the market to incorporate the imagined production structure. Forming a firm, which is how we can observe the implementation of the original entrepreneur's innovation, is not sufficient to disrupt the market. Only to the degree that the firm is successful and mimicked by others, and markets for the specialised factors utilised within it emerge, does the innovation disrupt the existent market. Disruption is in this sense constituted by a change, that is, intensification, to the division of labour utilised in the market, which is effectuated by the introduction of a productive innovation that causes a change to the extent of the market.

The tendency of the market, and thus the direction of the market process, therefore depends on the relative frequencies of all three types of entrepreneurial action, and the firm is necessary for the market's continued development. Without potentially disruptive innovation there are no firms and the market is then fully reliant on the price mechanism for resource allocation and consequently equilibrating in a Kirznerian fashion. With productive innovation the market's overall production structure undergoes changes that affect the 'direction' of the market process by expanding the market's extent through introducing more intensive specialisation under the division of labour. Such productive innovations ultimately facilitate increased resource utilisation and therefore wealth creation. Disruption is made possible only through the firm, since the firm enables productive action outside the extent of the market and thereby offers a means to escape the 'specialisation deadlock' – which is necessary for innovative, radical changes to the existing production structure. The firm, then, is a prerequisite for the evolution of the productive market process, since it is only through firms that productive innovations can be implemented and imitated, and factor markets consequently emerge.

It would be wrong to conclude that the existence of firms necessarily means disequilibration of the market, however. The formation of a firm is a sign of impending disruption of the market should other entrepreneurs establish firms to compete head on with the original firm's production process. From the point of view of the existing market, holding constant the extent of the market prior to the incorporation of the productive innovation in the market, the disruptive action of innovative entrepreneurs can indeed be disequilibrating. However, it should be noted that the original firm is not within the extent of the market; this is, after all, how we perceive of it as integrated and how it is distinguishable from market coordination of production. The competing firms, following the original firm to capture a share of the revealed profits, are also not acting within the market, but will bring about the creation of new market space for factors between them and the original firm. As their generated profits, which signal a potential for more socially efficient use of resources, attract capital investments from production processes within the previous extent of the market, the market's extent is expanded to include new capital and production structures. This means the market situation in which 'Kirznerian' entrepreneurs attempted arbitrage, thereby effectuating improvement and indicating an 'equilibrating' direction for the market, no longer exists. Opportunity costs have changed and with them relative market prices. In other words, the newly expanded market will tend in a different direction, towards a different end state or equilibrium. This tendency is established through profitable market action through arbitrage based on the new market data that have been revealed. This is not a case of disequilibration, unless we assess the direction of the newly expanded market using the market situation, and therefore its theoretical equilibrium, prior to the expansion. But doing so would be inaccurate, since we're comparing apples and oranges: the structure of the expanded market is different from the previous structure of the market, and so are their theoretical equilibria.

As soon as markets are created through the original- and imitator-entrepreneurs in a competitive discovery process, and the extent of the market consequently has been expanded to include the productive innovation, entrepreneurial arbitrage for profit brings about an equilibrating tendency. Whether this implies a shift from a single productive technology to another, or a fundamental reshuffling of capital and human resources, is of little import to our analysis of the function of the firm in the overall tendency of the market. With the expanded extent of the market, and the new production structures and other possibilities thereby placed within the reach of market exchange, the direction of the overall market process has shifted and with it other arbitrage opportunities will appear profitable.

We therefore see that even though we can distinguish between three different types of entrepreneurship that have different types of effect on the physical production apparatus of the market, they do not constitute different types of tendencies of the market. Rather, the entrepreneurship types interact to facilitate expansion of the extent of the market through an intensification of the division of labour, which shifts the position of a theoretical 'end point' for the market process should all errors in the present structure be corrected. Yet we should also expect the new extent of the market, which followed the entrepreneurially caused expansion, to be disrupted. The extent of the market will consequently expand further, again. The market structure is disrupted as often as entrepreneurs form new firms around the implementation of their productive innovations and imitator-entrepreneurs do their best to capture a share of the revealed profits. The extent of the market should therefore continue to expand, and thus upset the underlying market data that arbitrageur-entrepreneurs work with, though it may not be a smooth process. Market expansion happens as frequently as disruptive innovations make market actors adopt a more intensive specialisation under the division of labour. Each time this happens, the existing market's perceivable end point or 'state of rest' shifts.

What has here been drafted is a theory of the market process as ever changing both within its present extent, through entrepreneurial arbitrage, and in terms of its extent, through entrepreneurial productive innovations. The former is an ongoing process that is necessarily subject to the changes of the latter, since the latter shifts the direction of the market process by introducing changes to the fundamental structure of the market's productive apparatus. The implementation of a productive innovation – a 'firm' – changes the conditions for market exchange, since alternative production processes are made possible. This causes ripple effects brought about by market arbitrage for profit that shifts production towards the newly attainable level of productivity. In this sense, the instituting of a firm with its increased specialisation intensity can change the structure of the whole productive apparatus of the market. Entrepreneurship, it follows, is disruptive primarily through organising production within firms, which then incentivises competition that brings about change to the overall market structure – and this ultimately undoes the firm's rationale by incorporating its innovative discovery and subjects specialised production to efficient market coordination through the price mechanism. We can now see how the specialisation deadlock, while limiting to market coordination, does not in fact constitute an insurmountable barrier, since entrepreneurs eager for profit can and will choose non-market means to organise imagined production structures that utilise more intense specialisation that expand the division of labour, and – where successful – changes that very market structure. It should be noted, however, that it constitutes enough of a barrier to decentralised exchange to change the structure of production. But innovative entrepreneurship can through firms provide both disruptive and gradual improvements to production.

The question whether a specific market tends over time to get 'closer' to its end point or equilibrium, which has been subject to some debate, does not here become a question of theoretical significance. Our view of the firm as a means to by-pass the specialisation deadlock by implementing novel, disruptive production structures within firms outside the extent of the market incorporates tendencies that are often in the literature referred to as equilibrating, disequilibrating, and kaleidoscopic: equilibrating in the gradual and continuous improvement of production through arbitrage within the extent of the market, disequilibrating through the implementation of competing productive innovations in firms outside the market's extent, and kaleidoscopic in the effective unpredictability of implementing individual production plans based on productive innovation. Yet whereas all of these tendencies can be found in the dynamic of the market process, and the expansion of its extent through the formation of firms around productive innovations, they are immaterial for our understanding of the market process. In fact, they collaborate in the sense that they constitute different phases in the development and progression of the market towards achieving greater wants satisfaction. The process is effectuated by entrepreneurship and incentivised by profit, but whether the overall effect at any time period is deemed to be equilibrating, disequilibrating, or kaleidoscopic is based on the relative frequencies of each of the three types of entrepreneurship. The market process will appear gradually to approach its theoretical state of rest where entrepreneurial arbitrage is relatively more frequent and production innovations infrequent; it will appear disruptive where entrepreneurial imitation is common enough to change the conditions for arbitrageurs; and it will appear indeterminate in cases where entrepreneurial innovation is recurrent. The exact functioning and tendency of a particular market process at a particular point in time is entirely an empirical matter and is not the subject of this discussion. The contribution here is the role and function of the firm in the progression of the market process, which allows us to identify three distinct functions of entrepreneurship and how they relate to each other. The interaction of the different levels of economising and coordination in production, as well as the economic situations we find different types of entrepreneurship, show the symbiotic and mutually supportive nature of the different aspects of an economy. In our discussion, entrepreneurship cannot be understood without involving organisation and capital theory. Similarly, neither organisation theory nor capital theory would be complete without the other and entrepreneurship theory. While they address issues on different analytical levels, they are highly interdependent – to the degree they are not different sides of the same triangle. By addressing the working of the market process towards greater value creation, we can outline how they interact and indeed are interdependent – and together comprise a means to understand overall economic development.

Summing up

This chapter has adopted a different perspective from the discussion in Chapter 8, but elaborated on the implications and effects of the same process. From the point of view of the market process, rather than the comparatively 'micro' view we previously adopted, the firm plays a central role in the development of an economy. While it indeed has a lifecycle of its own that begins with the implementation of a productive innovation and ends with market-making, the firm provides a function that expedites the progression of the market process. We discussed how the original firm establishes a new type of production outside the extent of the market, and how imitating entrepreneurs engage in a discovery process. From the macro perspective, the discovery process and market-making as competition increases in the new production space and is subsumed by the market constitutes a type of entrepreneurial arbitrage between present and future states of the production structure: the market as it presently is, and the future market as it will be when adopting the productive innovation. Applying this perspective on the process that is started and brought to its conclusion by the economic function of the firm suggests an explanation for economic development and growth.

We also elaborated on how the three distinct types of entrepreneurship that are present in this model represent different 'directions' of the market process: equilibrating, disequilibrating, and kaleidoscopic, respectively. From the point of view of economic development, therefore, it is not a question of whether the market process is one or the other, but the progression of the market process indeed depends on components that represent all three.

Notes

1 See I. M. Kirzner, *Competition and Entrepreneurship* (Chicago, IL: University of Chicago Press, 1973).
2 See J. A. Schumpeter, *The Theory of Economic Development: An Inquiry into Profits, Capital, Credit, Interest, and the Business Cycle* (1911) (Cambridge, MA: Harvard University Press, 1934).

10 Policy implications

The discussion in previous chapters drafted a way of thinking about the dynamic market process that includes both within-market equilibration and disequilibrating market-making through imitating productive innovation. We saw that it is necessary to implement original productive innovations through a firm, even though it is conceived of not as a means to but as the outcome of such implementation. In other words, we observe a firm as an 'island of specialisation' because the implementation of a novel innovation by necessity appears both integrated, due to the strict productive interdependence that can lead to failure through incompleteness, and distinct from the market, as it is located outside the extent of the market and is structurally different. The firm therefore emerges as a phenomenon with a specific economic function: it establishes production outside the extent of the existing market and therefore out of the price mechanism's reach. It has a limited life span and is in its basic form, as we saw in Chapter 6, a temporary presence on the market landscape limited by the degree that the firm's accomplished profitability induces competitive imitation. As the market extent expands through competitive imitation and market-making, and therefore adopts universally the new division of labour, the firm's economic rationale diminishes and eventually vanishes.

Chapter 9 connected the micro-level firm-forming process around a productive innovation with the macro-level market process for economic development and growth. The firm, as we here see it, is the means by which the market expands beyond its previous extent, adopting more intensive specialisation under the divisions of labour and capital. Other market action, primarily in the form of 'Kirznerian' entrepreneurship through arbitrage, is limited by the extent of the market, just as Adam Smith noted. This limitation also applies to the division of labour to the degree it is utilised and applied in market-based production and therefore coordinated through exchange facilitated by the price mechanism. The economic function of the firm explicitly challenges this limitation by implementing productive innovations that rely on – or compose – more intensive specialisation that is supported by, or can be established through, market exchange. As a result, the market is in constant flux not only because of necessary adjustments of market production to changes that cause a shift in how resources should be allocated, but also in terms of market-making and disequilibrating expansion.

The latter changes the conditions for resource utilisation and market production coordinated through decentralised exchange, and thus the direction of market progression effectuated by the former.

The previous discussion suggests the market as a system is dynamic and responsive, and is equipped to deal with changes on several levels, of both endogenous and exogenous origin. Changing consumer preferences alert entrepreneurs by resulting in shortages and surpluses in certain lines of production, and therefore increased profits and losses, respectively. This rewards entrepreneurs who reallocate resources to their more profitable uses which, in turn, changes relative prices leading to further arbitrage. The market in that way responds to change 'spontaneously' or automatically – that is, without the need for central coordination – in such a way that the newly revealed errors in the market's present resource allocation are corrected. Entrepreneurs continuously attempt to predict and prepare for changes to the market. Their efforts to do so are constrained by the willingness and ability to risk capital assets, and this places entrepreneurial judgment at centre stage for the market's dynamic adaptability.

Other changes, including the discovery or innovation of new types of production and products that cause expansion of the extent of the market, bring about similar responses through individual entrepreneurs acting to capture profits. By responding to real changes and using their judgment to prepare for potential change, they realign the market's entire production structure with actual demand. The market is because of entrepreneurship a 'spontaneous' order that emerges from decentralised voluntary agreement and contract, and that 'automatically' adapts to change. Furthermore, the market continuously progresses through entrepreneurs' established productive innovations, and thus may not at any specific point in time be allocatively efficient. Allocative efficiency is a static concept that establishes the maximising allocation under the prevailing conditions. It is inapplicable where there are continuously changing, and expected future changes to, market conditions, since such changes require positioning in the present to meet the future structure of the market. What is optimal in the present may therefore be suboptimal when both the present and future states of the market are considered. The market process will therefore rarely be allocatively efficient in the present, but may find a maximising path through changes over time. The market process is however adaptively efficient when resource allocations are continuously adjusted to reflect all that is known about the present and what can reasonably be expected from the future.[1] The adjustments to a market's production structure are brought about by entrepreneurs, who allocate their capital and effort to maximise returns based on what they imagine will be the market's future conditions. These adjustments produce market prices that reflect entrepreneurs' combined understanding for the market, its production structure, and changes over time. Adaptive efficiency is therefore achieved in a market order that allows entrepreneurs to act fully on their judgment when allocating resources and investments.

The functioning of the market system brings about, or at least approaches, the 'best possible' use of the resources through the continuous adjustments made to the overall productive apparatus. This means the market is quite resilient to obstruction in the same way a river can 'deal with' a large rock placed in its way: it finds the path of least resistance around it, even if this path is not immediately or easily accessible. Of course, just like the river's flow is affected by a rock placed in its way, whether large or small, the market system's effectiveness in satisfying consumer wants is inhibited if subjected to obstruction. A natural disaster or other types of damage done to an economy's productive apparatus necessitates that capital resources are reproduced and production processes re-established – or that they are replaced by those better suited to the new market setting – which changes relative prices. To the extent that resources have been destroyed or made unusable, remaining resources will be reallocated towards the best possible overall solution. Because of the damage and loss of resources, this new productive solution will be of overall lesser value than the productive apparatus that would otherwise have remained intact. Destruction does not create value, even if it paves the way for a kind of production that was not previously considered.

As the market is in constant flux and subject to never-ceasing changes, there is no way of accurately evaluating the mechanism or calculating its overall efficiency. The only way to assess the functioning of a market process is through estimating its value-creating capabilities in comparison with plausible alternatives. As the properly decentralised market consists only of the individual or collaborate actions of entrepreneurs and other actors, who always aim to do better from the point of view of their subjective evaluation of the particular situation and their judgment about future conditions, and since profits are generated through satisfying real wants, through a process of time-consuming production, resource allocation through the price mechanism is maximised in the unhampered market economy. To make improvements to the market's entrepreneurially created resource allocation would require greater knowledge about the state of the market and possible future outcomes, as well as consumers' subjective valuations of those outcomes, than is revealed through the actions taken in the market and thus reflected in market prices. Such counterfactuals that produce outcomes that beat the progression of the market process *over time* are not realistic since they require immense knowledge of the present combined with impeccable foresight of the future. Schumpeter makes a similar point, stating that

> Since we are dealing with a process whose every element takes considerable time in revealing its true features and ultimate effects, there is no point in appraising the performance of that process *ex visu* of a given point of time; we must judge its performance over time, as it unfolds through decades or centuries.[2]

We can theoretically construct a higher performing counterfactual to the market process only by disregarding the shortcomings of man, for instance by assuming planning and direction by a benevolent dictator with perfect knowledge of all current circumstances relevant to using resources efficiently. But perfect knowledge of the present is not sufficient; one must also assume the power to enforce the dictator's vision for the market's future states. Even an initially flawlessly planned production process must be continuously adapted and adjusted to changing circumstances for it not to become hopelessly misaligned and maladapted. Therefore, even if the market is obstructed, as the rock placed in the river's way, it is still the best means of organising production – and more so with the progression of time and as conditions change. The 'invisible hand' works because it consists of myriad visible actions that react to any perceived change within the specific local settings, responsive to and affecting the relevant prices throughout the market. This generates a coordinated response from the bottom up, and reallocates resources towards better uses.

In order to find the best response to exogenous change from the top down, as though with a single mind, one must exercise perfect foresight regarding the courses of action as well as have sufficient influence to prepare for and direct productive resources accordingly. Yet even if this were possible, and all the knowledge necessary for perfect adjustment available, the collective discovery process through innovation and competitive imitation cannot be directed. Mises showed that this is the case in a powerful argument for the market economy based on private ownership,[3] and what we've learned in previous chapters about the dynamic complexity of the market process reinforces this argument. Indeed, the continuous expansion of the market's extent adds complexity on a different level, which is usually overlooked in attempts to outline a planned order that outdoes the market. As we've seen, the discovery process of the market is not only open-ended in terms of being unknown, but is unknowable since what is to be discovered is generated through repeated implementation and continuous experimenting. It is not only the case that there are a multitude of possible better ways of producing that are not yet supported through market exchange, but the details of these ways need to be figured out over time within a constantly changing market context. Adaptation and adjustment are ongoing in both the existing production apparatus and during the implementation of future production.

The question then becomes one of whether existing institutions support or hamper the exchange that is at the heart of the bottom-up adaptation and adjustment process in the market. Pure market institutions emerge spontaneously through market action, but can they be strengthened or supported by institutional design? This is where public policy comes in.

It hardly needs to be argued that policy can and does affect the workings of the market process and thereby affects also the outcome. To again use the market process as a river metaphor, we can think of policy as a rock either placed in or moved out of the river's way. In the former case, the rock is an added hindrance to the natural flow of the market, which has consequences for what is produced and how. It will also affect the value generated through the market process by affecting its overall performance. Resources in the market will be redirected towards dealing with and overcoming the obstacle that the rock represents. This constitutes a loss as compared to the situation prior to placing the rock in the river's way, since resources are not added but redirected and therefore are taken from productive uses.

But it is not necessarily the case that the rock is simply placed to stop or slow down the flow of the river. It is perceivable that it can also be intended as a means to force the flow in other directions and thereby – if successful – attain certain *political* goals. The latter case can, from the perspective of aiming to direct the market process towards certain ends, be seen as the other side of the coin. By clearing the river's path, the natural flow can potentially be 'improved' in the sense of becoming more steady and targeted. But by placing a new rock in or moving a rock within the river, the river's flow changes as an effect. These are the only ways in which policy can be used to effectuate a different type of market, presumably to achieve values of political (rather than economic) character. They necessarily constitute an economic loss as resources must be used to effectuate the change, but can produce a different kind of gain that, at least from the point of view of political decision-makers, is considered valuable.

What is relevant here is not the effect of policy on the market process per se, however, but how and in what ways it affects and, to the extent possible, can be used towards specific ends relating to the firm as an 'island of specialisation'. We thus focus specifically on the potential to use policy to influence how the firm revolutionises market structure and brings about an expansion of the limits of the market. As the market's extent is expanded, and it thus becomes equipped to deal with more intensive specialisation that facilitates increased productivity – creatively destroying the old, as it were – the economy 'grows' and can produce greater value. We can refer to this increase in value produced as the extent of the market expands as 'economic growth', which has implications of particular importance for policy-makers, such as the population's standard of living, the economy's overall employment of labour factors, and financing of the state. From this perspective, policy could, depending on its specific aims, attempt to increase or decrease the overall frequency of firm formation – or direct it towards certain industries or market segments to attempt to achieve particular or local effects. In other words, the questions asked here are: how can public policy affect the formation of firms? And, is this means appropriate for attaining stated ends? The particular cases we will discuss are policy measures taken specifically to change the *direction* or *speed* of the market process by manipulating the frequency of innovation. Depending on the end sought, such manipulation intends to produce changes either across the board or targeted towards certain parts of the market. There are two means available for policy-makers to effectuate such change: raising barriers (regulating, taxing, and prohibiting markets, actions, or actors) and lowering barriers (deregulating, subsidising, or permitting markets, actions, or actors).

Using policy to direct firm formation

Consider as a point of departure for the discussion in this and subsequent sections of the chapter a market impacted by different kinds of regulation, taxation, and so on to a degree that these measures do not significantly suppress market exchange or expansion. Assume furthermore that the effect of existing policy can, for our purposes, be considered neutral across the market landscape. In other words, we assume a market, under some type of modern government, that is fully functioning despite effects of different forms of political regulation. Apart from the added layer of regulation and policy effects, the model of the market is the same as what we have heretofore used in theorising on the firm.

From this situation, policy measures can be taken either to stimulate or to discourage productive innovations by entrepreneurs, which will therefore affect the frequency with which firms are being formed outside the present extent of the market. Both types of measures can be used either to produce an overall effect on the market, that is, to bring about faster or slower economic growth overall, or to steer the market one way or the other through producing a limited, localised effect. The latter simply targets the effects of the former type of measures to the specific parts of or certain activities in a market or industry that are preferred from a political point of view.

From our point of departure in the regulated market, it is conceivable to use policy measures such as tax exemptions for research and development or the creation of new firms, investments in education, and establishing government-funded business incubators and accelerators as well as innovation and research centres, and providing funding for research to stimulate innovation. Contrariwise, added taxes and fees on businesses, introducing restricting regulation, licensing and certification and other legal requirements, and outright prohibition of business can be used to discourage innovative entrepreneurs. All of these measures, and the ones not mentioned here, can also be used in targeted efforts to steer politically the direction of the market process.

For instance, if policy-makers believe the economy is 'overheating' in the sense of growing 'too fast' (too rapid expansion of the market's extent through frequent firm formation), and that this is undesirable, policy measures can be taken aiming at slowing down the overall growth rate. From our perspective, such measures would need to raise barriers for entrepreneurs to implement new innovations outside the extent of the market as well as for entrepreneurs striving to compete with original firms through emulation and competitive discovery. But policy can also subsidise the status quo, both directly through granting specific privileges to existing market actors and indirectly through institutional support and infrastructure investments, and thereby make novelty relatively more expensive and so make established market production less costly. By making it costlier to form firms, productive innovations become less attractive and fewer entrepreneurs will therefore attempt to implement their imagined innovations. As fewer resources are used to form firms, the relative resources available for arbitrage within the market increases. This causes a shift from innovation and market-making to within-market exchange and could therefore, if we assume that arbitrage is not adversely affected, potentially increase the rapidity of within-market adjustment to exogenous change.

Policy measures, whether aimed to stimulate or discourage the formation of firms, must do so by either making it cheaper or more costly to produce or implement productive innovations. They can thereby influence the *frequency* of future firm formation. However, as the frequency depends ultimately on how entrepreneurs perceive the value of their imagined productive innovations, which informs their decisions to attempt implementation, the frequencies – both with and without policy measures – are uncertain. It also means we cannot know the exact effect of policy on the future frequency of firm formation. We do not know exactly how entrepreneurs react to the changing conditions. For instance, in certain situations a policy stimulation that entails only a minor improvement, monetarily speaking, could bring about a major shift in entrepreneurs' valuation of opportunities. The opposite may also be true, where a policy change expected to have a major effect may only marginally affect firm formation frequency.

Policy effects are also subject to what Robert Higgs terms 'regime uncertainty',[4] or the trust entrepreneurs have in the political system and institutions of the market. According to Higgs's analysis, entrepreneurs' expectations about changes to the institutional setting for market action, or the 'rules of the game', as it were, have a significant effect on their decisions to invest for future gain. Regime uncertainty entails entrepreneurs' expectations about whether the political regime will move towards greater violations of private property and the market or lesser violations. If entrepreneurs distrust the intentions of policy-makers and suspect that policy will change for the worse, that enforcement will be to the detriment of business, or that policy measures will be interpreted increasingly unfavourably (and perhaps unpredictably), they will refrain from investing. Stimulating policy may therefore have an effect that is opposite to its ostensible goal: entrepreneurs may refrain from forming new firms despite stimulating policy because they distrust policy-makers and suspect that the regime will become increasingly hostile towards the market. This suggests that there is fundamental uncertainty to using policy to bring about specific changes to the frequency of entrepreneurship.

In addition to using policy to change the overall frequency of firm formation, whether to 'cool down' or stimulate economic growth, policy-makers may find a certain sector of the economy especially advantageous or desirable, and tailor policy measures to stimulate innovation specifically in this area. For instance, responding to political pressure or a perceived opportunity for growth in the widgets-producing sector that is left unexploited, policy can be designed with the intention to reward entrepreneurial investments supporting only the production of widgets. By rewarding activity in widget production, policy-makers can create artificial profit opportunities that attract entrepreneurs and labour from other sectors of the market. Policy can also increase the firm formation frequency by lowering the costs of implementing productive innovations that relate to development or production of widgets. This can be done in a variety ways, for example through subsidies, tax deductions, monopoly privileges, or public matching of private investments.

Policy measures can only redistribute entrepreneurial action by directing entrepreneurs towards certain industries or tasks through changing the incentive structure of the market. As policy cannot add real value, which is created through production that satisfies actual demand and is not a result of regulation, policy needs, first, to remove in order to add. To incentivise widget production, policy-makers must either lessen the regulatory burden in the market disproportionately to benefit widget producers specifically, or increase the burden on all but widget production. Even direct subsidies need to be financed somehow, and the money used to subsidise widget producers must therefore be extracted from somewhere. Since policy can only increase or decrease the regulatory burden, the effect and precision of policy measures is necessarily limited. And, as we saw above, the magnitudes and even nature of outcomes is very difficult to predict. Policy is therefore a very blunt instrument for attempting to establish a preferred market structure. One can as easily overshoot as undershoot the targeted frequency, and due to unknown factors that also influence entrepreneurs' decisions, such as regime uncertainty, some policies can even backfire and produce a situation that is worse from the point of view of the end aimed for.

The seen, the unseen, and the unrealised

We have already seen that policy is a blunt tool with imprecisely predictable outcomes, and that the result can sometimes be the very opposite of what was intended and expected. Policy measures have uncertain outcomes because the economic system is constantly in flux and its structure and progress is an effect of using dispersed and imperfect knowledge in decentralised decision-making. This knowledge is then revealed in action and becomes reflected in price changes, which makes the price mechanism a means to inform market actors about social opportunity costs that help guide their allocations of resources. This dynamic process continuously adjusts to exogenous changes. In other words, the exact path of the market process is impossible to foresee.

Furthermore, as the economy is in many respects a closed system, limited to the extent of market exchange, the determination of market prices and the alloca-tion of scarce and valuable resources in specific quantities, there are always two sides to any coin. There is a trade-off to any action. As we noted above, policy that aims to stimulate the production of widgets cannot do so without at the same time discouraging other production. Also, even if we for a moment disregard the special role of policy in the market, any local increase in economic activity is made possible only through a shift in effort and resource availability from one sector to another. An increase in the production of widgets, which depends on the use of scarce resources and therefore has trade-offs, means that the inflow of resources must be taken from elsewhere where fewer are left to be used. The price mechanism, when unaffected by arbitrary or uneconomic measures, steers the market process by bringing about resource allocations that are better compat-ible with value-creating production. Policy is likewise bound by the limited availability of resources, which means any policy measure taken to either stimu-late or discourage certain activity has a corresponding opposite effect elsewhere. Stimulating firm formation, therefore, means a shift in resource allocation. Whether or not policy directly shifts resources from one market sector to another, resources are shifted by entrepreneurs from market production to establishing new productive innovations. What is produced in the market will therefore need to produce with less.

This other side of the coin is what the French economist Frédéric Bastiat termed the 'unseen' and forms the basic lesson in the parable of the broken window.[5] In Bastiat's story, the breaking of a window is praised by the naive for leading to beneficial economic activity as replacing it creates new income for the glazier, who can then spend the money to purchase other goods, hire more people, etc. However, notes Bastiat, this is only the 'seen'. What is 'unseen' is what the money used to replace the broken window had otherwise been used for. This economic activity is lost when the owner of the window reprioritises among his ends in order to instead replace the broken window (supposedly a more pressing and therefore more highly valued use of his resources). Whereas replacing the broken window constitutes a net income for the glazier it is an added cost for the owner of the window. But it is in fact a net loss from the point of view of the economy, since the 'unseen' activity – the value-creating activities that would have taken place instead of replacing the broken window – is lost in the effort merely to restore what was destroyed. This is why we above noted that destruction does not create value – even if it increases seen activity to replace what is lost, this 'gain' is at the cost of the destroyed values.

In a dynamic market process there is more to the story than what is 'seen' and what is 'unseen'. As the market extent expands through implementation of productive innovation, any loss of productive activity, such as the 'unseen' economic activity that will now not occur, ultimately slows down the progress of the market process. A broken window is ultimately a lost resource, which could (and probably would) have played some part in supporting the formation of new firms, the emulation of an original innovation, or the arbitrage activities of entrepreneurs within the extent of the market. The investment necessary to cover costs of implementing a productive innovation is made based on the accumulated capital in an economy, which is made available to the capitalist-entrepreneur either through saving up profits earned in exchange (his or her savings) or borrowing in financial markets (other people's savings). In both cases, the availability of productive resources in the market is a prerequisite for investment. An unavoidable result of the loss of resources is therefore the limiting effect it has on the expansion of the market, and therefore the intensification of specialisation through the division of labour. Market progress is slowed down as resources are lost, which means less wealth is ultimately produced.

The same effect is noticeable where the course of the market process is forced in a different direction from what we would otherwise have seen. Any direction other than that brought about by entrepreneurs aiming to profit from serving actual consumer wants is suboptimal as the most eagerly held wants will no longer be satisfied or at least not satisfied as soon. We have already seen that the market process functions even in the face of exogenous shocks, arbitrary or ad hoc restrictions, and under other suboptimal conditions. It is therefore the case that the new direction, effectuated by a loss from destruction or exogenous shock or new policy, will also produce value – but by satisfying *other* wants. These other wants are not the same ones that were voluntarily chosen by consumers in the previous market situation. They expressed their urgency for want satisfaction by increasing their willingness to pay, or producers selecting the most valued use of resources, under specific circumstances. As the production ability of the market is restricted by destruction or policy, or becomes maladapted due to an exogenous shock, it can no longer satisfy as many wants. The outcome is therefore of comparatively lesser value. The market process will consequently progress more slowly in terms of wealth creation in the new direction, which is the one that appears as most value-creating after the rock was placed in the river's way. The direction of the market process without the rock in its way would be superior (would create more value), but it is no longer possible.

It follows that although policy can be used to pursue specific social or political ends that are deemed unlikely to be attained if the market is not directed, such measures do not only have uncertain outcomes but ultimately slows down the overall progression of the market process. As the market process slows down, the economy will become less specialised and for this reason less productive than would otherwise have been the case. It therefore produces less value. Policy-makers always face the trade-off between the estimated political or social value of the policy and the loss of value-creation due to the hampered or 'redirected' market process.

The loss of value created as the market process is forced in a new direction is not easily measurable. A direct consequence of redirecting the market process is the loss of productivity through innovation and specialisation, which can be expressed in terms of consumptive power and the availability of consumer goods. Of greater concern, and much more closely aligned with the discussion in this book, is the effect on the progression of the market process, and thereby the expansion of the extent of the market. This is primarily structural in the sense that the market with a lower frequency of firm formation will more slowly adopt the more intensive division of labour, which suggests two consequences of major import to market actors. First, new and more productive tasks and processes remain unrealised and therefore labourers stay relatively unproductive. This means they not only earn relatively lower wages, but also that the new and 'better' jobs, more saleable skills, and attractive market positions that would have emerged will not do so. And, second, the choice set of available consumer products and services is limited as new offerings will not come to be. These effects on both production and consumption, which constitute a loss of value through limiting the alternatives available in choice situations, make both producers and consumers worse off. They lose potentially more valuable options and therefore cannot maximise their welfare to the degree they otherwise would have; they also lose the freedom to choose between a wide range of products, services, and market activities as the choice set is restricted through the hampered market process. The 'unrealised' has a significantly impoverishing effect on the welfare of people.

Empowering markets through policy

Despite the mounting and immeasurable cost of the 'unrealised', which consists of lost values, choices, and opportunities that affect the continued progression of the market and consequently cannot be regained, policy is oftentimes used with the intention to increase economic growth. As economic growth is achieved through the progression of the market process and expansion of the market, the market's natural tendency towards expansion can be strengthened by subsidising or otherwise stimulating the adoption rate of productive innovation. This was mentioned above as increasing the frequency of firm formation, and is primarily possible through removing the 'rocks' that block the path of the market process or that force it in a comparatively suboptimal direction. Such policy measures are targeted to facilitate market exchange and increase the market's ability to adopt productive innovations by bringing about lower costs of transacting or limiting the uncertainty of entrepreneurial endeavours by providing supporting and reliable institutions. To be effective, growth-increasing measures should target enabling or empowering the market to 'break free' from its limiting extent – the specialisation deadlock – by removing obstacles and lowering costs of entrepreneurship.

However, policy has historically been used instead to increase the productivity of the labour force and support businesses under the guise of fighting unemployment. In order to achieve the former, massive public investments in (higher) education attempt to stimulate an increase in the level of education and therefore the productive knowledge of common workers. Countries like Sweden invested early in providing public general education, followed by public higher education, in order to make the workforce more productive and thereby raise their relative value in international production. Whereas such investments have diminishing marginal returns, since going from illiterate to literate or from a few years of education to high school degree raises one's productivity more than going from high school degree to university degree, they are also measures that show increases in statistical aggregates. Education in itself, even if we assume that education is a proper proxy for knowledge and skills of workers, does not necessarily raise the productivity of a specific individual, whereas the educational level of the workforce is strongly correlated with the latter's productivity. For any individual to become more employable or productive in the market, it is necessary that education efforts strengthen the particular individual with respect to existing skills, interests, market position, and local demand in the production structure. Education will only have value to an individual within a production system if it contributes specifically to that individual's productivity, whereas education that is not particularly suited to this individual's situation is at best a waste of time (unless it will improve the individual in future situations).

For the workforce as a statistical aggregate the issue may appear differently, however, since neither workers nor education is treated specifically. Just like 'workforce' is too general to tell us anything about the workforce, 'education' is too general to tell us anything about the knowledge (or even degrees) acquired.

In other words, a state investing in education to make a country's illiterate workforce literate would seem to boost productivity, especially if the increase is relative to that of other countries or markets and therefore can increase the inflow of capital investments. Yet the real effect (and, indeed, the wanted outcome) is not 'literacy', but that specific skills are added through specific education, and that this raises the productivity of individual workers. One reason there is diminishing returns to investing in education (the education level of a workforce, that is, the general statistic, not an individual's choice to pursue specific education) is that the higher the level of education achieved the more specific it generally is: a graduate school degree is more specific than a college degree, which is more specific than a high school education. In other words, for the measure to be effective, the higher the level of education achieved requires greater matching between, on the one hand, the individual and their skills, interests, and opportunities, and, on the other hand, the form and topic of the educational effort.

In addition to productivity-enhancing measures that target the workforce specifically, policy measures can be taken to support businesses by establishing a 'business friendly' political climate with supporting institutions and well-functioning infrastructure that lowers the cost of transacting. Such measures aim to lower barriers for exchange, which can thereby increase the frequency of market exchanges and consequently speed up the equilibration process within a market. Barriers can consist of any types of costs to carry out exchanges, from difficulty to discover relevant market prices across a varied market landscape to costs of transportation over spatial distances. Policy measures can be intended to lower such barriers by establishing regulation and industry standards, and investing in infrastructure and technology. A national public road system and therefore an implicit subsidy of road transportation, as is also often the case with railroads, is a common means by which policy is used to 'tie together' distant parts of the same country and boost domestic trade. But, as discussed above, such investments come at a cost. Whereas explicitly aiming to lower transaction costs in the market, these policies tend to focus on that which is 'seen' while overlooking effects that are 'unseen' or 'unrealised' (or both).

These types of stimulating policy intended to increase productivity and lower barriers, both of which are very common in policy all over the world, target primarily the existing market. While they can have an indirect effect on the frequency of attempts to implement productive innovations through firm formation, the policy measures are highly inefficient to this end. One reason is that policy-makers are at least as unable to foresee where productive innovations may be successful as market actors, and therefore efforts to stimulate firm formation are necessarily unguided or, at best, based on hunches. It is quite impossible to predict where entrepreneurs will imagine ways to improve production processes or new products to be offered in the marketplace. Even if policy-makers knew what innovations entrepreneurs would take, it would be excessively difficult for them to predict what supporting measures would stimulate entrepreneurs to take appropriate actions. Even if this were possible, the how, when, and in what way the market's extent can, will, or indeed should be expanded is neither known nor knowable. It will only be figured out as a joint effort when entrepreneurs engage in competitive discovery to improve on the original productive innovation.

But firm formation itself can of course be supported through different kinds of subsidies or by easing the regulatory burden on doing business. The danger here is that while these types of policy measures may increase the frequency of entrepreneurs attempting to form firms as 'islands of specialisation', there is no certainty that these entrepreneurial endeavours are the proper ones – whether they would have been chosen in an unhampered market. Indeed, by lowering the threshold or even covering part of the cost for entrepreneurial enterprises, policies intended to stimulate economic growth may instead increase overall uncertainty by attracting a number of hotheads and adventurers who could otherwise not afford the undertaking. As their implementations of potentially (but perhaps more likely un-) productive innovations claim resources that would otherwise have been used more prudently elsewhere, primarily in proper productive efforts, the net effect of well-meaning but poorly designed policy can be capital-consuming and therefore lead to a lower standard of living instead of driving economic growth.

Summing up

What we have seen, then, in this chapter is an application of the theory of the firm as an 'island of specialisation', and especially what it teaches us on how and why firms are formed and what this implies in terms of economic development, on policy. As the firm is formed around a productive innovation, policy does not have the means to affect the nature of these innovations – they are the result of the imagination and judgment of entrepreneurs. But policy can affect the frequency of firm formation by subsidising or raising obstacles to new firms, either in the market overall or with regard to specific sectors of the market. By doing so, however, we found that there are costs that are not easily seen but that affect the progression of the market process. We identified those costs as the unseen economic undertakings that are lost and the unrealised options that never come to be and that may affect the long-term progression of the market process. These often overlooked costs contributed to the following discussion on the possibility of using policy to empower markets.

Notes

1 For more on adaptive efficiency, see D. C. North, 'Institutions and a Transaction–Cost Theory of Exchange', in J. E. Alt and K. A. Shepsle (eds) *Perspectives on Positive Political Economy* (New York: Cambridge University Press, 1990), pp. 182–194; P. Moran and S. Ghoshal, 'Markets, Firms, and the Process of Economic Development', *Academy of Management Review*, 24:3 (1999), pp. 390–412.
2 J. A. Schumpeter, *Socialism, Capitalism and Democracy* (New York: Harper & Bros., 1942), p. 83.
3 See L. v. Mises, 'Economic Calculation in the Socialist Commonwealth', in F. A. v. Hayek (ed.) *Collectivist Economic Planning* (London: George Routledge & Sons, 1935), pp. 87–130.

4 R. Higgs, 'Regime Uncertainty: Why the Great Depression Lasted so Long and Why Prosperity Resumed after the War', *Independent Review*, 1:4 (1997), pp. 561–590.

5 F. Bastiat, *That Which is Seen, and That Which is Not Seen: An Economic Essay* (1850) (World Library Classics, 2010).

11 What the future holds

The previous chapters attempted to outline a new theory of the firm. What distinguishes the particular approach in this book from previous attempts to explain economic organisation is its starting point and approach: the dynamic and expanding market process as a structure aimed towards wants-satisfying production. Rather than establishing the empirical fact (or, as would be more accurate, the *apparent* fact) that there are both markets and firms, as does for example Ronald Coase in his Nobel-winning article on the nature of the firm, we started by asking where the market process would be without firms. More to the point, the question posed was what the firm's function in a market process would be. Another way of phrasing this is to ask what specific problem to the market process is or can be solved by integrated production. Specifically what is the economic *function* of the firm?

The problem was found in production as a symptom of, as well as driving force for, economic growth and development, specifically as specialisation under the division of labour intensifies and the extent of the market consequently expands. Adam Smith teaches that the division of labour, by which an economy can dramatically increase its output, is limited by the extent of the market. Yet, at the same time, we know historically and empirically that the division of labour increases, that specialisation intensifies, and that the market expands as economies grow. What type of activities or processes facilitate this process? We discussed this question in Chapters 2 and 3 and found that markets, consisting of decentralised exchange, seem to lack the means to expand their reach more than gradually, which would be insufficient to explain expansion of the scale, degree, and speed we have seen over the past couple of centuries. Markets equilibrate through trade and can support increased specialisation as market density increases (primarily, as is commonly identified, through a growing population), but this constitutes only gradual shifts towards higher levels of productivity. In contrast, the introduction of new products, new production technologies, and other types of disruptive innovations do not entail gradual change. They are radical, creative and destructive, and take leaps forward that require both up front financing (Chapter 7) and entrepreneurship (Chapter 4). The originality of productive innovations is unsupported in the existing market. The firm, therefore, emerges as a way of establishing such innovations by implementing them where they can only be realised: outside the extent of the market. The firm then amounts to an 'island of specialisation' that is integrated by relying only, or at least to a significant extent, on strictly interdependent parts. This means that the firm is the observable result of an entrepreneurial undertaking to break free from the type of 'specialisation deadlock' (Chapter 3) that we found would inhibit development and growth within the extent of the market. This suggests the firm is a temporary measure (Chapter 6), subject to and eventually dissolved through the competitive discovery process (Chapter 8), and it helps explain the nature of the market process and how markets expand and increase productivity by adopting more intensive specialisation and division of labour (Chapter 9).

The theory makes several interesting contributions, but perhaps the most important relates to its theoretical positioning. First, it is integrative by finding an economic function of the firm that has value and implications on the micro level of exchange and production and the macro level of the market process, market structure, and economic growth in addition to the meso level of organisations, institutions, and advanced coordination. The firm represents a solution to the 'specialisation deadlock' that arises due to the inability of decentralised exchange to surpass the limits of or increase the extent of the market; it thereby helps intensify market specialisation and the division of labour; and it is therefore an important contributor to, if not a component of, economic growth and development.

Second, by investigating the firm's economic function within the realm of market production we have avoided making errors by including legal and other non-economic aspects of the actual market. This meant a departure from most theorising on the firm in two ways that are both important and valuable. First, the approach is deductive instead of empirical. By concentrating on the function of the firm conceptually, it transcends the limitations of experience and observations of what the institution of the firm has been. Second, the approach began without a definition of the firm. In fact, part of the inquiry was to find a definition of the firm to be explained. Not having a definition of the object of one's study may sound problematic or even paradoxical. But as there are several accepted and acceptable definitions in the literature, all of which have major shortcomings, it was necessary to start without a (or, if one prefers, with an open-ended) definition. Starting with neither definition nor explanation was thus deliberate. We wanted to solve a problem inherent to the market that could be solved by an economic function that we could intuitively think of as a firm. This approach, in which the economic problem and function took precedence over subjective experience and familiarity of what usually constitutes a firm, expedited analytical deduction virtually free from experiential biases. Of course, a firm is still something, though it can persuasively be argued that it is only or primarily a legal rather than an economic entity – a legal fiction. But once we assume that it indeed exists, is it defined by the employment relation or coordination or planning or hierarchy or legal status or something else? The exact definition of the firm in our analysis was not permitted to steer the analysis of its function, so we started without one. Instead, we allowed the firm to be what provides the function that firms would plausibly have in the evolving production structure of a dynamic market process. The definition of the firm thus emerged from the function necessitated by the economic problem.

Theories of the firm in the extant literature, in rather stark contrast, tend to begin with a definition, which often includes a tension or even contradiction. The definitions of the firm – and there are several – consequently have major shortcomings, are inconsistent or contradictory, and may even be theoretically dubious. One reason is that a definition based simply on the subjective, inductive understanding for what a firm 'is', perhaps based on personal experience, necessarily includes a number of non-economic aspects such as legal definitions, procedural rules, artificial or arbitrary institutions, a notion of hierarchy, a distinction between market and other 'types' of contracting – or what amounts to seemingly arbitrary assertions rather than argument. Consider, for example, Coase's fundamental assertion that the firm is a planned hierarchy, and his conclusion that this is both the firm's value and how it is different from the market. Or consider Sanford J. Grossman and Oliver D. Hart's definition of the firm as 'consist[ing] of those assets that it owns or over which it has control'.[1] Coase claims that the firm is defined by its asserted value; Grossman and Hart fail to provide a definition altogether (what is 'it' in their stated definition?). These types of problems are often overlooked in the literature. Instead, the definition is accepted at face value, and theorising is then aimed at elaborating on and comparing theoretical insights. The contributions of these theories therefore stand and fall with the accuracy of the definition, which should be highly problematic to the degree the firm is defined arbitrarily or imprecisely. A definition that simply describes a characteristic of the observed empirical phenomenon, that mixes economic with legal and political aspects, that comprises assertions without basis or theoretical relationship, or that offers no theoretical explanation beyond the stated definition, should not be acceptable as starting points for theory. The theory drafted in the previous chapters avoids this type of problem completely.

Needless to say, the theory outlined in this book is a draft and it remains incomplete and underdeveloped even as we have reached the last chapter. But it offers great promise as it provides the firm with an economic function in the market process, suggests an explanation for market expansion and economic progress, and avoids many common pitfalls in firm theorising. Furthermore, it provides a dynamic view of market organisation and market change that neither contradicts nor replaces but is consistent with and contributes to theories in entrepreneurship and management as well as economic theory aiming to explain the dynamics of the market. In effect, it complements much of what is known in these literatures by offering an additional argument and integrative component for explaining the progression of the market process.

Accomplishments aside, parts of the theory still need to be fleshed out and it will likely have to be expanded to be properly assessed and tested, and it needs to be applied in order to see how it can explain empirical situations. Its limitations are in this regard unknown. As it is a draft, there are questions that need answers, arguments that need to be scrutinised, definitions that need clarification, weaknesses that need to be addressed, and areas in need of further study. I will here focus on some of those areas as well as on how what has been discussed in this book complements specifically the Austrian economic theory of the market as a process.

Areas for further study

Chapters 8 and 9 extended the analysis of the firm beyond its definition and emergence to provide an explanation for the firm's lifecycle. The argument was made that the firm has a specific and temporary function in realising productive innovation that cannot be implemented through market exchange within the extent of the market. This function, and consequently the value of the individual firm to the economic system, ends as the market 'catches up' with the innovation by adopting the more intensive specialisation and adjusting the division of labour throughout the market's production apparatus. This produces a more efficient allocation of resources that is made possible through the expanded extent of the market that comes with the new specialisation. Whereas this completes the process of creative destruction through firm formation, at least from the perspective of the market process, it does not address issues on the level of the individual firm.

We know from history that firms are not as temporary a phenomenon as the theory suggests they should be. Whereas part of the explanation for the longevity of actual firms can likely be found in legal and political causes, there is room for explaining how and why firms can survive past their initial function as an 'island of specialisation'. A possible explanation for why firms survive past what our framework seems to explain is that we have not considered strategies adopted by individual firms to extend their lifespan and extract value from their positioning outside the extent of the decentralised market. It should be in the interest of the individual firm to raise barriers to entry into the created production space such that a first-mover advantage is created and profitable production can be prolonged. Such strategies to deter new entrants or make entry economically unfeasible can range from organisational measures to encapsulate fully or make the production process opaque, to gaining control of the supply of necessary resources or sources of input. These are indeed two of the five cases in which Schumpeter would predict the development of 'new combinations' in firms.[2] Our framework would suggest that they contribute to the longevity of the firm as a strategy, but not that they are causes of firms.

Whereas the original firm would not be able to become internally efficient without competitive discovery and market-making, the firm's aim is not efficiency for its own sake: it is profits through productive innovation. Upholding an inefficient yet profitable monopoly situation can consequently be a valuable tactic as an alternative to a competitive process with a highly uncertain outcome. Such strategies could extend the life of a firm far beyond the period of transition between one market state and another facilitated by integrated productive innovation. They can also slow down the progression of the transition, and thereby extend the temporal life of the productive innovation that composes the firm.

Barriers to entry can be raised by the firm itself, but can also inadvertently result from its actions. Note that the concept of the firm here developed is the fact that there is no market to support the structure of the specific productive innovation, which suggests that there is a necessary delay between the original firm's formation and the arrival of competitors to compete for profits in the new production space. The lack of a market bars market actors from directly competing with the original firm, and even as competitors are formed there will remain frictions until the new productive space becomes integrated into the existing market through general adoption of the new degree and kind of division of labour.

The original firm and its competitors are, as we saw in previous chapters, differentiated because of their differing implementations of the productive innovation. This is due to a lack of knowledge of how best to organise production, as well as their varying skills, experiences, and access to production factors, and the competitive discovery process leads towards convergence around the most efficient production structure. But as competition intensifies, firms can also engage in differentiation as a competitive measure in order to create specific niches with sufficient customer base to support the firm's distinctive profit goals. Branding, specific design, quality customer service, and massive advertising campaigns are examples of such strategies that differentiate firms within the new production space and thereby help resist and delay the firms' eventual dissolution.

In addition to such economic means to prolong the firm's lifespan as a profitable unit of production, the framework of legal institutions further hinders the emergence of individual competitors as well as the escalation of competitive discovery. Legal requirements raise barriers to implementing productive innovation, thereby making the original firm less likely to experience the arrival of competitors after a new production space has been formed. Legal limitations to production methods, resource extraction and use, and sale of goods, licensing and certification requirements, environmental restrictions and emission regulations, and limitations to bargaining rights raise barriers and increase costs overall, and could therefore potentially protect an entrant from competitors by making entry too costly. In addition to such artificially created economic monopolies, legal institutions provide a plethora of competition-limiting tools for the original firm to use. Examples include patents that outlaw direct competition and copyrights that protect innovations and mandate payment of royalties by imitating firms that engage in competitive production.

As we saw in the previous chapter, policy measures tend to restrict the scope of profitable innovation in the market and thereby inhibit overall growth. But while this raises the bar for entry into or creation of new productive spaces outside the extent of the existing market, it can also effectuate or increase the first-mover advantage and provide sanctuary for those firms that successfully enter it. If the cost to enter a specific space is high, it will attract and can accommodate fewer producers who may then earn a larger share of the profits. With restricted or hindered entry and increased profitability, the productive lifespan of the firm increases while the overall rate of market absorption of the intensive specialisation utilised in the productive innovation decreases. It seems the firm gains in both longevity and profitability what society loses in economic growth and prosperity. This tendency may be counteracted by other mechanisms, but the regulated market should be a fertile area for applying the basic theory drafted here.

Implications of the theory

The theoretical framework we have here drafted provides the firm with a distinct function in the market process, but the definition of firm that follows from the theory seems very narrow. The reader may already have wondered about the degree to which the firm as an 'island of specialisation' can explain the prevalence of firms in the actual marketplace. We thus have to ask what purpose the definition of the firm as a productive innovation implemented outside the extent of the market, and therefore the means by which the market process deals with and overcomes the specialisation deadlock, can serve.

It is indeed the case that firms are a more common occurrence in the modern market than our theory accounts for. In this regard, the theory seems to explain less than most existing theories of the firm, which provide explanations for why firms are so plentiful. This should not be seen as a problem for this theory, however, for reasons we have briefly touched on above. We explicitly set out to explain the economic function of the firm, and derived a definition of the firm from the explanation of this function. The result is a theoretical framework that unambiguously explains how we can understand firms, including the role they play in the market and the impact firm formation has on the production structure, on exclusively economic terms. The economic firm may differ from actual firms to the degree that the latter are defined using non-economic means. To be sure, firms observed in the actual market are recognisable as registered legal entities that conduct business protected by specific legal privileges. Oliver E. Williamson has called attention to the fact that firms and markets exist in different institutional environments as they fall under different legal doctrines. Whereas markets are regulated through contract law and disputes between parties therefore can be settled in courts, firms' internal matters cannot:

> The implicit contract law of internal organization is that of forbearance. Thus, whereas courts routinely grant standing to firms should there be disputes over prices, the damages to be ascribed to delays, failures of quality, and the like, courts will refuse to hear disputes between one internal division and another over identical technical issues. Access to the courts being denied, the parties must resolve their differences internally. Accordingly, hierarchy is its own court of ultimate appeal.[3]

Whereas this provides a potential explanation for the actual firm in the market, it is a legal explanation. As business transactions that are organised using contracts that are legally categorised as 'employment' contracts are legally mandated to be organised as a legal firm, the prevalence of firms in the market is a direct function of legal definitions. In this sense, the firm is indeed a legal fiction as the difference between market and firm is primarily a matter of law. What is observed as a firm in the actual marketplace may therefore completely lack economic rationale or function, and has economic ramifications only contingent on the legally determined institutional environment.

This is not the type of phenomenon we attempted to explain, and for this reason, the economic theory of the firm as an 'island of specialisation' provides an explanation that differs from what can be observed in the market. The economic definition of the firm is different from what people in general would refer to as a firm for the simple reason that it looks exclusively to its economic function. This is not different from how many other economic phenomena are treated in economic analyses as opposed to how they are commonly perceived in a specific and complex empirical setting.[4]

This is not to say that the definitions lack value, however. It means only that they have different uses and support different types of analyses. Williamson's legal definition serves its purpose when studying the impact of institutional design and governance choice for specific transactions in different market settings. But as it is a legal definition, it cannot provide an economic explanation for the firm. Indeed, the legal firm has no economic function.

Our definition, in contrast, is a strictly economic definition and is therefore particularly suitable for economic analysis. Whereas the theory developed in this book cannot be used to make predictions about legal firms, it explains the economic nature of firms and therefore provides a framework for studying the implications of changes that affect the economic firm. As we identified that firms are the manifestation of productive innovations implemented outside of the market's extent, and therefore that they are core to how the market adopts a more intensive division of labour, we can make predictions about the development of real markets based on how changes affect the economic function of the firm. We can also explain the outcome and effects of certain exogenous or endogenous events on market structure, economic growth, and efficiency.

For example, as we saw in Chapter 10, policy can affect – and is often designed to have an effect on – how the economic function of the firm is carried out. Regime uncertainty affects entrepreneurs' willingness to establish firms. Exogenous shocks to the economic system change relative prices and therefore the attractiveness of new firm formation relative to other market action. The implementation of productive innovations, but more importantly the ensuing competitive discovery process, suggests a dynamic with which economic development can take place. The relative frequencies of productive innovation, imitation, and arbitrage events in a market affect how fast an economy can grow and for how long. The particular structure of a market's existing production apparatus is a result of previously established firms, and it both facilitates and restricts the scope of future entrepreneurship. The availability of accumulated savings affect the frequency of implemented productive innovations and therefore the growth of the economy and the expansion of the market's extent. As the firm here takes an important role in the progression of the market, what affects the firm has repercussions on the future development of the market. We can therefore, based on the definition of the firm as an 'island of specialisation', trace the *economic* implications of changes, including legal such, that affect the economic firm.

The firm in Austrian economics

What we did in the previous ten chapters was produce an argument for what the firm can be and what function or role it has in the market process. We started by constructing a model of the market and its dynamic: how it coordinates specialised production through the price mechanism and how it responds to changes of both exogenous and endogenous origin. The market model is 'Austrian' in the sense that it embraces the market as a process, because it focuses on production of value, and because it recognises the decentralised and bottom-up dynamic of an entrepreneurially driven market process. We also added insights about the nature of specialisation under the division of labour from primarily Adam Smith and Emile Durkheim. The result is a theoretical framework that captures the economic nature of the specialised exchange market that is also limited by the extent of the market through productive reality.

Chapter 3 discussed how productive reality sets a limit for further development of the market through adopting more intensive specialisation under the division of labour, and we found that the market is indeed limited by a 'specialisation deadlock' that arises because market actors must maintain compatibility with the market structure. This inhibits actors as they strive to find more productive ways to produce goods, since the market cannot support the outright splitting of tasks to bring about more intensively specialised production processes. Standard production stages can be split only in rather obvious and simple ways, and existing stages can only gradually be narrowed. This leaves novel, entrepreneurial, and imagined production processes unsupported by the existing market, which is the reason we found that implementations necessarily fall outside the extent of the market. As they are outside the extent of the market and therefore cannot benefit from market exchange or the price mechanism, the tasks and those performing the tasks suffer from the incompleteness problem. This produces an integrated 'island of specialisation' that is necessarily integrated and separate, and that is important for the market to take steps towards more intensive specialisation through the division of labour that are more than gradual. This distinct economic phenomenon resembles a firm.

This places the firm at the centre of the expanding market and it contributes strongly to the evolution and progression of the market process. As such, the firm is where novel and advanced capital goods used in production are necessarily manufactured. The market can only produce capital goods that can be assembled using parts and production-aiding capital goods already available or appropriable through exchange transactions. The 'specialisation deadlock' is therefore equally applicable on specific labour skills, production processes, and the production of capital goods. The firm and the economic function that it fulfils is in this sense core to how we can understand capital theory, the evolution and continuous adjustments to a market's capital structure, and the production structure respond to change in for example the interest rate. Without the firm, the production and adaptation of productive capital structures would be significantly impeded. The firm should therefore also be a necessary component when explaining the readjustment process following exogenous shocks to the market system.

It thus seems likely that the firm as an 'island of specialisation' plays an important part in the Austrian theory of the business cycle, both in terms of the inertia in readjusting the capital structure to the new conditions of the market and the means by which such readjustment takes place. At any given time, a fraction of the market's capital structure is bound up within firms in specific entrepreneurial production ventures intended to outdo the market by implementing a different degree and kind of division of labour. These firms were formed by entrepreneurs relying on their judgment and thus interpretation of available market data and expectations of the future states of the market. If the underlying market data are the result of manipulation, for instance through the artificial expansion of credit, these entrepreneurs have made their bets on the future based on false information. As new capital goods have been produced to support the firms' production processes, market-saleable inputs have been procured and transformed through the firms' unique production processes and investments made in production processes that should otherwise have been deemed unlikely to succeed, these resources are in positions that are neither fully compatible with market exchange nor of much value in existing exchange.

This suggests insights into the formation of unsustainable booms and the problem of correcting produced capital structures as the accurate market data are revealed. The correction process necessitates that new firms are formed that can profitably make use of capital goods that were transformed in now defunct production processes. This, in turn, requires access to investment capital, willingness of capitalists and entrepreneurs to invest in and form new firms as accurate market data are revealed, and entrepreneurial imagination to find uses for already intensively specialised capital goods that were no longer useful as the true state of the market was discovered. The bust and correction process that must follow an unsustainable boom can be generically explained by referring to the economic function of the entrepreneur who bids for resources, but the specificity and origin of the capital structures and therefore the details of the correction process are not available until the role of the firm is recognised and included in the analysis.

The correction process following an unsustainable boom is not categorically different from the continuous adjustment of the market's production structure, however. Business cycles are but exaggerated manifestations of the normal types of shifts within the production structure of the market that repeatedly occur on a smaller scale. Under normal circumstances, the market's production structure is continuously revolutionised by firms implementing new degrees and kinds of the division of labour. Some firms are successful and their innovations adopted by the market after the competitive discovery process; other firms fail, and therefore have little impact on the structure and extent of the market. The boom and bust cycle is caused by specific interference with the normal market process that brings about clusters of firm formation based on misleading market data, followed by large-scale failure of those clusters.

Without interference, the market process rarely reallocates a comparatively large share of productive resources towards a specific market or type of production. When this occurs, it is presumably in response to a shift in consumer demand, due to for example a revolutionising innovation, or changes across the board in consumer behaviour. Such adjustments to the production structure are fundamentally different from the massive investments being done as part of an unsustainable boom, however, since they are caused by a real or expected shift in consumer demand. It is the result of capitalists responding to the underlying market data in ways that to them appear most appropriate, and innovations in those lines of business thereby receive the funding needed. Hence, firms form in greater numbers in that specific production space. In contrast, what signifies the boom–bust cycle is that there is no real change in consumer behaviour that causes the boom, but capitalists' and entrepreneurs' expectations about consumer behaviour have shifted due to interference that has changed available market data.

Whereas much of this is already known and is incorporated in the theoretical framework of Austrian economics, the role of the firm as a vehicle for implementing innovation beyond the extent of the market provides more details to the processes. Recognising how the extent of the actual market is limited by the degree and kind of division of labour that it has already adopted underscores the effect of the 'specialisation deadlock'. It explains the inertia we see in changes to the production structure and directs our attention to the economic function of the firm. The progression of the market process, and what we may refer to as economic development and growth, depends on the firm as an 'island of specialisation'. In other words, the evolution of market structure and the ability of market sectors to produce growth and respond to or incorporate change depends on the functioning of the firm lifecycle. The formation of firms around productive innovations, the competitive discovery process through entrepreneurial imitation, and the dissolution of firms as the market catches up, are all necessary to explain how the extent of the market is expanded. There should therefore be a place for the firm in Austrian theory, and from what we've learned in previous chapters the function of the firm may be core to the functioning of the dynamic and wealth-producing market process.

The firm as the implementation of a productive innovation also points to a possible means to tease out and account for theoretical differences between Austrian notions of the entrepreneurial function. We saw in Chapter 9 how we can think of the entrepreneurship function as three distinct types: the Kirznerian arbitrageur-entrepreneur who supplies the equilibrating function within the extent of the market by reallocating resources through exchange for profit; the Schumpeterian disruptive entrepreneur who potentially disequilibrates the existing market structure by implementing a productive innovation outside the extent of the market; and the mimicking entrepreneurs who fulfil the disruptive potential of the Schumpeterian entrepreneur by bringing about a competitive discovery process that brings the innovation to the market.

A market with only Kirznerian arbitrageur-entrepreneurs will largely be devoid of disruption, and will therefore always be equilibrating. Such a market should soon approach a situation resembling the perfectly competitive model were it not for exogenous changes that require adjustment of the production structure. As exogenous changes are expected, the market process aims for a moving target that it will not reach.

A market with only innovator-entrepreneurs and imitator-entrepreneurs lacks the ability to respond to change, and it should therefore always be in disequilibrium and is unlikely to be equilibrating. But it will be consistently disruptive, perhaps to such a degree that the market process never is able to recover from the introduced innovations and therefore faces prohibitively large coordination costs and a severe knowledge problem. The effect of innovation on market structure depends ultimately on the relative frequency of productive innovations implemented, the frequency of imitator-entrepreneurs, and what exogenous changes the market suffers. But a market that is subject to disruptive innovation but lacks the means to equilibrate through exchange would have a defective price mechanism, which raises the question of whether it can be considered a market – or at least it will remain one.

Nevertheless, a strictly 'Kirznerian' market should be unable to move beyond its extent due to the specialisation deadlock and its lack of imaginative entrepreneurship to establish innovative production structure outside the extent of the market. A model consisting of exchange-based arbitrage that brings the market closer to its 'end point' and that constantly adjusts resource allocation in response to exogenous change is an unrealistic and flawed model of the market. We know from experience that production becomes ever more specialised, so the model must be able to account for how the market, through endogenous means, expands beyond its prior extent. The model we have discussed in this book does just that, by combining equilibrating forces within the extent of the market with innovative disruption and competitive discovery to expand specialised production beyond the extent of the market.

Many of the details of our model will require elaboration and clarification. The model is also likely to raise questions both about applicability and compatibility with Austrian theory since it introduces new aspects and challenges held beliefs. These and similar questions need to be properly answered. There may also be errors in need of correction. All of this will contribute to the ongoing discussion and continued discovery of the nature of the market process and production. But if there is one contribution of this book, it should be that there is a role for a purely economic firm – and that it may be important for how we perceive of and understand the market process.

Notes

1 S. J. Grossman and O. D. Hart, 'The Costs and Benefits of Ownership: A Theory of Vertical and Lateral Integration', *Journal of Political Economy*, 94:4 (1986), pp. 691–719, p. 693.
2 See J. A. Schumpeter, *The Theory of Economic Development: An Inquiry into Profits, Capital, Credit, Interest, and the Business Cycle* (1911) (Cambridge, MA: Harvard University Press, 1934), p. 66.
3 O. E. Williamson, 'Comparative Economic Organization: The Analysis of Discrete Structural Alternatives', *Administrative Science Quarterly*, 36:2 (1991), pp. 269–296, p. 274.
4 Money, cost, and demand are examples that have different meanings in economic analysis and in colloquial speech.

References

Alchian, A. A. and H. Demsetz, 'Production, Information Costs and Economic Organization', *American Economic Review*, 62:5 (1972), pp. 777–795.

Bastiat, F., *That Which is Seen, and That Which is Not Seen: An Economic Essay* (1850) (World Library Classics, 2010).

Baumol, W. J., 'Entrepreneurship in Economic Theory', *American Economic Review*, 58:2 (1968), pp. 64–71.

Böhm-Bawerk, E. v., *Positive Theory of Capital* (1889) (South Holland, IL: Libertarian Press, 1959).

Bylund, P. L., 'Division of Labor and the Firm: An Austrian Attempt at Explaining the Firm in the Market', *Quarterly Journal of Austrian Economics*, 14:2 (2011), pp. 188–215.

Bylund, P. L., 'Toward a Framework for Behavioral Strategy: What We Can Learn from Austrian Economics', in T. K. Das (ed.) *Behavioral Strategy: Emerging Perspectives* (Charlotte, NC: Information Age Publishing, 2014), pp. 205–232.

Bylund, P. L., 'Ronald Coase's "Nature of the Firm" and the Argument for Economic Planning', *Journal of the History of Economic Thought*, 36:3 (2014), pp. 305–329.

Bylund, P. L., 'The Firm and the Authority Relation: Hierarchy vs. Organization', in G. L. Nell (ed.) *Austrian Theory and Economic Organization: Reaching Beyond Free Market Boundaries* (New York: Palgrave Macmillan, 2014), pp. 97–120.

Bylund, P. L., 'Signifying Williamson's Contribution to the Transaction Cost Approach: An Agent-Based Simulation of Coasean Transaction Costs and Specialization', *Journal of Management Studies*, 52:1 (2015), pp. 148–174.

Bylund, P. L., 'Explaining Firm Emergence: Specialization, Transaction Costs, and the Integration Process', *Managerial and Decision Economics*, 36:4 (2015), pp. 221–238.

Bylund, P. L. and R. Wuebker, *Where Do Factor Markets Come From? Toward a Resource-Based Theory of the Entrepreneurial Firm* (Keystone, CO, Entrepreneurship exemplars conference, 2014).

Cantillon, R., *Essai Sur La Nature Du Commerce En Général* (1755) (London: Macmillan & Co., 1931).

Coase, R. H., 'The Nature of the Firm', *Economica*, 4:16 (1937), pp. 386–405.

Coase, R. H., 'The Nature of the Firm: Origin', *Journal of Law, Economics and Organization*, 4:1 (1988), pp. 3–17.

Connell, C. M., 'Fritz Machlup's Methodology and the Theory of the Growth of the Firm', *Quarterly Journal of Austrian Economics*, 10:4 (2007), pp. 300–312.

Demsetz, H., 'R. H. Coase and the Neoclassical Model of the Economic System', *Journal of Law and Economics*, 54:4 (2011), pp. S7–S13.

Durkheim, E., *The Division of Labor in Society* (1892) (New York: Free Press, 1933).

Foss, N. J. and P. G. Klein, *Organizing Entrepreneurial Judgment: A New Approach to the Firm* (Cambridge: Cambridge University Press, 2012).

Grossman, S. J. and O. D. Hart, 'The Costs and Benefits of Ownership: A Theory of Vertical and Lateral Integration', *Journal of Political Economy*, 94:4 (1986), pp. 691–719.

Hart, O. D., 'An Economist's Perspective on the Theory of the Firm', *Columbia Law Review*, (1989), pp. 1757–1774.

Hart, O. D. and J. Moore, 'Property Rights and the Nature of the Firm', *Journal of Political Economy*, 98:6 (1990), pp. 1119–1158.

Hayek, F. A. v., 'Economics and Knowledge', *Economica*, 4:13 (1937), pp. 33–54.

Hayek, F. A. v., *The Pure Theory of Capital* (London: Routledge & Kegan Paul, 1941).

Hayek, F. A. v., 'The Use of Knowledge in Society', *American Economic Review*, 35:4 (1945), pp. 519–530.

Hayek, F. A. v., 'Competition as a Discovery Process', *New Studies in Philosophy, Politics, Economics, and the History of Ideas*, (1978), pp. 179–190.

Higgs, R., 'Regime Uncertainty: Why the Great Depression Lasted So Long and Why Prosperity Resumed after the War', *Independent Review*, 1:4 (1997), pp. 561–590.

Jacobsen, L. R., 'On Robinson, Coase and "The Nature of the Firm"', *Journal of the History of Economic Thought*, 30:1 (2008), pp. 65–80.

Jacobsen, L. R., 'On Robinson, Penrose, and the Resource-Based View', *European Journal of the History of Economic Thought*, 20:1 (2011), pp. 125–147.

Jacobson, R., 'The "Austrian" School of Strategy', *Academy of Management Review*, 17:4 (1992), pp. 782–807.

Jensen, M. C. and W. H. Meckling, 'Theory of the Firm: Managerial Behavior, Agency Costs, and Capital Structure', *Journal of Financial Economics*, 3:4 (1976), pp. 305–360.

Kirzner, I. M., *An Essay on Capital* (New York: Augustus M. Kelley Publishers, 1966).

Kirzner, I. M., *Competition and Entrepreneurship* (Chicago, IL: University of Chicago Press, 1973).

Kirzner, I. M., 'Economics and Error', in L. M. Spadaro (ed.) *New Directions in Austrian Economics* (Kansas City, MO: Sheed Andrews & McMeel, 1978), pp. 57–76.

Klein, B., R. A. Crawford, and A. A. Alchian, 'Vertical Integration, Appropriable Rents, and the Competitive Contracting Process', *Journal of Law and Economics*, 21:2 (1978), pp. 297–326.

Klein, P. G., 'Opportunity Discovery, Entrepreneurial Action, and Economic Organization', *Strategic Entrepreneurship Journal*, 2:3 (2008), pp. 175–190.

Klein, P. G. and P. L. Bylund, 'The Place of Austrian Economics in Contemporary Entrepreneurship Research', *Review of Austrian Economics*, 27:3 (2014), pp. 259–279.

Knight, F. H., *Risk, Uncertainty and Profit* (1921) (Chicago, IL: University of Chicago Press, 1985).

Lachmann, L. M., 'Complementarity and Substitution in the Theory of Capital', *Economica*, 14:54 (1947), pp. 108–119.

Lachmann, L. M., *Capital and Its Structure* (1956) (Kansas City, MO: Sheed Andrews & McMeel, 1978).

Lewin, P., *Capital in Disequilibrium: The Role of Capital in a Changing World* (London and New York: Routledge, 1999).

Marshall, A., *Principles of Economics*, 8th edition (1890) (New York: Macmillan, 1920).

Marx, K., *Capital: A Critique of Political Economy* (1867) (New York: Charles H. Kerr & Company, 1906).

Menger, C., 'On the Origin of Money', *Economic Journal*, 2:6 (1892), pp. 239–255.

Mises, L. v., 'Economic Calculation in the Socialist Commonwealth', in F. A. v. Hayek (ed.) *Collectivist Economic Planning* (London: George Routledge & Sons, 1935), pp. 87–130.

Mises, L. v., *Planned Chaos* (Irvington-on-Hudson, NY: Foundation for Economic Education, 1947).

Mises, L. v., *Socialism: An Economic and Sociological Analysis* (1936) (New Haven, CT: Yale University Press, 1951).

Mises, L. v., *Human Action: A Treatise on Economics. The Scholar's Edition* (1949) (Auburn, AL: Ludwig von Mises Institute, 1998).

Mises, L. v., 'Profit and Loss', in *Planning for Freedom: Let the Market System Work* (Indianapolis, IN: Liberty Fund, 2008), pp. 143–172.

Moran, P. and S. Ghoshal, 'Markets, Firms, and the Process of Economic Development', *Academy of Management Review*, 24:3 (1999), pp. 390–412.

North, D. C., 'Institutions and a Transaction–Cost Theory of Exchange', in J. E. Alt and K. A. Shepsle (eds) *Perspectives on Positive Political Economy* (New York: Cambridge University Press, 1990), pp. 182–194.

Penrose, E. T., *The Theory of the Growth of the Firm* (New York: John Wiley & Sons, 1959).

Pfeffer, J., *Power in Organizations* (Boston, MA: Pitman, 1981).

Porter, M. E., *Competitive Strategy: Techniques for Analyzing Industries and Competitors* (New York: Free Press, 1980).

Porter, M. E., 'The Contributions of Industrial Organization to Strategic Management', *Academy of Management Review*, 6:4 (1981), pp. 609–620.

Porter, M. E., *Competitive Advantage: Creating and Sustaining Superior Performance* (New York: Free Press, 1985).

Robbins, L. C., 'The Representative Firm', *Economic Journal*, 38:151 (1928), pp. 387–404.

Robinson, E. A. G., *The Structure of Competitive Industry* (London: Nisbet, 1931).

Robinson, E. A. G., 'The Problem of Management and the Size of Firms', *Economic Journal*, 44:174 (1934), pp. 242–257.

Rothbard, M. N., *An Austrian Perspective on the History of Economic Thought, Volume I: Economic Thought before Adam Smith* (Auburn AL: Ludwig von Mises Institute, 1995).

Rothbard, M. N., *An Austrian Perspective on the History of Economic Thought, Volume Ii: Classical Economics* (Auburn AL: Ludwig von Mises Institute, 1995).

Rothbard, M. N., *Man, Economy, and State with Power and Market. Scholar's Edition* (1962) (Auburn, AL: Ludwig von Mises Institute, 2004).

Sautet, F. E., *An Entrepreneurial Theory of the Firm* (London: Routledge, 2000).

Say, J.-B., *A Treatise on Political Economy or the Production, Distribution and Consumption of Wealth* (1821) (Auburn, AL: Ludwig von Mises Institute, 2008).

Schumpeter, J. A., *The Theory of Economic Development: An Inquiry into Profits, Capital, Credit, Interest, and the Business Cycle* (1911) (Cambridge, MA: Harvard University Press, 1934).

Schumpeter, J. A., *Socialism, Capitalism and Democracy* (New York: Harper & Bros., 1942).

Shane, S. A., *A General Theory of Entrepreneurship: The Individual–Opportunity Nexus* (Cheltenham: Edward Elgar, 2003).

Shane, S. A. and S. Venkataraman, 'The Promise of Entrepreneurship as a Field of Research', *Academy of Management Review*, 25:1 (2000), pp. 217–226.

Simon, H. A., 'A Formal Theory of the Employment Relationship', *Econometrica: Journal of the Econometric Society*, 19:3 (1951), pp. 293–305.

Simon, H. A., 'The Architecture of Complexity', *Proceedings of the American Philosophical Society*, 106:6 (1962), pp. 467–482.

Skousen, M., *The Structure of Production* (New York: New York University Press, 1990).

Smith, A., *An Inquiry into the Nature and Causes of the Wealth of Nations* (1776) (Chicago, IL: University of Chicago Press, 1976).

Spulber, D. F., *The Theory of the Firm: Microeconomics with Endogenous Entrepreneurs, Firms, Markets, and Organizations* (Cambridge: Cambridge University Press, 2008).

Stigler, G. J., 'The Division of Labor is Limited by the Extent of the Market', *Journal of Political Economy*, 59:3 (1951), pp. 185–193.

Strigl, R. v., *Capital & Production* (1934) (Auburn, AL: Ludwig von Mises Institute, 2000).

Williamson, O. E., *Markets and Hierarchies, Analysis and Antitrust Implications: A Study in the Economics of Internal Organization* (New York: Free Press, 1975).

Williamson, O. E., 'Transaction Cost Economics: The Governance of Contractual Relations', *Journal of Law and Economics*, 22:2 (1979), pp. 233–261.

Williamson, O. E., *The Economic Institutions of Capitalism* (New York: Free Press, 1985).

Williamson, O. E., 'The Logic of Economic Organization', *Journal of Law, Economics, and Organization*, 4:1 (1988), pp. 65–93.

Williamson, O. E., 'Comparative Economic Organization: The Analysis of Discrete Structural Alternatives', *Administrative Science Quarterly*, 36:2 (1991), pp. 269–296.

Williamson O. E., *The Mechanisms of Governance* (Oxford: Oxford University Press, 1996).

Index